T0282764

"America's Elites strangled our country with managed —— —— posed for close to 40 years. The Populist Nationalist Movement galvanized around a former Democrat billionaire from Queens in 2015, hammering through long odds to elect him President. That Movement— now an emerging majority of the nation is the subject of an incredible book by two of its leaders. *The Emerging Populist Majority* is the action plan for both electoral victory and effective governance in the decades to come. Written by young firebrands, it is a must-read for everyone concerned about the salvation and rejuvenation of our Republic."

—Steve Bannon, Chief White House Strategist, Host of *War Room*

"The left is going to hate this book, but that says it all."

—Richard Baris, Director, BIG DATA POLL

"Olson and Wax have thrown the old playbook out the window and now present a new plan forward for the GOP, should its leaders realize the importance of capturing a growing groundswell around the country. They understand the American body politic more than most of the high-priced beltway consultants who spend their nights on CNN panels."

—Joe Borelli, New York City Council Republican Minority Leader

"Gavin Wax has been long dedicated to building up the New Right to save the Republic. Beltway elitists have listened to the 'Chamber of Consultants' for far too long, and it's time we rely on creative outsiders to come in and start representing the will of the American people. Wax outlines exactly how the Party needs to align with American interests to build new coalitions of voters who don't trust the media, politicians, and legacy political parties."

—Tyler Bowyer, Chief Operating Officer Turning Point Action

"*The Emerging Populist Majority* is a must-read for anyone searching for a clear roadmap on growing the MAGA movement, restoring American prosperity, and saving our Republic. Gavin Wax and Troy Olson provide the most detailed chronology yet of how we got to this point—and why the America First agenda has the so-called elites pressing the panic button."

—Alex Bruesewitz, CEO X-Strategies

"Gavin Wax and Troy Olson are not only good at reading the tea leaves, they have also done a remarkable job explaining them— even for folks who are not politically savvy. *The Emerging Populist Majority* is a great book that will prepare you to help get our country back on track!"

— Mike Collins, US House of Representatives (GA-10)

"Gavin is a political mastermind—he's a trailblazer that just gets it. Gavin is right when he says this movement is far from over. We are just getting started, and what we have here does not end with President Trump. There's an awakening happening in this country, and we're going to make sure it's heard. This book is the anecdote for Republican doomerism and will enrage Democrat partisans who think they have it wrapped up and are the party of the future."

—Ryan Fournier, Founder Students for Trump

"Authors Troy Olson and Gavin Wax masterfully distill their transformative impact on America's political scene in this brilliant book. *The Emerging Populist Majority* is must read for every battle-ready conservative preparing to join the fight to save America.

—Matt Gaetz, US House of Representatives (FL-1)

"From the trenches of protests to save Teddy Roosevelt's statue in New York, to knocking on doors and organizing, nobody has been on the front lines of the populist movement like Wax. Do you want to know how this whole thing happened? He tells you from a thrilling front-row perspective."

—**David Marcus Author of *Charade: The Covid Lies That Crushed a Nation***

"Gavin is emerging as one of the leading voices of the next generation of the political right. He has an acute instinct for what the key issues are for the country and has his finger on the pulse of his generation. This will be the first of many important works that we all need to heed as guidance through this uncharted territory we now find our ourselves and our country in."

—**Amanda Milius, *Producer & Director of The Plot Against the President***

"Gavin Wax is one of America's most effective political activists. He is the steroid injection that transformed the New York Young Republican Club from an organization of some 50 people that could have met on a Subway car into a 1,000-member colossus that now fills ballrooms. He also is a keen observer and clear thinker on domestic affairs and public relations. I can think of few people better equipped to dive deeply into the future of American conservatism. And, conveniently, he has placed his thoughts between the covers of this book. It deserves a close and immediate read by anyone who wonders whether America will stay afloat or sink beneath the relentless waves of Wokism."

—**Deroy Murdock, Fox News Contributor**

"Gavin Wax is exactly the kind of firebrand we need to hold the establishment accountable, and *The Emerging Populist Majority* lays out a cogent roadmap for the future success of our nation."

—**Vickie Paladino, New York City Councilwoman**

"*The Emerging Populist Majority* will white pill republicans, enrage the America Last libs and neocons, and provide insight to international partners fighting the same fights abroad against the same foe."

—Jack Posobiec, Senior Editor Human Events

"Just as Kevin Philips' seminal book, *The Emerging Republican Majority* was a blueprint for the majority coalition birthed by Barry Goldwater, expanded by Richard Nixon, and brought to fulfillment by Ronald Reagan—Gavin Wax's book, *The Emerging Populist Majority*, is a blueprint for the new Republican populist coalition that will return the GOP to majority status. Wax's understanding of Donald Trump's ability to ignore Wall Street and the country club elites who dominated the party in the Bush years, to form a coalition of anti-globalist small business people, blue-collar families, suburban middle-class voters, and ever-increasing numbers of Hispanic and African-Americans, is the formula for the future!"

—Roger Stone, *New York Times* Bestselling Author

"In south Brooklyn, an emerging populist majority has already emerged. The very diverse district I represent in the New York City Council has gone from heavily Democrat to heavily Republican over the past half-decade. This would be news to many, so I'm glad this story is getting out to a wider audience."

—Inna Vernikov, New York City Councilwoman

THE EMERGING POPULIST MAJORITY

THE EMERGING POPULIST MAJORITY

Troy M. Olson & Gavin M. Wax

BOMBARDIER
BOOKS

Published by Bombardier Books
An Imprint of Post Hill Press
ISBN: 979-8-88845-224-0
ISBN (eBook): 979-8-88845-225-7

The Emerging Populist Majority
© 2024 by Troy M. Olson and Gavin M. Wax
All Rights Reserved

Cover Design by Conroy Accord

Post Hill Press
New York • Nashville
posthillpress.com

Published in the United States of America
1 2 3 4 5 6 7 8 9 10

Dedicated to those with commitment and love for this country.

"Far better it is to dare mighty things, to win glorious triumphs, even though checkered by failure, than to take rank with those poor spirits who neither enjoy much nor suffer much, because they live in the gray twilight that knows not victory nor defeat."

—Theodore Roosevelt, twenty-sixth president of the United States

TABLE OF CONTENTS

FOREWORD

BY RAHEEM KASSAM

This book is not "easy reading." Nor should it be. This book is not your typical, ghostwritten, political puffery published by some television talking head with a view of making a quick buck on a bestseller before Christmas. Nor should it be.

What Gavin Wax and Troy Olson have created with *The Emerging Populist Majority* is a deeply serious, deeply thoughtful, and deeply nerdy dive into America's political settlement...or lack thereof.

In this book, what you'll come away with—if you put the time and effort into internalizing the critical concepts contained herein—is a wealth of information that will undergird a thesis scarcely advanced: that populism is the natural and default status of America's body politick, not centralized neoliberalism or progressivism. And certainly not corporate globalism.

This book is neither a screed nor a manifesto. It is not a "roadmap." You will not finish the final chapter thinking that everything is under control and that these very smart people are handling the fate of your nation so you don't have to. It is quite the opposite.

The Emerging Populist Majority will arm *you* personally with the historic framework required to put your shoulder to the wheel for a massive intellectual and political reassertion of the country's founding principles and, equally critically, what they mean for today.

Critics may blast this necessary assertion of otherwise poorly documented American political history as "the right's 1619 project"—which will both confirm their own attempts to alter the past through revision and coercion while telling you everything about how much the current ruling class is petrified of such important truths.

The corporate center of America—the "uniparty"—often positions itself as the West's rightful "governing class." Oftentimes, rightists make the mistake of adopting their language, handing them the moral and political high ground in a bid to be the underdog, and lowering their expectations to the point where Republicans on Capitol Hill have very little to do at all.

But right-wingers must be more forceful than simply touring the nation and its television studios, declaring themselves to be "unwoke" or whatever the latest middle-of-the-road moniker is for the globalist and increasingly demonic left *and* "right."

Simply put: these are quite evidently *not* the best positioned people to form America's governing party in the twenty-first century.

In fact, Wax and Olson seem to hint at the possibility of a range of contingencies except the continuation of the tired status quo.

In a book that I believe already begs for a sequel or a second volume, the authors reassert a great many concepts and ideas sprinkled throughout the American political tradition that have almost been lost today. These can come at no better time given America's fast march to one of its most fractious elections ever.

The Emerging Populist Majority is a necessary and well-stated anecdote to much of the political commentary today that sacrifices the big picture and long-term trajectory of America for a narrow, two-party horse race.

Olson and Wax conclude on a thesis that says the populists are slowly, persistently, and gradually winning, going through the most expedient and viable legal vessel they can.

It was my great pleasure to read it and to recommend it to you. I hope you do the same for others, for that is how victory goes viral.

PREFACE

The story of how this book came into existence is as unlikely as the populist movements and developments it covers. How does a former busboy born and raised in Queens come to coauthor a book with a former cook from a small town in Minnesota? The story of how and why that can happen is in some ways a microcosm of the conservative, traditionalist, patriotic, and populist fusion project currently changing the face of American politics. It's also a microcosm of the potential going forward of an urban and rural populist fusion that would create the strongest, deepest, and broadest political coalition in nearly a century. What may come to America's political future is one reason this book exists. The other reason is our recent and not-so-recent past.

For the better part of the past two decades, the media and cultural establishment in America have time and again declared the Republican Party dead or on its deathbed, and declared an ascendant and forever Democratic Party majority because of the country's changing demographics. Whether called the "coalition of the ascendant," the "wired workers" of tech, our biggest societal development during that time, "demographic inevitability," or this book's subgenre—the emerging Democratic majority—this thesis has been deeply harmful to our political discourse. This book will show just how much it has not come to pass, and the more it does not come to pass, the more poisoned the discourse has become. An era of negative partisanship and ideological polarization has left this land

and its people in a seemingly perpetual struggle at the 50-yard line, content to kick long field goals. It is clear we cannot and will not go on much longer like this. We have arrived at a pivotal moment of transition. In fact, we're already halfway through it.

We attempted to make this book as fact-driven as possible, discussing recent and historical trends while pulling no punches with the past or present in service of trying to lay out a possible future extrapolated from these trends that could change the trajectory of America. And this is where we make our bias clear. Both authors love this country a great deal but believe this country is in a real and relative decline. Worse, that decline is managed by indifferent elites that have every incentive to keep us divided along racial, economic, ideological, religious, and tribal lines.

This book has three intended audiences. One, if you're a Republican base partisan, you'll no doubt like much of what you read here. Whether you're a hack or a doomer, we hope this book goes beyond the typical "red meat" to a political base variety. Two, for those who are Democratic partisans or politicos, we welcome the "blue rage" reading to come or the intellectually curious exploration. Either way, thank you for giving us a shot. One of us not only used to vote Democrat after all, but also knocked on doors for Barack Obama in Iowa in 2007–08. In addition to being a military veteran and from a small town, he is a relatively on-the-nose cultural stand-in for the Obama-to-Trump voters who represent the critical difference between a potential "emerging democratic" coalition that could have been but never developed—and *why*. The other author is a cultural stand-in for what is happening throughout urban America. Surrounded by a dominant cultural progressivism, the new counterculture in America is patriotic, traditional, populist, and overwhelmingly from working- and middle-class backgrounds. Both of us are first-generation university graduates, neither went to an Ivy League school, and a generation or two ago we would be considered prime examples of the Democratic base.

This is the real "it switched!"

Finally, the last intended audience is the frustrated and exhausted American who wants to throw both major parties into the sea, and the interested parties abroad who understand how important a workable and competent America is for the world and further understand that history has continued.

To our friends and detractors—thank you for reading, and we hope to see you soon.

INTRODUCTION

I magine being an American politico or insider in the lead-up to the 1936 election. The country is still mired in the Great Depression, and there is controversy, and in some quarters, intense backlash to the New Deal. The alphabet soup of agencies and programs coming out of the first hundred days set an impossible standard for the beginnings of presidential administrations to follow. In the midst of this emergency, there was great uncertainty across America: financial and economic uncertainty, political instability and crisis, and a society in desperate need of a calm and steady hand.

We look back on this era with a couple of realizations with the benefit of history, hindsight, and some final outcomes like our shared experiences in the Second World War that tie this era into a triumphant bow of crisis and hard times leadership before bringing about a two-decade high. As transformative a president as Franklin Roosevelt ended up being, presiding over American life and culture for so long that many of those who served in the war could not recall another president, we tend to forget how tumultuous the domestic 1930s were. We also tend to forget what preceded Roosevelt. The victor of a paradigm writes a new history and rewrites the old one as much as is possible, just as the Houses of York and Lancaster tried to do to win legitimacy over the civic and social order during the War of the Roses in fifteenth-century England.

For progressives this era becomes a more successful realization of the vision and view of governance articulated by Woodrow Wilson, in whose shadow we live in so many ways. For conservatives and more specifically Republicans, this era meant the eventual upsetting of the apple cart and of being displaced as America's natural ruling and dominant party—a position the party has never truly reclaimed. From Wilson to Roosevelt to Johnson (because Truman and Kennedy were accidentally and insufficiently committed to the secular progressive religion) to Obama (Carter and Clinton were also insufficiently committed, with Clinton's standing being the most complicated) to whoever is next but probably not Biden (even though Joe Biden is in many ways the most progressive president ever, whatever that means now), the events of the previous turning from one civic and social order to another marked the origin story of the progressive administrative state and view of government without restraint, with the Constitution as a hindrance at best, something to strive to do away with entirely at worst or most. For the progressives of the Third Civic Order as we'll call it here, it has always been the State of New York motto of Excelsior (Ever Upward). In the view of this cultural elite and the majority of institutions aligned with it, any other path is simply illegitimate—as illegitimate as the House of York if you're a Lancaster, or House of Lancaster if you're a York. In its simplest form, civic orders are the mere periodization of American history (emphasis on politics), like one would teach in an Advanced Placement (AP) high school history class, and in more complex terms represent the social understanding and legally codified notions of the relationship between the People and the Constitution, the People and the Government, and the Constitution and the Government. In the preamble to the United States Constitution it says, "We the People," not "We the government." Civic orders operate legally between these forces but are most importantly reinforced socially and culturally by the notions of the period.

The First Civic Order, preferably called Jeffersonian democracy and seen at its height historically as the "Era of Good Feelings" or the early American Republic, represents a solid notion of the new nation forged in liberty and in our founding charters of freedom. The internal contradictions in that founding represent not a flaw of that nation, as all nations and peoples have flaws, nor something wrong with that Constitution and the political system and organizational structure it lays out, since the founders accounted for means of changing it in various ways, but rather the internal contradictions and flaws represent what will eventually undo and break apart that civic order. Jeffersonian democracy worked well for forging a new nation conceived in liberty, but the notion that all men were created equal and the Constitution's compromise with the institution of slavery and subsequent developments unforeseen during the founding charter period—like the invention of the cotton gin specifically and the general development of a more agrarian society in the South alongside a more merchant and industrialized society in the North—meant that this civic order would dramatically see itself to the door.

The flaw and seeds of the undoing of the civic order are there from the start, and this is seen again with the Second Civic Order, preferably called the Republican Union. The Republican Union flips the dominant and natural governing party in the system and country and, unlike the Era of Good Feelings, creates martial law in the South and Reconstruction initiatives. The dominant party, the natural governing party—while challenged by the oppositional party, as well as occasionally by a viable third party contributing ideas and in the case of the Federalists and Whigs, getting replaced by a new party altogether—is ultimately responsible for driving the constitutional republic forward and forging the new social consensus, understanding, and relationship between the three above. As with Jeffersonian democracy, the undoing of the Republican Union civic order is also found in its seeds and beginnings: *industrialization*. Gone are the parallel economies developing throughout the early republic and Jeffersonian and Jacksonian democracy to be replaced with the rapid pace of industrialization, which creates a genuine middle class in American life, raises the standard of living, puts America on the top as first an economic then later a diplomatic and world power, but also sees high levels of inequality and undeniably human traits of greed, envy, and excess.

In addition to this industrialization at home, the industrial democracies developing in Europe and the consequence of technological change and innovation—the so-called "flattening of the world"—raise the stakes for international politics and world order. Therefore, it is not the Great Depression or the market crash of 1929 that created the lasting civic order that replaced the one of the Republican Union but rather the Second World War. Just as the First World War upended the civic orders in Europe and around the world, the more triumphant and satisfying end to the Second World War forged a new civic order throughout American life.

The coalition that supports the social consensus is best understood from a social class perspective and analysis. The less industrialized South, with higher levels of poverty, united in a coalition against the Republican Union with the lower classes of the more industrialized North. Furthermore, the Republican Union civic order was unable to add new states out west halfway through this civic order, which means the McKinley triumph of 1896 was most similar to the Jacksonian first populist moment in the 1820s and '30s. By the standards of their day, the Republican Union civic order included all the elites, most of the most progressive Americans by the standards of the day, but none of that was enough to keep black Americans from realigning to the same party as the Ku Klux Klan and the party of the Confederacy—the Democratic Party. While modern Democrats will say that the parties were very different then, while at the same time draw some straight-line analysis from both the issues and various states of that day, the flaw in that line of thinking is (a) people do not live forever, and (b) lots of other things change, too, but the parties themselves within a civic order change gradually and change more in accordance with competing companies within a marketplace rather than the moralistic, social, and culturally driven values coming from the people.

This book will argue that our current civic order that was forged out of our shared wartime experiences will ultimately and gradually be undone by many of the seeds of its founding, as is already happening. The institutions of the liberal international order itself and the process of globalization that the victorious Western democracies doubled down on started to speed up after the end of the Cold War. The beginning of our story of an emerging and new majority thus first begins on what drives it into a political coalition. This process is far more gradual and less triumphant than the in-retrospect narratives that each civic order writes into the record as their quasi-origin story.

It is a story within a broader narrative, not unlike the country itself. And it is notable that for each order-crisis-seed of the next story, interested civic Americans define themselves first by what they are against, defining themselves against an opposing force, before jumping off and figuring out what they are for—but nearly always in the direction of greater freedom. In *The American Crisis* where Thomas Paine scolded and cautioned against being a summer soldier or a sunshine patriot, the country's revolutionaries were being tested from the Continental Army to the Continental Congress to the financiers, to the no greater than one-third of the colonies that supported the cause and had enough of British rule. By declaring independence in 1776, they defined themselves first and foremost as being against something. It would take arguably another cohort or half cohort before a proper founding had been put into place on the second try after the failed Articles of Confederation. This original thirteen-or-so-year period between the Declaration of Independence in 1776 and the Constitution (written in 1787, ratified in 1788, in operation since 1789) along with the Bill of Rights we know as the founding period, and the interpretation of this period and relationship to its meta-narrative serves as a constant reference and jumping-off point for all further stories, influenced heavily by social developments in culture and technology, economics, education, politics, philosophy, religion, and the distribution of information.

Jeffersonian democracy defined itself as against the administration or against the Federalists, America's first political party. America's first political parties were classified as cadre parties, meaning parties dominated by a political elite group of activists. Regardless of the dominant party that took hold, an anti-Adams, anti-administration (President John Adams), or anti-Federalist position was the jumping-off point for a story dominated first by Thomas Jefferson and natural successors through the state of Virginia and the Office of Secretary of State, thus the first true American political party was born around Jefferson. And as "the First Political Party"[i] points out, along with it comes party-building around this story, and although founders like James Madison did not set out to start a political party, in fact writing against them as causing corruption and encouraging war in *Federalist #10*, all who cautioned against factions, including General George Washington, first president of the United States, inevitably ended up joining them. Madison took up the same commitment to study and research and ultimately wrote essays as he did with his contributions to *The Federalist Papers*. In laying out what became the platform and viewpoint of their party, it would define "him and his allies as agrarian, expansionist, pacific, and populist."[ii] They would dominate American politics for the next two and a half decades, and arguably, those same sentiments would dominate the next two and a half decades after that with only occasional and fleeting exceptions. Beyond merely contributing to the creation of the first real party, the outgoing Adams administration contributed to early American partisanship through the Judiciary Act of 1801, which created six new federal circuit courts and proceeded to staff them entirely with Federalists, from the judges down to the clerks.[iii] The judiciary would remain a Federalist redoubt for a couple of decades because of these outgoing acts. However, at the ballot box, America became a de facto one-party state during the Era of Good Feelings.

Supposedly, this de facto one-party state was broken up by the 1824 election and the populist Andrew Jackson. But while Jackson upset the political establishment of the day, he was still far more in tune with the spirit of Jeffersonian democracy than his detractors and more in line with the idea and the story of that lineage. Supported by the people, he won three straight popular votes and served two terms as president, and his chosen successor, Democrat Martin Van Buren, served one more after Jackson's retirement.

The next story also defines itself in its beginnings as being against something: either against disunion (for the moderate or conservative Republicans like Lincoln and company) or against the institution of slavery itself (like the abolitionists and radical Republicans). Notably, the more a faction defines itself as being against something first and foremost, the more likely it is to prevail both in upsetting and breaking from the established story and order while also winning out against internal deliberations with the emergent coalition. Although notably, this alone is not sufficient. The emerging coalition must also be comfortable with exercising executive and presidential power especially, even if it carries a philosophy suspicious of it. This is the fate that befell the Whigs.

Like the others, the Whigs were founded as an against party, an anti-Jacksonian party. This Whig retreat from using executive power[iv] is noted by presidential historian Jon Meacham in the chapter "The Confidence of the Whole People" from his book *The Soul of America: The Battle for Our Better Angels*, and it was one reason why the Whigs were a poorly conceived opposition party. Instead, to upturn the civic order a coalition more comfortable with the use of executive power would have to prevail. Despite many similarities to the populist streak and spirit of Jackson, including facing a Congress hostile at times, as Jackson remains the only president censured by the US Senate[v]—the broader Trumpian comparison to Jackson[vi] falls short on the key marker of affiliation with the main dominant streak of American life at the time, Jeffersonian, and Donald Trump's nonaffiliation with the current ruling order of his time. In another timeline, Trump could have perhaps been an affiliated populist Democrat running against a Wall Street and neoconservative-heavy Republican Party. Trump had at one time or another been a Republican and a Democrat, and his biggest prior political involvement was the Reform Party of first Ross Perot and later Patrick Buchanan, where he received his first vote for president in the California primary in 2000.

While the party of Lincoln prevailed in winning the American Civil War, preserving the union and ending the institution of slavery, it was the radical Republicans whose ideas ultimately drove the civic order-turning, even if their preferred candidates did not.

As the victory began to fade in the hearts and minds of the Republican Union, rather than an Era of Good Feelings, America went through two decades of hard-fought close elections from the end of Reconstruction to the election of 1896. That election saw a renewal of the Republican Union in the same ways Jackson's victories and empowerment of a whole new group of voters saw a renewal of the Jeffersonian impulse and Madisonian party. Jackson bears one more affirmative comparison to the presidency of Donald Trump in that his election broke a continuous streak of coastal executives. By that time, all the nation's chief executives had hailed either from the southern coastal state of Virginia or from the northern coastal state of Massachusetts.[vii] Jackson, the first populist president, was also the first western president and the West came to increasingly be defined by the populist strain of American thought as the country moved further westward and further away from the centers of power in Washington.

Finally, our last example of this "against" trend as the first step to our new story is the breaking from over a century of established American foreign policy going back to Washington and his suspicion and warnings against foreign entanglements and taking part in Europe's wars. Far more so than the coalition against the excesses of the Industrial Age, which created America's first middle class, the Second World War and its finality locked into being what had been first articulated by Woodrow Wilson, a vision of national government that begins moving beyond the constraints placed on it by the Constitution. Although he mostly failed politically in his time, Wilson's vision of government was given a second life between the era of the stock market crash of 1929 and the industrial and administrative demands of the Second World War. Throughout this chaotic time, much of political rhetoric was defining itself as against something before being *for* something: against fascism and Nazism, against communism, against the New Deal or Rooseveltism,[1] or against entrance into the war through the America First committee.

What was set in motion by the New Deal but never fully bought into by the electorate, as we'll discuss later, was locked into the story and system by the shared experiences of the war and the material prosperity that came along with being one of the two powers left standing by war's end and the only powerful Western democratic capitalist society left standing. America's position coming out of the war was not only at a high, but also one of heightened responsibility over international affairs. And it is from this birth that we can see the seeds of the next destruction, winding down, or mere end of our current story. Just as the compromise with slavery in the founding contained the seeds for the undoing of Jeffersonian democracy, and the vastly different experiences in industrial patterns that eventually created a solid Democratic South and northern labor and urban coalition in the 1930s and 1940s upturned that order, so, too, are the seeds of the end of the vast progressive administrative state being pushed to the forefront in the last decade and next in the form of the breaking of the liberal international order and the revolt against globalization and global and coastal elites.

Civic Order	Inciting Crisis	Seeds of Destruction
Jeffersonian democracy (US Constitution)	Civil War	Institution of slavery, differing regional economies
Republican Union	World War II Great Depression	Industrialization
Progressive administrative state	The clash and decline of civilization	Liberal international order and globalization
The Emerging Populist Majority?		

---

[1]   It's notable that any "ism" added to a president's name whether you like them or not is the first sign of relevance.

For President Roosevelt of the first term, who in many ways continued the policies of action and tinkering with the economy through government experimentation in an economic crisis that his Republican predecessor, Herbert Hoover, had tried, there was actually much more going on. Neither history nor demographics were inevitable in this era. To the south in Louisiana was a populist called Huey Long who entered the workforce as a traveling salesman before entering law and later becoming governor of Louisiana and then a US senator. Huey Long was a rural populist and from the working class. To the west was a Canadian-born Catholic priest called Father Charles Coughlin who was the original political talk radio star before being banned from the airways at the outbreak of the war. Father Coughlin was also the original "social justice warrior" and from 1936 to 1942 published and distributed *Social Justice*, a topical, political periodical that garnered much attention and controversy. Coughlin at his public peak received eighty thousand letters per week. For the lead-up to 1936, Coughlin backed populist Huey Long until his assassination in 1935. Although Coughlin started off as a Roosevelt and New Deal supporter, by 1934 he had turned into a harsh critic. Much of this history and Coughlin's connections to the political left are lost to history and overshadowed by his increasing reputation and accusations of anti-Semitism throughout the decade. More than any figure from this era though, the progressive activists that the *Hidden Tribes* report, published by the UK group More in Common, refer to take their lineage in many respects from Coughlin more than from Roosevelt or Huey Long or other forgotten figures like Floyd B. Olson (no relation to coauthor) of Minnesota.

In the Midwest, Floyd B. Olson was to Minnesota what Roosevelt was to the nation, and there was also much talk about Olson forging a third-party campaign for 1936. Olson became governor of Minnesota on the Farmer-Labor third-party ticket, which in the 1920s was more accurate perhaps to describe them as the second party after the Republicans. In some elections the state Democratic Party in Minnesota was down to 5 percent of the vote. Since the Civil War the state had been dominated by the Republican Party. Olson's third-party run and challenge from the left against Roosevelt was not to be, as he opted to run for the US Senate instead. After winning the Farmer-Labor primary, Olson died of stomach cancer prior to the 1936 general election.

Between Long and more forgotten or regional figures like Coughlin and Olson, back east in Washington, Roosevelt, the original triangulator and every bit of the master politician that Abraham Lincoln was, put the eastern establishment (then conservative and traditional, now progressive) into a rearguard action just as his cousin, Republican president Theodore Roosevelt, had done a generation before him. More than any Democrat, Franklin Roosevelt had modeled his rise and political career after his cousin Theodore. But in the lead-up to the 1936 election, the establishment elites of the day were nearly united in the certainty that Franklin would be a one-term president, whereas Theodore Roosevelt had cruised to reelection in 1904 and would have in 1908 had he decided to run again.

The Social Register crowd and entrenched power would, as FDR would say, unite in their hatred against him, and he "welcomed their hatred." This certainty from the nation's ruling class in its righteous politics was similarly seen in the popular culture of the day. Famed and prolific composer and songwriter Cole Porter penned "You're the Top" in 1934, which waxed nostalgic about the strength of the Coolidge dollar and in its ode to all things on top, the GOP included.

A widely read periodical, the *Literary Digest*, the "FiveThirtyEight of its time," claimed their "scientific" poll pointed to a clear victory for Alf Landon, the governor of Kansas. When the results were in, Roosevelt had achieved his peak victory, an even bigger electoral and popular vote margin than in 1932, carrying all but two states (Vermont and Maine). Within its sample, the *Literary Digest* (which was more or less taken down and discredited by this scandalous inaccuracy to predict the future, going out of circulation shortly after) poll probably was scientific, but its methodology exposed the bias of the day from the ruling class and the detachment between realities on the ground and elite opinion. The poll was based on three sample populations: (1) those who had an automobile and license plate, (2) those who had a landline phone, and (3) those who had a subscription to the *Literary Digest*. Just as most pollsters would miss the 2016 and, really, the 2020 elections (which predicted a Biden landslide win by modern standards) because of a failure to understand the society and electorate they're trying to model, the *Literary Digest* was incapable of understanding the fact that government experiments or not, many Americans without landlines, without automobiles, and without the spare change to spend on a subscription had responded favorably to the economic turnaround attempts of the first Roosevelt administration. There was a pollster who did get it right that year though, George Gallup, whose Gallup poll more or less invented the modern polling industry. Notably, Gallup stopped its horse race polling of presidential politics in the lead-up to the 2016 presidential election.

The much talked and written about but seldom understood New Deal coalition fell apart in either 1968 or 1980 depending on whom you ask. But the effects of it are still with us. The New Deal was a political success but had very mixed results as a matter of policy. The New Deal did not end the Great Depression; rather the shared experiences and industrial might of the country during the Second World War did. The war also locked in what this writing will call the Third Civic Order. And in the aftermath of the war, with most of the peer competitor economies around the world devastated by it, the United States stood alone as an unchallenged economic power, with only its wartime ally the Soviet Union and the geopolitics of the Cold War challenging overall.

For a decade and a half after the war, there was an American High of broadly shared economic prosperity and some of the most peaceful times of domestic tranquility in terms of American family and community life. This era was not perfect, but it had a lot going for it (in which America does not do well today). While President Eisenhower had two FDR-like landslide victories of his own, Eisenhower was an institutionalist, not an ideologue. That job went to his vice president, Richard Nixon, whose anti-communist credentials were established early and often in his career. Nixon's life and career arc are what bring us to the first book of the "emerging" political writing and analyst tradition that forecasted the future of American politics through a deep dive of past elections, trends, swings against the trend, and looking closely at American geography, demography, and ideology. *The Emerging Republican Majority*, written by Bronx-born and -raised Kevin Phillips, who was a staffer on the 1968 Nixon for President campaign, made a deep splash across the political and media landscape.

To this day, the Phillips book has been incorrectly tied to the "southern strategy" associated with Nixon's '68 and '72 campaigns. But what the intellectual gatekeepers of the new American consensus really disliked was a kind of "right-wing populism"[viii] they saw in Nixon, not unlike how Beltway court and clerisy commentators discuss Congressman Matt Gaetz today. Just as first Wilson's long shadow and Roosevelt's Caesar-esque reign over American politics became the founding myth of the liberal class and progressive administrative state, so, too, did Richard Nixon come to characterize the beginning of its true opposition to this class. "To the cosmopolitan liberals, hating Richard Nixon, congratulating yourself for seeing through Richard Nixon and the elaborate political poker bluffs with which he hooked the sentimental rubes, was becoming part and parcel of a political identity."[ix] Sound familiar?

In truth, neither Phillips nor anyone else was a master of the so-called strategy. The 1972 Republican victory of the once solidly Democratic South was notable because the South had either uniformly or mostly voted against the Republican Party, the party of Lincoln, for a century. What makes the Phillips book notable is merely explaining and analyzing these trends and forecasting from them. It is not just something Phillips did for the American South, but something he did for the entire country. Published in 1969, the projected electoral map was, if anything, underestimating the '72 Nixon landslide (where he won forty-nine out of fifty states, including Minnesota, which has not been won by a Republican presidential candidate since). The only state the doomed McGovern campaign carried was Massachusetts. The university and research hub that Boston had turned into, in addition to the Kennedy machine developed over the prior generation, had made the state the de facto capital of Democratic politics, previously held by New York, which was also for a long time the de facto capital of Republican politics. It was from the Phillips book and the doomed McGovern campaign written off as "acid, amnesty, and abortion" that traumatized a generation of 1960s enthusiasts and the parts of the baby boomer generation involved in Democratic politics and left-wing activism.

Perhaps that's why just over three decades later its retort came from two Democratic campaign consultants and writers (Ruy Teixeira and John Judis) in the form of 2002's *The Emerging Democratic Majority*, which years later received a de facto nickname in the "revenge of the George McGovern" coalition. Just as *The Emerging Republican Majority* developed a connection with the "southern strategy" so, too, would *The Emerging Democratic Majority* develop a connection that became the stuff of myth and legend with the emerging professional-class and progressive coalition (which they called a progressive center coalition) that first was born from some of McGovern's strongest supporters and campaigners. One of those campaigners was a young Bill Clinton of Oxford and Yale Law School.

While this book here owes its namesake and tradition to those two books, its contents are just as equally inspired by two previous refutations of *The Emerging Democratic Majority* and much of subsequent media and political culture of the last few decades: *The Lost Majority* by Sean Trende (2012) and *The Great Revolt: Inside the Populist Coalition Reshaping American Politics* by Salena Zito and Brad Todd (2018). For a deeper analysis into why the "demographic inevitability" coalition or professional-class, pro-globalization coalition fell apart, both of those books in many ways are better precursors to this one than either from the "emerging" tradition.

The Emerging Populist Majority is part refutation of the demographic inevitability thesis that makes two critical mistakes and has had one devastating consequence. Mistake one: it makes a straight-line analysis based around demographics and assumes that prior trends will continue when most of American political and election history shows that "coalitions of everybody" rarely if ever last more than a few cycles. Mistake two: it makes the assumption that the Republican Party had the structural advantage at the time of writing at the beginning of the twentieth century. Just like in the 1950s, dominant parties, coalitions, and cultures are more than just who is up and who is down in the last few election cycles. Whether it is the much talked about but seldom understood "Overton Window of acceptable conversation," or who is by and large in control of and running our major institutions, there is a lot more going on than just the makeup of Congress and the presidency. And finally, the tragic consequence of demographic inevitability theory made famous by *The Emerging Democratic Majority* but made ubiquitous by subsequent media and culture is that it has contributed greatly to the divisiveness of our times and been a toxic cancer on the national conversation. And that divisiveness at best or our unrecognizable country at worst is at least part of the reason why the 2002 emerging thesis is stubbornly refusing to emerge. This writing rejects that prior thesis but does not wholesale reject "demographics as destiny" either. Rather, it seeks to show that the demographic trends are now trending the other direction, without assuming a forever trend.

The Emerging Populist Majority is also part rejection of critical election and realignment theory broadly or at least the most common and known in our popular culture version of it. This writing will show that the critical elections and realignments most talked about throughout much of our culture, media, and a lot of our university social science are not really critical elections or realignments at all by any meaningful and consistent definition of the terms. Instead, we will touch on institutions, the role and rights of citizens in American life and how that interacts with our constitutional republican founding, the generational theory of history advanced by William Strauss and Neil Howe in books like *The Fourth Turning*, and look at some of the best social science from across the pond on America's various ideological groups in our increasingly tribal times—the *Hidden Tribes* report (2018 and subsequent updates) from More in Common (UK).

We will look at the origins of our modern political divide and their roots at the end of the last civic order and the beginning of this one—the progressive administrative state created out of necessity by the Second World War. Furthermore, we will argue that America's next rendezvous with destiny cannot be managed, led by, or won by our current ruling class of political practitioners and their backers. No matter how much they seem in charge today and have directed much of American government and politics since the war and prior, this is the end of the line for them, and the real battle is between a successor ideology that has been taking over the Democratic Party and a coalition of Americans nostalgic for the high, who recognize real and relative decline in our time and are intent on and committed to navigating the country through a long crisis and winning the right to become the dominant party and coalition over the next civic order.

Just as the America Franklin D. Roosevelt presided over featured a changeover in the progressive direction of a bigger and more activist government, the America of the 1930s was also traditional, less connected, more religious, and featured more intact families. The New Deal coalition was made up of seemingly contradictory and downright hostile parts to one another. It was a coalition so large that it included southern white Democrats whose militant political arm was the KKK and also featured newly realigned African Americans, especially those who had gone to the urban north during the Great Migration. This "coalition of everybody" had its policy-making and political heyday from 1932 to 1938 and again after Lyndon Johnson's win in 1964 that lasted for just two years—the last *true* landslide win for a Democratic presidential candidate. What follows will not try to rewrite history or wholly exist in the pantheon of the "emerging" trilogy, but it is inspired and influenced by ideas, theories, and declarations often made null and void by the next election or the march of American time.

Instead, what follows aims to get across four themes. One: that America's present realignment has been both very long and gradual, as most realignments tend to be over time, and it only just passed the 50-yard line recently. Two: America's present dichotomy is not a political left versus a political right but rather between the elite and the people, between a top-down and grass tops versus a Main Street and grass roots. The present dichotomy is more appropriately understood not by race, gender, sexuality, or anything that dominates elite culture but rather understood through social class, not necessarily by economic class (although also correlated and important). Three: that Hispanics and Asians are and will continue to realign into the Republican Party in direct contradiction with the thesis of *The Emerging Democratic Majority*, which its coauthor, Teixeira, has notably since denounced as finished. Newer generations of Americans and recent citizen arrivals want and expect the America that was promised, and the Democrats are not offering that. And finally, four: unlike the previous civic order change, which was over government and its role in American life and the citizen relationship to the Constitution, this one is on a level beyond government and beyond politics itself, and is driven first and foremost by civilizational concerns. Like the previous books of the "emerging" tradition, there is a major political party that stands to benefit—but the *why* is far more interesting than the *who*. While what follows stands to be of interest to Republican partisans and movement conservatives and populists, it is perhaps of even more interest to the many concerned and silent Democrats wondering what happened to their party or to the Democratic partisan wondering why their party cannot achieve a triumphant FDR or LBJ-style victory over the hated Republicans.

CHAPTER 1

OUR LAST "RETURN TO NORMALCY"

The year was 1920, not 2020, and the country was coming out of not just a pandemic, called the Spanish influenza, but also the Great War, the first fundamental break from the Monroe Doctrine in US history. Outgoing president Woodrow Wilson was stricken with a stroke and not seeking a third term, but the truth is his ideas had been rejected as well. The country was returning to normalcy. The Democratic Party was in shambles, and the 1920 presidential election, the first election where women in all US states could vote, began to reveal a major party that was about to be replaced by a third party. The same thing had happened to the Whigs seven decades prior. The "return to normalcy" of 1920 was a rejection of Wilsonism, a rejection of going beyond the Constitution as an inconvenience and an outdated document as Wilson had suggested in his writings and had shown throughout his presidency, and a rejection of outcomes related to both the war, the influenza, and the economic turmoil that results from both happening in a succession of years.

The Democratic Party looked like it was near extinction throughout the 1920s, and in some states it was. However, it still maintained, with few exceptions, the solid South that the party had held since the end of Reconstruction. The only exception was the election of Warren Harding and his vice president, Calvin Coolidge, in 1920. While Harding was at the top of the ticket for the election that won states in every region of the country and won by 26 percent in the popular vote, Coolidge, because of Harding's death a few years later, became more associated with the Roaring Twenties. Some scholars consider the decade the zenith of American conservatism. That would be incorrect. Others write it off as an era of runaway capitalism. This is also incorrect and narrow. The Republican Party that presided over the 1920s wasn't just a return to normalcy for its dominant position in American politics, it was also a return to normalcy, especially under Calvin Coolidge, with the political alignment that was hard-fought and -won first by William McKinley around two key issues: currency and tariffs.

In 1896 prior to William McKinley's election, the preceding two decades of American politics looked very similar to our previous two decades. Today, we have had an information age tech revolution, and the downstream societal effects of that have tremendously impacted American politics. In the final quarter of the nineteenth century, it was the American version of the Industrial Revolution that created such turmoil. From the end of Reconstruction in 1876—an election where the Republican candidate, Rutherford B. Hayes, lost by 3 percent of the popular vote but won the Electoral College by one vote, and whose victory was secured through a promise to pull federal troops out of the former Confederate United States, effectively ending a decade of postwar reconstruction— until William McKinley's triumph in 1896, US presidential elections were incredibly close affairs. In that twenty-year span all but one (1896) were nearly fifty-fifty elections, just like in our prior twenty-year span since 2000 all but one (2008) have been close, nearly fifty-fifty elections. Both involved a split popular-electoral vote; in fact, in each twenty-year span it happened twice. In the nineteenth century it happened in the aforementioned 1876 and also 1888 presidential elections, and in the first two decades of the twenty-first century it has happened in 2000 and 2016. There are many other similarities between these two eras and a few more that we could very well see in the coming decade. Historians refer to the era of 1873 (when one economic crisis hit) to either 1879 or 1896 (just after another panic hit), depending on the metrics used, as the Long Depression.[x] The Long Depression is analogous to the economic conditions felt by middle- and working-class Americans the past two decades, with the exception of 2017 to 2019, when the bottom 60 percent grew at a faster rate than the top 1 percent for the first time in decades.

McKinley's victory in 1896 is considered by many political historians, especially the subscribers to "party systems" theory, which we will not subscribe to here, to be a realignment election. And it absolutely was in the sense twenty years of close elections stopped and were followed by sixteen years of political stability with a dominant Republican Party reestablishing its post–Civil War position. Technological change and economic conditions brought forth the currency and tariff issues that made McKinley an ideal candidate for the time. McKinley was pro-tariff and pro–sound currency, whereas his Democratic opponent—the western prairie populist William Jennings Bryan, who had run in fusion with the latest third-party challenge from the People's Party (commonly known as the populists), who won 8.5 percent of the vote and five western states in 1892—had split his coalition on the currency issue as a free silver and free trade candidate. In this sense many Americans today are confused on just what populism is. Some say it is defined by what it is against, and others try to draw straight lines from the populism of yesterday to the populism of today. The history of anti-populism, always stemming from elites, has also always been with us as long as populism has. Dr. Victor Davis Hanson writing for the Hoover Institution made mention of "Dueling Populisms," which originated in classical times, one redistributionist and tied to the politics of urban mobs, and the other stemming from the conservative and often rural quarters of the middle classes.[xi] It is the latter form of populism that gets disparaged in the liberal press today, while the former is celebrated.

In *The People, No*, Thomas Frank commented that from the very beginning populism has had two meanings—one as its proponents understood it, meaning a movement in which ordinary citizens demanded democratic *economic* reforms, and then the populism as its enemies characterized it: a dangerous movement of groundless resentment in which demagogues led the disreputable.[xii]

The dictionary definition of populism is "support for the concerns of ordinary people." That McKinley, a Republican affiliated with the party of Lincoln who drew support from both business and labor, and Bryan, affiliated with concerns of western populists of the nineteenth century, would find themselves on opposite sides of the term today gets to the central paradox of populism. It is not a political ideology in the same way traditional conservatism, liberalism, and progressivism are, but rather it can be affiliated and associated with any of those depending on the concerns, issues, and demands of the day. It is a flexible ideology that is dependent on events and the response to those events by elected leaders and political parties. The Democratic Party of Bryan and later Franklin Roosevelt had no monopoly on populism just as the Republican Party of Theodore Roosevelt had no monopoly on progressivism during the progressive era when both major parties laid claim to it.

While McKinley's victories were indeed electoral triumphs, they fall short of the realignment claimed by historians. McKinley was very strong electorally and appealed to a wide variety of people, but his 4 percent and 6 percent (in 1900) victories are overshadowed by Theodore Roosevelt's landslide win of 19 percent; Harding's landslide "return to normalcy" victory in which normalcy won by more than it ever had, 26 percent; Coolidge's 25 percent victory; and finally Hoover's 17.5 percent victory. William H. Taft, the outgoing president's (Theodore Roosevelt) chosen successor and good friend, had a more humble 8.5 percent victory, which would exceed every victory of our modern era today. However, McKinley, assassinated in the first year of his second term, should get great credit for running in many ways the first sophisticated and modern campaign, closing the chapter on the nineteenth century and welcoming America into the twentieth century both politically, economically, and socially. America was a burgeoning economic superpower that was about to become a military power over the coming decades, and it was because of that military strength and victories that we became an accidental superpower abroad and created a new civic order at home from our shared wartime experiences.

One can see just after the panic of 1893, which affected every sector of the American economy, that a strengthened political coalition was born thirty-eight years before it would sweep that coalition out of power. The Republican sweep of 1894, winning 116 House seats and five Senate seats, is to this day the largest midterm wipeout on record. Democrats lost seats in their southern strongholds of Alabama, Texas, Tennessee, and North Carolina. In these areas, just as Democrats and Populists endorsed the same candidates in the West, Republicans and Populists endorsed the same candidate in the South. While not eventually successful in overturning one of the two major parties, this fusion ballot strategy of the Populists of the 1890s was the last viable and feasible third-party attempt that wasn't just splitting up the favored or dominant party and spoiling the election. Any third-party attempt today should look to the Populists and understand that in our system, only by being against the established party in a given jurisdiction can you actually break up either the two-party monopoly or the more realistic one-party monopoly in the many areas where there is no effective political competition. As this book will show, this strategy looks less and less viable as the years go by, and the populist and conservative fusion united by patriotism and commitment to the founding and the American republic gets solidified.

The 1894 map and later victories by Harding, Coolidge, and Hoover look very, very similar and stable. Wilson's eight years via the wrong type of third-party challenge, taken up by one of our best presidents in American history in his worst political mistake, albeit a spirited one, split the Republican coalition and foisted Woodrow Wilson onto the country—a proto-civic order president. These years are seldom understood well anymore because the media, cultural, and political system of today has little incentive to make them understood, but instead pushes a narrative that reflects the vision of America they want people to see and believe, not unlike the propaganda a York would push to support their claim to the Plantagenet dynasty against a Lancaster and vice versa. Wilson serves as precursor and articulator of the new civic order, largely rejected in his own time, but more influential than the presidents around him, winning both elections while never once receiving a majority percentage of the popular vote. While mostly unsuccessful politically in his day, a recent biography by A. Scott Berg sums it up best: "In one decade after another, one sees that the silhouette of history that spreads across the capital city of the United States of America is not just that of its national cathedral but increasingly that of the President who is buried therein. It is the lengthening shadow of Wilson."[xiii]

It is also important to understand the throughline starting with Wilson that will help describe the renewed fervor of today's interventionists—of the nature of progressivism and its zest for war: "Progressive intellectuals' view of war as a golden opportunity for replacing traditional American individual economic and social decision-making processes with collectivist control...."[xiv] When one looks at twentieth-century American history and entrances and exits from major wars, you see a progressive Democrat in Wilson entering war, Harry Truman entering war, and a Republican Eisenhower exiting it; a progressive Democrat Lyndon Johnson entering and escalating to war, and a Republican Nixon exiting it. This pattern was decidedly broken with the end of the Cold War and entered a more bipartisan consensus toward a volunteer and professional force–backed war machine. Yet the latent power in war-making powers remains central to the progressive project and is historically scrutinized by the traditionally conservative project; despite the patriotism and tendency in culture for one side to exalt the veteran and military service member far more often, this feature should not mistake the relationship between American political philosophy strains and their coalitional support and likelihood toward war.

While a stable political map finally emerged in 1894 and 1896 to support the Republican Union civic order led by the party of Lincoln (characterized first by Midwest and Northeast Yankeedom but then by solidifying a hold on the western states through McKinley's defeat of the populist and free silver challenge) and held for many decades to come, there were also great changes taking place in the country, most notably around immigration rates. This again bears resemblance to our own times over the past few decades. During the very successful six years of the Coolidge presidency, there were two political successes that he and Congress ushered forth: first, the rollback of tax and spending World War I policies that reduced the new income tax to very low rates, and second, an immigration law that lasted for four and a half decades and contributed greatly to helping the great American mixture become Americanized and simmer to both a more perfect union and more tightly knit patchwork quilt (the more accurate metaphor). In another portion of Third Civic Order propaganda, more immigration favored the nonruling party, the Democrats. There is some truth to it, like many things, but it's also a very inaccurate picture of the times.

In the late nineteenth and early twentieth centuries, it's more accurate to say that the political parties alternated new arrival and immigrant populations in terms of voting patterns and outreach, and that secondly, this outreach was highly region-specific. In Minnesota—which neighbors Wisconsin, the founding place of the Republican Party (and therefore Second Civic Order)—the state was settled by Union Civil War veterans and predominantly Scandinavian immigrants. And those immigrants were as diehard Republican as the veterans were. Before favoring Franklin D. Roosevelt in 1932, Minnesota had only once given its electoral votes to anyone other than the Republican Party standard-bearer: to FDR's cousin Theodore Roosevelt's "Bull Moose" third-party run in 1912. Throughout its early history, immigrants outnumbered settlers, especially in the Greater Minnesota regions of the state. In New York City, however, the dominant party from the days of Tammany Hall up through today has been always the Democratic Party. The city voted against Abraham Lincoln and against Donald Trump. While individual boroughs have at times given their votes to the Republican candidate, it has been one of the most consistent Democratic voting regions of the country, the New Netherlands "free" trading post if you will, just as much as Upstate New York has been one of the most consistent Republican voting regions, especially outside its major cities. Upstate larger cities, however, did emulate the Tammany Hall machine politics of the downstate largest city in America. Machine politics came first, and immigrant politics was second and the most clear and identifiable recruitment depot to maintain political power and control and operate the transactional spoils system that follows. To this very day—with considerable assistance from the DC metro, San Francisco, and Los Angeles—identity politics in America was born from and is beholden to machine politics, either through the direct party apparatus or affiliated partner organizations. Yet still in this era, many big cities had Republican mayors,[xv] and it was not until 1932 that Democrats won a majority in New York state or carried Illinois.

Another trend started with McKinley's reinforcement of the Second Civic Order was a Republican tradition and preference of quick, clear, and decisive wars[2] with America's entrance into the Spanish-American War. Although McKinley was very mixed on this conflict, its quick victory helped catapult the next Republican president, Theodore Roosevelt, first to the New York governor's seat and two years later to the presidency in 1901.

Roosevelt, like Coolidge later on, essentially got two terms. Both refused to run for a third in keeping with the example of George Washington. Washington, Jefferson, Lincoln, and later Theodore Roosevelt himself became the enduring spirit of the Republican vision of what the United States of America and our founding charters of freedom are understood as and symbolized as at Mount Rushmore, authorized to be built under the Coolidge administration. Many admirers of Coolidge wanted his

---

[2] This tradition was decidedly broken under President George W. Bush with Iraq and Afghanistan. He took the country to war like a Democrat would and indeed chastised Democrats as "betraying the party of Franklin Roosevelt and Harry Truman" once his administration's policy toward Iraq underwent significant criticism.

visage and features on Mount Rushmore alongside Washington, Jefferson, Lincoln, and Roosevelt, but "silent Cal" was humble until the end and perhaps to a fault for his overall legacy. Coolidge was forgotten and often lambasted in later years but has recently undergone a well-deserved reevaluation by historians like Amity Shlaes.[xvi]

Coolidge is perhaps the best president who has undergone severe criticism, mostly by lazy retrospective and little-read armchair historians and politicos who see the Third Civic Order as a natural progression of American life and view history in a linear onward and upward trajectory. Coolidge has become synonymous with the economic troubles that followed his presidency but which took hold under his successor, Herbert Hoover. In truth, Coolidge called Hoover a "wonder boy" who tinkered too much. Coolidge had seen the coming collapse of 1929 and was increasingly nervous about it in his final year. He felt the economy was too overheated, and a correction was in store. Hoover, like Roosevelt who followed him, tinkered with the economy far more than Coolidge ever would have—yet in the revisionist history of the Third Civic Order, all blame must be set on the Yorks if you're a Lancaster or all blame on the Lancasters if you're a York.

In the county-by-county map below, one can see just how similar to the 1894 midterm Republican sweep the 1920 results were, a trend that continued with the exception of one state in 1924 (Wisconsin) and one in 1928 (Massachusetts). In these years the Democratic Party looked like a rump party and was in danger of being replaced by a third party just as the Republicans had replaced the Whigs and their last-ditch attempt to remain a second party in the system through their 1856 fusion with the Know-Nothings, an anti-immigrant party that was quite strong in New York City and against the ruling Tammany Hall Democratic machine. This either/or nature and trade-off feature of arriving groups of Americans that sort into in-group/out-group is nothing new in American politics but rather is a constant. For instance, the Anglo-Saxon whites were the foundation of three different political parties: the Federalists, Whigs, and Republicans.[xvii]

The Irish arrived and joined the Democratic Party, while the Italians generally joined the Republican Party. Puerto Ricans became Democrats, and Cubans both at first and now once again became Republicans and so forth.[xviii] This pattern of American politics does not lend itself well to the type of coalition Democrats seek to build today, focused so intently on race and trying to fashion a new melting pot, when in reality the breakdown over time more resembles sorting through ethnicity and nationality over race and a patchwork quilt or a mosaic as we'll see throughout.

Notable in the 1924 results though were just how strong La Follette's numbers were out in the northern west. Despite McKinley's triumph and expansion a generation prior, there was still a great hunger and popularity to an anti-eastern establishment candidate, then conservative and affiliated with Coolidge, the "tops" if you will. It was a strength that benefited directly from the constitutional rules themselves, the founders' fear of rural and smaller town populations being dominated by larger states and concentrated populations while under the same union. Like many electoral signals we'll see throughout, it was a precursor of things to come.

1920

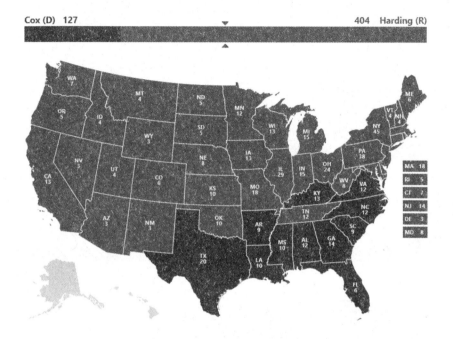

Cox (D)   127   404   Harding (R)

Presidential Election	Rep. Electoral Votes (Dem., Third Party)	Rep. Popular Vote	Dem. Popular Vote
1920	404 (127)	60.4	34.1
1924	382 (136, 13[3])	54.0	28.8
1928	444 (87)	58.2	40.8
1932	59 (472)	39.6	57.4
1936	8 (523)	36.5	60.8

The course of the changeover electorally that disempowered one civic order and began to chart the course of another can be seen over sixteen

---

[3] Wisconsin Republican senator and third-party Progressive Party nominee Robert La Follette received thirteen electoral votes (winning his home state as a favorite son) and received 16.6 percent of the popular vote, a margin that has since only been exceeded by a third-party or independent candidate one time, in 1992 by Ross Perot, who received 18.9 percent of the vote.

years and five elections above, yet one understands why Cole Porter and company would in the mid-1930s still associate the Republican Party with "the top." And this Republican-led civic order was one of a coalitional majority that was a pro-tariff party. The Grand Old Party now held nine out of ten seats outside the South, a total of 302 seats, nearly 70 percent of the House of Representatives[xix] where budgeting and spending bills start. The results of the first postwar election were a smashing success for "normalcy," a far bigger endorsement than the normalcy election of 2020 one hundred years later.

1924

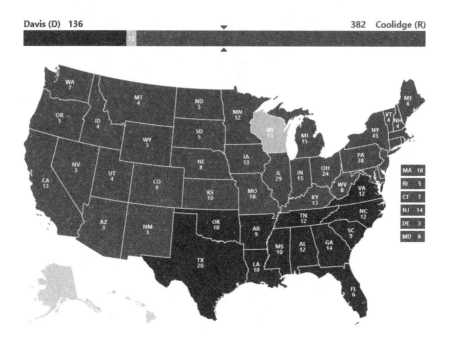

The balance of power was at its low point. This is what happens when the oppositional party reaches noncompetitiveness; a third party or new regional parties rise up in opposition to the opposition, promising a better argument and better representation of interests. The Coolidge-led party was not just a tax-cut party as his detractors and historical revisionists of the next civic order would allege; rather it was, as Amity Shlaes put it, a "devotion to service that struck people. His ideas and the culture were in harmony."[xx]

The Democratic Party nomination in 1924 went to a Wall Street banker at J. P. Morgan, John W. Davis; but at first it looked like William McAdoo— Wilson's treasury secretary and son-in-law, and the preferred candidate of the Ku Klux Klan wing of the Democratic Party—would emerge.

La Follette, an Independent Progressive and Republican, held his own convention for a third-party run. The Progressives went further than Roosevelt's Bull Moose run and presidency, and now free from the larger party, went forth with a platform that included public ownership of railroads, higher taxes for the rich, and the abolition of interventions in labor disputes of the kind President Harding had used.[xxi] Even with the third-party breakaway, Coolidge still received 54 percent of the vote and beat the Democratic vote by over 25 percent. This was less than Harding in 1920 but still impressively high given the break from both the farm bloc and that independent third-party run, which historically tends to (and in this case actually did) break off from the dominant and incumbent party in the system. Harry Truman would face a similar two-bloc and party breakaway twenty-four years later and not fare nearly as well on the way to his upset victory. After Coolidge was reelected, a budget-responsible America saw its stock market rise upward to many gains that were very real in the next half-decade.

1928

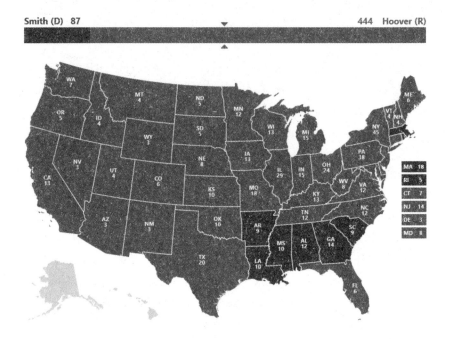

Smith (D) 87   444 Hoover (R)

Few could have predicted the 1932 victor would have been the running mate on a ticket that twelve years earlier in the "return to normalcy" election of 1920 received just 34 percent of the popular vote and won just 127 electoral votes, all of them in the South. The election results of 1928 did not show much of any dent in the Republican Union civic order either. If anything it was strengthened throughout the decade. Hoover, a self-made man, an engineer, and considered the ideal president for an economic crisis, distinguished himself by running food relief during the Great War and had been a cabinet member for both Harding and Coolidge. While Hoover was instinctively distrusted philosophically by Coolidge, there was no doubting the future stability of the coalition of the dominant party in the civic order in 1928, winning over 58 percent of the popular vote and 444 electoral votes.

The Democratic candidate, Al Smith, in political defeat is often credited as a precursor to what FDR was able to achieve in political victory. This is due to his New York City status—which will always shine brightly across the population and land, as it is a top media market and de facto cultural and actual financial capital of America and indeed the world in many respects—and due to his immigrant and Catholic heritage. Thirty-two years later, Catholic John F. Kennedy would achieve the victory first trailblazed by Smith. Outside of these comparisons though, Al Smith makes little sense as a proto- or precursor to FDR. One, his politics were more conservative than the Democratic Party became over the next decade or two (at least in the Northeast) and two, he would go on to be a harsh critic and denounce much of the New Deal throughout the 1930s. As mentioned, the fusion of machine and immigrant identity politics had been true in northern cities for some time, and while Smith achieved greater margins in this respect, viewing his coalition as a precursor to FDR's is dubious and makes little ideological sense. The more accurate ideological precursor to FDR, and by extension what becomes the Third Civic Order, is in fact Woodrow Wilson's combination of extra-constitutional behavior; increased global involvement, especially using the military abroad; and his use of culture and identity as a wedge between a united population and substituting a means and material measure of equality for a political and rights-given one.

What was first articulated by Woodrow Wilson in power, though he failed miserably by the end of his presidency, was perfected politically through President Franklin Roosevelt, but first he needed what all successful candidates and political coalitions need—a major event, crisis, and opportunity. To this day, apart from his World War II leadership, FDR's greatest successes were political successes as leader of his party and its growing coalition. Roosevelt felt himself the true heir of his cousin Theodore's political legacy rather than Theodore's son Theodore Roosevelt III. Roosevelt III narrowly lost the New York governor's race to Al Smith in 1924, a job later won in 1928 narrowly by Franklin Roosevelt. Theodore III had lost in a good Republican year, and Franklin had won in a bad Democratic year (which were most of the years of the 1920s). In those two narrow elections for New York governor, back in an era when most New York elections were much closer regardless of political party, the state that had come to dominate American politics dominated it in part because it was not just a large state but rather a large state that was also up for grabs in election after election and trended far closer to the national outcome, just as Florida does today.

Franklin Roosevelt, like Barack Obama would later do in 2008, campaigned as a chameleon in 1932 where he was everything at once to everyone. Roosevelt campaigned on a "balanced budget" and many other conservative talking points that would be more associated with Calvin Coolidge or Al Smith than incumbent President Herbert Hoover. Yet, he also promised an intense program of experimentation until things improved. Roosevelt had the confidence of a patrician and with grades more in line with Joe Biden. He also helped the country's electoral system enter a new age of vicious partisan attacks, and his attacks got returned not by Hoover, who campaigned in line with his predecessors and tried to stay above the fray, but by surrogates and the era's equivalence of influencers. The attacks would get returned from both the right and the left: by the Father Coughlins and Huey Longs of the world and by the industrialists or, as Franklin Roosevelt would later call them, the economic royalists.

What truly happened in those years after the Great Crash of 1929 and the early years of the Depression that followed the "return to normalcy" and Roaring Twenties was not just the beginning of the end of one civic order, for that was never known until years later, but rather a rare instance in American life where the ruling social and political elite got caught off guard. They had backed the wrong horse and put their money in the wrong place. On one hand, Roosevelt set off to save capitalism in America; on the other hand, he also forced the then-conservative northeastern establishment into a rearguard action, the same rearguard action the liberal and progressive establishment of the Northeast is slowly being forced into today. Prior to FDR in 1930, where the Democratic Party had its first solid midterm gains in years, picking up the Senate and nearly the House, and then just prior to World War II in 1938 when Republicans in combination with anti–New Deal Democrats forged a new congressional coalition to curb the power of Roosevelt and the presidency itself after an attempted court-packing scheme and double-dip recession, a closer look at the 1930s does not reveal an easy and solidified new coalition but rather a country teetering on the edge politically like much of the world at the time. The years of '33 to '38 were an era of active governance, given a thumbs-up approval by the electorate in 1936 especially in the greatest victory the Democrats have ever had (along with 1964), but by the '38 midterms there were already signals that it was time to slow down before the war, another big crisis and event, had interrupted the normal course of what is trending and swinging, and what is emerging and what is a return to normal.

1932

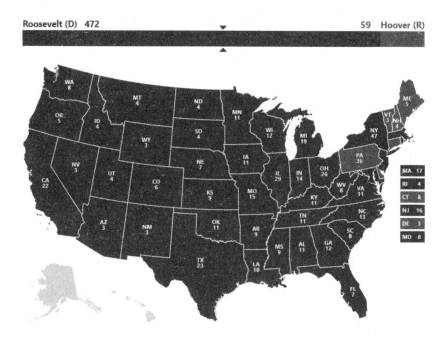

The presidential election results by county of 1932 and to a lesser extent, 1936, show a northeastern establishment being pushed into a rear-guard action.

1936

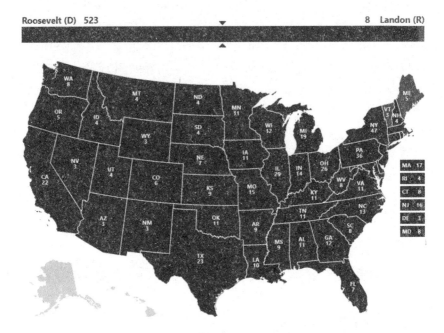

Roosevelt (D) 523   8 Landon (R)

House of Representatives Vote under the "Return to Normalcy" Second Civic Order

Year	Rep. Vote Share (%)	Dem. Vote Share (%)	Rep. Seats	Dem. Seats	Trend
1920 (Harding)	58.82	35.38	303 (+63)	131 (-61)	Solid Republican
1922 (Harding)	51.86	44.64	225 (-77)	207 (+76)	Lean Republican
1924 (Coolidge)	56.06	40.22	247 (+22)	183 (-24)	Solid Republican
1926 (Coolidge)	57.11	40.09	238 (-9)	194 (+11)	Solid Republican
1928 (Hoover)	56.73	41.97	270 (+32)	164 (-30)	Solid Republican
1930 (Hoover)	53.04	44.50	218 (-52)	216 (+52)[4]	Lean Republican

---

[4] The 1930 Democratic gains were in West Virginia, Kentucky, Ohio, Indiana, and Missouri, much like the recent populist-conservative fusion gains of the "Emerging Populist Majority" in the last decade or so.

Beyond looking at presidential elections, where personalities come into play much more, it is most helpful to look at the House vote and not the Senate vote when assessing party strength and trends. The decade of the 1930s shows the growing rural strength of the Democratic Party and the constitutional advantages the founders had set up. Any party that moves too far away from the small town and rural areas of the country and performs poorly yet continues onward does so at their own peril.

House of Representatives Vote under the First Decade of the *Would-Be* Third Civic Order

Year	Rep. Vote Share (%)	Dem. Vote Share (%)	Rep. Seats	Dem. Seats	Trend
1932 (FDR)	42.08	54.48	117 (-101)	313 (+97)	Solid Democratic
1934 (FDR)	41.29	53.92	103 (-14)	322 (+9)	Solid Democratic
1936 (FDR)	39.67	55.93	88 (-15)	334 (+12)	Solid Democratic
1938 (FDR)[5]	47.5	48.7	169 (+81)	262 (-72)	Toss-Up
1940 (FDR)	45.6	51.4	162 (-7)	267 (+5)	Lean Democratic
1942 (FDR)	50.8	47.0	209 (+47)	222 (-45)	Lean Republican

Just as it had since the Civil War, the heart of the Republican Party in these years revolved around New York and Ohio. No Republican has won the presidency without winning the state of Ohio. The Republican Party had picked up eighty-one seats in the House in the 1938 midterms, a sign

---

[5] After the 1936 election, FDR overreached with court-packing and the like, the country went into a double-dip recession, and politically he and Democrats moved to begin to slowly purge the party of southern Democrats. Like today, they sought to build a progressive party in a country that has *rarely*, if *ever*, *truly* had a progressive majority. For progressivism to work, it needs to be populist; it needs to be patriotic rather than elitist liberal and leftist. From 1938 to 1964 the Conservative Coalition rose in earnest to dominate Congress after this attempt by Roosevelt, inspired by Wilson more than Theodore Roosevelt, to lock in a one-party state. In time, the court-packing proved unnecessary anyway as a majority of the court soon became FDR-appointed justices.

of regaining its lost rural and traditional small-town Heartland and western strength. Much of these same areas resisted or were wary of the possibility of the first third-term presidency in American history. The election of 1940 was between two internationalists, President Roosevelt and Wendell Willkie, who was briefly considered a favorite in the summer before being more heavily scrutinized and fading in the fall. Within five years, both President Roosevelt and Willkie would be dead. Another candidate, the closest leader to a conservative standard-bearer, President and Supreme Court Chief Justice William H. Taft's son Robert Taft, senator of Ohio, sought and was denied the Republican nomination in 1940, just as he would be in 1944, 1948, and 1952 as well. In many respects Taft embodied the Heartland conservative and isolationist sensibility: isolationist in peace, willing to fight in war. Taft was a critic of both Japanese American internment camps that were set up during the war and also the Nuremberg trials, which he considered ex post facto law enforced by the victors. The victory that Taft and the conservative movement sought just before the war that prioritized national sovereignty and the Monroe Doctrine over the internationalism of Wilson and later Roosevelt, and most American politicians after, would never get its day in front of the electorate, but the sentiment of it remained powerful in the nation's Heartland and interior that sent so many of its sons to war.

In so many ways World War II changed the course for America and the world. And now eighty years on, that change is aging out more and more as we'll discuss in the next chapter. World War II not only got the country out of the Great Depression and into the booming times associated with the American High, but it is also the real foundational crisis of the Third Civic Order, not the crash of 1929, subsequent activist government of either Hoover or Roosevelt, or the Great Depression era generally, although it was very much part of the crisis era that finished off the late Second Civic Order.

Indeed, the "return to normalcy" was a roaring decade romanticized in literature by lost generation writers such as F. Scott Fitzgerald and that featured a calm before the storm not equaled for another three decades until the pastoral and family-focused 1950s. What was then the Roaring Twenties is now the not-so-roaring twenties in the twenty-first century. But the analogy to a return to normalcy was still made just after a pandemic and dropped by an American winning coalition far weaker and increasingly tattered and frayed compared to that one.

Thus, one of the central themes of this book comes into the fray. The return to normalcy that wasn't particularly wanted at all or, to the extent that it was, was not received by the electorate, and was not given and offered after victory by the ruling establishment elite.

Much has been made in Third Civic Order literature of the myth of the "great party switch" of the southern United States. In truth, only two Republican presidents have ever been dependent on the South to win the White House: George W. Bush and to a lesser extent Donald Trump. Today, the Midwest is now again the most Republican voting region in the country over the South when it passed it last year (2021). In contrast, every Democratic president after the Civil War until FDR was dependent on the South to become president. FDR's strongest base of support was in the South, and after the peak of early Third Civic Order governance from the dominant party—the Democratic Party—John F. Kennedy, Jimmy Carter, and Bill Clinton were dependent on the South to become president. Party affiliation in the South was still Democratic well into the 1990s. By and large, this is a club northern liberals have long liked to use to first exert their moral superiority over the South and then in a partisan way do it over Republicans. But the truth is that the heart and birth of the Republican Party was in the Midwest; it reached its zenith with a Yankeedom (Northeast and Midwest) and western coalition, and has only won the presidency with southern electoral votes as its critical margin to put it over 270 one-fourth as many times as the ruling party of the Third Civic Order has. In the midwestern zeitgeist state of Kansas, where Dorothy and Clark Kent hailed from, and as Thomas Frank points out: "Republicanism has always been central to the state's identity...it has not sent a Democrat to the U.S. Senate since 1932,"[xxii] and furthermore it is culturally much more similar to Minnesota than it is to Alabama.

The switch theory was always bonkers and negatively partisan though, because no one alive then is alive and voting now. In American life especially, people move in and out of regions, and new voters and aspirants come in. And in American life—like FDR's comeback triumph in 1932, twelve years after losing in a landslide as the Democratic vice presidential candidate and eleven years after contracting polio, which confined him to a wheelchair for the rest of his life—there are always second acts and even sometimes third acts. This, too, is true and extends to American politics.

What has really switched throughout the now late Third Civic Order is what was once populist Democrats and progressive Republicans a century or so ago are now progressive Democrats and populist Republicans.

More on that change in the next chapter, and how both of our last two presidents, Barack Obama and Donald Trump, are a version of Woodrow Wilson—a proto-civic order president and pre-50-yard line marker, which we'll call the "normalcy" or "return to normalcy" marker: the point at which we know we're descending from one civic order and entering another in an emerging, aligning, resorting, and realigning majority.

CHAPTER 2

THIRD CIVIC ORDER (1940 TO PRESENT)

What is this civic order that keeps being mentioned? What is the Third Civic Order? What were the first two? How long until the fourth, if any at all? Intellectually and on a big-picture basis, this forms the background of much of what will be discussed here, yet for purposes of chronology and the larger emerging populist majority thesis, *only* this chapter will dive in on what civic orders are.

They are defined by three features: One, constitutional structure and the citizen and political systems relationship to and treatment of the constitution; two, as an epoch that literally mirrors America's history since the American Revolution. Think of it as the way you might break up and teach a high school or middle school history class over the course of a year— from the revolution to the Civil War, from the Civil War to World War II, and finally the "modern" postwar era. And three, it closely mirrors a long human lifespan and accounts for four living generations. In this manner, unlike the party systems, regime, and other theories of realignment, civic order thinking has more in common with Strauss and Howe's generational theory of history than it does with any political or social science.

Consider the constitutional structure. Post-founding documents,[6] the country had a dominant ruling order and framework that for our purposes here we're going to characterize as Jeffersonian democracy. The first three administrations after the ratification of the Constitution, necessary after the failures of the Articles of Confederation between the victorious colonial states and the British Empire, were decidedly nonpartisan, and at the end of Washington's second term, a term he reluctantly took on before retiring for good, he warned against factionalism and partisanship.

The third administration, that of the second US president, John Adams, warned against it, too, and mentioned that an equally contentious partisanship of two major blocs would ruin the tenets of the fledgling American Republic. Benjamin Franklin, when asked by a curious onlooker after the Constitution was forged what form of government we had, he replied, "We have a republic, if you can keep it." The preamble of the Constitution laid down its intentions clearly: "In order to form a more perfect union." This founding period and early days spent after the American crisis is the First Civic Order, an order that became best represented by Thomas Jefferson's two terms and the political organization that formed around him whether he wished for it or not, and the developments out of those years. While John Adams warned against two equally potent sides and was likely correct that it would have split the young republic apart like so many civil wars and conflicts had in world history, what saved the young republic from this fate is the First Civic Order, which we'll call Jeffersonian democracy. Jefferson and Adams fought two closely contested elections to succeed General Washington, with Adams winning the first, Jefferson the second. The early factional battle between the Jeffersonian Democratic-Republicans and the Federalist Party of Adams and Hamilton was over before it got started, with the Federalists vanquished as a political

---

6   "Founding documents" refers to the Declaration of Independence, the US Constitution, and the first ten amendments to the Constitution, the Bill of Rights. See the *Federalist Papers* for the most important insight into this era and rationale for why the founders saw fit to make the United States of America a federalist system (as opposed to unitary or confederate) and republican form of government (as opposed to a more direct form of democracy).

force, Adams being the young republic's first one-term president, and Hamilton shot dead in a duel by Vice President Aaron Burr. Starting in 1804 there were no competitive presidential elections, and a de facto Virginian succession took place with two terms of Jefferson to Madison to Monroe. Twenty-four years of a one-party state called the "Era of Good Feelings" that even when broken, was broken by an internal party split over the election of Andrew Jackson over another one-term presidency of the Adams family, John Quincy Adams, the son of the second president. Up until the last decade or so, the Democratic Party traced their founding back to Thomas Jefferson and Andrew Jackson and would host Jefferson-Jackson dinners alongside the Republicans' Lincoln dinners.

Just as Jeffersonian democracy is the First Civic Order, the next unit in history class that covers the sectional crisis of the Civil War, the capital R, Republican Union, civic order makes up the second.

The Second Civic Order is the Civil War amendments and reconciliation of the compromised nature of our founding itself, especially the compromise between the states to create the Constitution and the conflict with the revolutionary and egalitarian natural rights spirit of the Declaration of Independence. This civic order, like the first, was won with blood, toil, tears, and carnage, but we emerged a better nation, "a more perfect union." The Gettysburg Address by the first Republican president, Abraham Lincoln, directly tied the effort that the nation was engaged in, that the House was divided over, that left countless thousands of dead on the battlefield, to the founding of the nation itself. When it was all said and done, he, too, would give his life for the establishment of this Second Civic Order. Each civic order reestablishes order from chaos just as countries have done throughout history as a way of self-preservation on one hand and out of a sense of shared national purpose and destiny on the other. The work of one civic order starts at the beginning and infancy of a long American life, and it begins to fade away at the end of that life—giving way to those who are better equipped to grapple with and understand the work left undone or poorly done, or conditions that did not yet exist during the establishment of the previous civic order. The long lifespan represents the "social time."

Civic orders need not be analyzed by political party strength, subtle realignments, or trends and swings that are always taking place as events happen and party coalitions react to those events and make choices that create new allies and alienate old ones. Civic orders are assumption-based and mini-foundational in and of themselves. It is the explanation for why today's Democratic coalition and their media allies assume they are forever entitled to rule and consider opposition only acceptable when it is in the rearview mirror or manufactured opposition. Today's Democratic Party and yesterday's Republican Party in many ways were affiliated with the ruling Third Civic Order.

The postwar American life and accidental superpower status brought on by the war is the Third Civic Order, or the "progressive civic order," of the administrative state, first conceived in power during the Progressive Era by Woodrow Wilson and to some extent in his own way also by Theodore Roosevelt—never fully a *new* civic order until well into the Franklin Roosevelt presidency and not during the New Deal either but rather World War II. World War II is the actual crisis. While civic orders often split over political and economic issues, they are far more united around social, cultural, and narrative issues. They may differ on tax rates, but their sense of civilization, civil society, and civics has great continuity. For instance, America prospered under Republican rule throughout the Gilded Age even though Republicans themselves were split between an eastern and a western branch, just as the prior Democrat-led civic order was split between North and South. Easterners preferred high tariff walls that protected manufacturing from foreign competition while Midwesterners—beholden to the Easterners for credit to buy machinery and finance mortgages—wanted free trade. Years later, the issues and emphasis would change. As eastern entrepreneurs became an eastern establishment, they came to prefer a settled economic order to a wide-open one; as America became an equal partner with Europe, the eastern business titans became free-trade internationalists while Republicans in the Heartland were protectionist, isolationist, and more laissez-faire.[xxiii]

Just as Woodrow Wilson was a proto–civic order leader, our upcoming Fourth Civic Order leaders have already emerged and already been president. As with Wilson, they do not emerge to lead their respective sides but to *articulate* the options of where we go from here. Just as Wilson was two decades dead by the time the country began living in his intellectual shadow and articulation, we currently exist in an emerging shadow of already articulated visions of the future.

One is of the "fundamental transformation" of America that came to be represented first by the presidency of Barack Obama and its attempted acceleration by the Biden administration, and the other is the "Make America Great Again" of Donald Trump, a slogan first used by Ronald Reagan, and America First, a slogan that first existed in common usage just prior to the final transition into the Third Civic Order of the *progressive* administrative state.

Just as the "return to normalcy" establishment elite of the 1920s was affiliated with the established civic order, that was then conservative and Republican, so, too, is our recent "return to normalcy" establishment elite of the 2020s affiliated with the established civic order, but today's establishment is a progressive center that assumes a forever legitimacy and right to rule. The "fundamental transformation" is not the progressive liberal center holding but rather a successor ideology winning out, one that has already seemed to grow wary of its founder every bit as much as the current civic order grew distant from Wilson.

There are four potential versions of how the Fourth Civic Order plays out, and we won't know for years still, but it's looking more and more like a choice between a fundamental transformation successor ideology and a republic if we can keep it, if you will. Either of these articulations can go by many names, slogans, and leaders. But a singular leader is distinctive and the "great man theory of history," analogous to the generational theory of history and historical (over political and social science) paradigm we're playing in here.

The Strauss-Howe generational theory spoke of eighty-seven years (with about twenty-one or twenty-two for each living generation and the total representing a long human life span) as being the social time that passes from generation to generation before a new paradigm is entered into. Unlike the common progressive scientific articulation of history as "ever upward" or bending toward something that is always in the direction of "progress," whether morally and culturally defined or scientifically defined, the generational theory of Strauss and Howe, and therefore civic orders, sees history as seasonal and cyclical, with things in common but falling short of literal history repeating itself—a mode of understanding more than a predictive model that succeeds in one election until it fails in the next. The social time, shared experiences of the individual citizens, gets reinforced under one civic order in ways that it would not in another. In their book *The Fourth Turning: An American Prophecy—What the Cycles of History Tell Us about America's Next Rendezvous with Destiny* Strauss and Howe discuss four generational archetypes and four generational cycles of history that are interplaying and interacting. To back up their theory, centuries of not just American history but Western and other civilizational and cultural history, such as the mythological synthesization work of Joseph Campbell[xxiv] and others, were thoroughly researched and organized.

For their generational theory, four generational archetypes (hero, artist, prophet, and nomad) interplay with times of crisis, high, awakening, and unraveling. They look at both the secular institutional world and the spiritual world as well as the role of individuals.

The First Turning is a *high*, an upbeat era of strengthening institutions and weakening individualism, when a *new civic order* implants, and the old values regime decays.

The Second Turning is an *awakening*, a passionate era of spiritual upheaval, when the *civic order* comes under attack from a new values regime.

The Third Turning is an *unraveling*, a downcast era of strengthening individualism and weakening institutions, when the *old civic order* decays, and the new values regime implants.

The Fourth Turning is a *crisis*, a decisive era of secular upheaval, when the values regime propels the replacement of the *old civic order* with a new one.[xxv]

These definitions and overview of Strauss and Howe are critical to the thesis of this book and critical to understanding why American politics seems so chaotic right now. It's not just social media and the ubiquitous nature of technology. While that and other new paradigms are important, it's not what is driving our times. What is driving our life and times is written in the stars far more than we care to admit. In other words, American politics has been long overdue for a shakeup, and the Third Civic Order is in its own political "fourth turning," which means we're in a decisive era of secular upheaval, when the values regime propels the replacement of the old civic order with a new one. And that is where *The Emerging Populist Majority* comes in, arguing that a set of ideas and worldview will win out rather than reducing it merely to a party like past "emerging" books have done. In a sense this crisis has been going on a bit longer than we think even or seems to have overlapped with the "unraveling" phase. See the graph below.

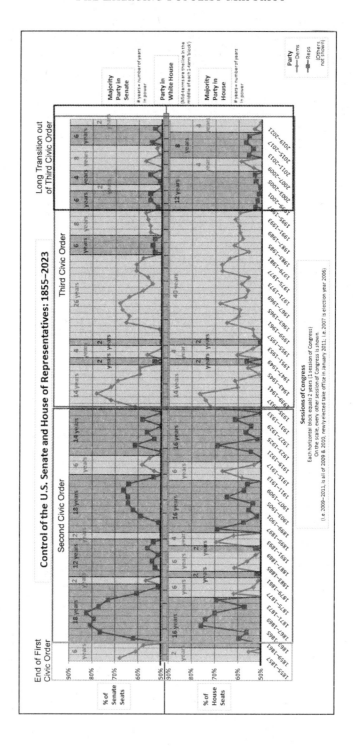

Control of the U.S. Senate and House of Representatives: 1855–2023

Blocked out in darker shading is an era of profound congressional domination that covers the Second Civic Order, the Republican Union one if you will, and the Third Civic Order is covered in lighter shading for many years with slight exceptions through 1994. What made the foundational Third Civic Order more dominant and popular is precisely what is making it so weak today. The FDR coalition had liberal intellectuals, urban workers, progressive reformers, rural and agrarian populists, and African Americans who realigned after the Great Depression over economics more than culture. The FDR landslides of 1932 and his biggest one in '36 suffered a setback in the '38 midterms, but the coalition still proved durable enough to win a third and a fourth term. Moreover, it was what happened in the 1940 election internally to the Republican Party, ensuring a victory for Wendell Willkie the internationalist over Senator Taft the more isolationist, and further rejection of that posture after the war but, most important, the war itself that remade America and ensured the final rise of a new civic order out of a crisis.

Civic Orders and Generational Theory of History of Strauss and Howe (The Fourth Turning and the Spirit of '76, or a Long Human Lifespan)

Civic Order	Foundational Crisis	Generational Alignment	Dominant Party	Oppositional Party
First	American Revolution and the Founding	high, awakening, unraveling, *crisis*	Jefferson-Jackson Democrats	Federalists, then Whigs
Second	Civil War	high, awakening, unraveling, *crisis*	Republicans	Democrats, Populists, Progressives
Third	World War II	high, awakening, unraveling, *crisis*	Democrats	Republicans, Reform

Throughout each civic order is an inflection point that comes to define the unraveling and crisis ahead. It is the moment where opposition to the ruling and dominant paradigm of the civic order looks like it's going to stress to the point of breaking, but because of the timing in society, the civic order instead makes an adjustment, even though the opposition gets clarified and perhaps solidified. For Jeffersonian democracy and its de facto one-party Era of Good Feelings, it was the split of that one party around the personality and presidency of Andrew Jackson, in many respects America's first populist. For the civic order of the Republican Union it was William McKinley. Prior to McKinley's 1896 triumph with the issues of sound gold-backed currency and pro-tariff approach, America had experienced twenty years of close elections, and the Republican Party was running out of new states to create out west to stay in power (not unlike the Democrats' push to create new states and new senators, or to abolish the Electoral College today), yet in the thirty-six years after McKinley's 1896 victory, the Republican Party dominated every election except for when it split in 1912 and narrowly lost to an incumbent Wilson in 1916. For our current civic order of the progressive administrative state, it was early on, and it was with a popular war hero figure, Eisenhower, who like U. S. Grant nearly a hundred years prior, became president under the national hero model and manner, and in many ways was a reset of the country's political system. For movement conservatives of the Taft variety, Eisenhower's failure to roll back the New Deal was a disappointment; to New Dealers, it was a relief. Yet, for progressives and liberal intellectuals themselves, Eisenhower represented the beginning of a frustrating era in which the structures of the progressive administrative state would remain, but their best-laid plans of building a "Great Society" would get continually frustrated in their eyes either by obstructionists, do-nothing Congresses, or most accurately, the limits of the academic way of running a country itself. The pastoral American High of the postwar "I Like Ike" years would be outcomes just about any American would take economically and in foreign policy today—a confidence in the country and in home and family life that have not been seen since.

Those who subscribe to party systems theory will claim that Nixon in 1968 and Reagan in 1980 represented the country turning to a more conservative direction and represented the rise of a new dominant political coalition, a new civic order if you will. But this is not the case. The outcomes of both the 1968 and 1980 presidential elections by county, the strength of the parties down ballot in Congress and in the states, and the increasing assumption from the cultural centers of information bear out a Third Civic Order that still agreed to the structures of the New Deal, its new direction and relation to the Constitution.

In so many ways, the 1940 election, between two internationalist candidates in a country that had to be thoroughly convinced, with hardcore opponents to entering World War I jailed by a presidential administration, was the first election under the Third Civic Order. The constitutional norm breaking of a third Roosevelt term represented the social consensus for a new civic order, just as the institutional line being drawn with presidential term limits afterward represented the desire by the political establishment and public to still adhere to the basic framework of the country, but with new, more bendable wood as picture frame.

Willkie got thoroughly defeated, yet already by 1940 there was evidence of an increasing Republican rebirth and revitalization that adjusted to the new political and civic order—united and thoroughly patriotic. Even those against American entry to the war were nevertheless active participants after Pearl Harbor. In the 1940 results, you can see North and South Dakota saying no to a third term that went beyond the precedent of Washington, as well as Nebraska, Kansas, Colorado, and Iowa. Two industrial midwestern states joined the no vote in Indiana and Michigan. In the beginning years of the Third Civic Order, one key part of the coalition, the agrarian and rural populists and working middle-class Midwesterners, were already having some second thoughts.

1940

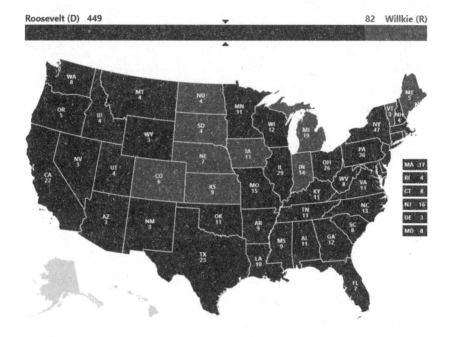

With Willkie running essentially in cooperation with FDR on international affairs, a once polling lead, impressive for a candidate who had never held elected public office, became a slim fifty-two to forty-eight lead for the incumbent Roosevelt in the final Gallup poll. The chapter "Four More Years" in Jean Edward Smith's biography of Roosevelt pointed out that his "traditional preelection poll taken by the White House press pool showed him with 315 electoral votes to Willkie's 216."[xxvi] A voter turnout at the highest level in more than three decades (over 62 percent) eventually reelected the president to a third term. Alternative history only knows what would have happened had the Republican Party nominated a candidate who offered more of a genuine alternative rather than an echo, which would be the ongoing dilemma over the next decade or so. Even so, had Willkie carried the industrial Midwest, he would have still come up short at 311 to 220. A similar election would take place eight years later with those popular vote margins. The durability of the coalition and changeover of civic orders became more and more clear. To win, Willkie would have needed to resemble all of the prior Republican coalition or at least most of it, pushing westward into the McKinley-Theodore Roosevelt strong states, into New England where good governance and public servant Calvin Coolidge did well, and sweeping further into the industrial Midwest into the farm belt Midwest to add Minnesota and Wisconsin to the totals. Not until 1952, with a still mostly solid Democratic South, would Willkie's path to victory be accomplished.

By 1940 it became more and more apparent that with war on the horizon, the old civic order was over, and the new emerging administration would have an opportunity with the war to lock in far more than the New Deal could have ever dreamed of accomplishing. For a new, but undeniably old American tradition emerged around the figures and party of the New Deal, if not necessarily the ideas. It was the image of the great American adventure. Once synonymous with Theodore Roosevelt, his son, Theodore Roosevelt III, heir to the adventurer's spirit had narrowly missed out on the governorship of New York, failing to capture Coolidge's coattails in an era with more split-ticket voting. Instead, four years later it was another Roosevelt, Franklin, from another party, the Democratic Party, the party of Jefferson and Jackson, who got quoted no longer, who had emerged as the adventurer, taking small and company town Republicans and farm and labor Democrats to war as Americans. As Amity Shlaes noted in "Willkie's Wager" in her new history of the New Deal era, *The Forgotten Man*, "It was the adventurer's America too that the soldiers would shortly be defending. And no one wanted to serve more than the Forgotten Man."[xxvii]

While Willkie and later Dewey helped bridge the revitalization that was a precursor to winning back Congress for a brief moment in 1946 and Eisenhower's win in 1952, the 1940 and 1944 elections were still landslide victories for FDR that would be treated as the largest of landslides in the contest that we're accustomed to today. And part of the reason why these landslides seemed to come so easily, beyond the magnetic pull and steady-hand leadership of Roosevelt in these crisis years, was the fact that the solid South for the Democrats who were on the outs during the Second Civic Order became a guaranteed set of electoral votes for the third. In these years the Republicans began with no such "solid" anything or any sort of wall. The Yankeedom and Heartland coalition of the Second Civic Order had shattered, and the Northeast had been put into a rear-guard action that it still resisted more or less outside of New York City and the wealthier areas of the Boston to Washington, DC, Beltway.

Republican standard-bearer Governor Thomas Dewey of New York, but born and raised in the Midwest, seemed an ideal candidate to return the party to the White House and was heavily favored in 1948 after his 1944 showing, yet even he fell short as President Harry Truman won one of the more impressive campaigns in American political history. Challenged from both the solid Democratic South (Strom Thurmond) and from the progressive left (Henry Wallace), Truman's coming-from-behind victory, running against a Republican Congress, is perhaps the clearest example of the durability of the coalition that first came together in 1932. But like most strings of victories in presidential politics, it would be the final time.

1944

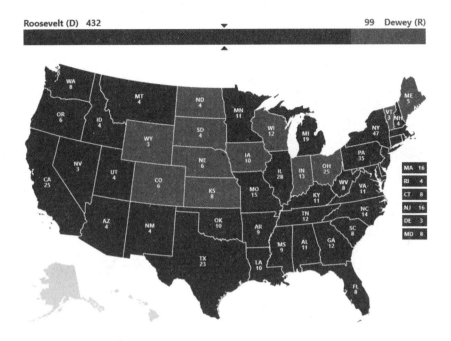

Roosevelt (D)   432   99   Dewey (R)

The House of Representatives vote, freed from the confines of senatorial and state political dynamics and closest to the people, along with the state legislatures themselves, shows an even clearer picture. President Roosevelt in his final election runs ahead of the Democratic share of the popular vote and, if anything, keeps the party in the majority because of that top-of-the-ticket strength. After a brutal midterm defeat in 1946, where Republicans won the House vote by over 8 percent, President Truman flipped it around, helping to lead the ticket and party to pick up seventy-five seats. Because of much greater rural strength, and being strong enough in nearly every state, Democratic popular vote wins translated to more electoral wins, and Republican popular vote wins translated to fewer electoral wins.

1948

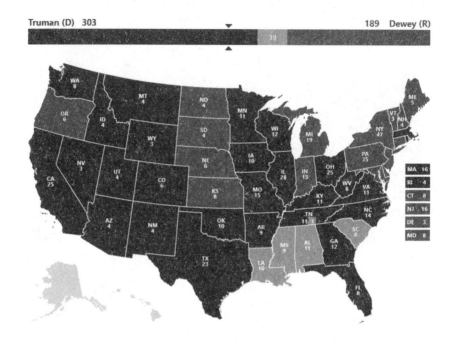

House of Representatives Vote from WWII to Cold War-Era into the War Generation Alignment

Year	Rep. Vote Share (%)	Dem. Vote Share (%)	Rep. Seats	Dem. Seats	Trend
1944 (FDR)	47.1	51.8	189 (-20)	244 (+22)	**Lean Democratic**
1946 (Truman)	53.5	45.0	246 (+55)	188 (-54)	**Solid Republican**
1948 (Truman)	45.4	52.6	171 (-75)	263 (+75)	**Lean Democratic**
1950 (Truman)	48.9	49.6	199 (+28)	235 (-28)	**Toss-Up**
1952 (Eisenhower)	49.3	49.8	221 (+22)	213 (-22)	**Toss-Up**

The second and final Truman years' midterm, an era sadly ignored by too many, began to turn this concept on its head. In both 1950 and 1952, with nearly equal popular vote shares in the House of Representatives, we got two wildly different House results. One, this is reflective of how much midterms go against the party holding the White House because of differing levels in party enthusiasm, turnout, and targeting. Two, we begin an alignment that becomes all too common over the next forty years that make up the War Generation, or Cold War Alignment, Republican presidential landslide figures that have limited coattails downstream to the House and to the states. This is not to say Eisenhower did not work and campaign hard, beginning a barnstorming trend his vice president, Nixon, would carry forth eight years later (possibly to his detriment). With a campaign headquarters in his wife's hometown of Denver and a family home at 60 Morningside Drive, New York City, from his previous position as president of Columbia University, Eisenhower traveled over thirty thousand miles by air, twenty thousand miles by rail, and appeared in 232 towns and cities over forty-five states.[xxviii]

General Eisenhower exceeded four hundred electoral votes and won the popular vote by over 11 percent, yet only twenty-two seats in the House were picked up. Today, the House vote will more closely align with the presidential vote. There has been a significant decline in split-ticket voting that began to accelerate during the unraveling and into the crisis of the Third Civic Order but was very present during the American High and Awakening. Outgoing President Truman, whose presidency has aged quite well today by historical considerations, represented the peak of the old Democratic coalition at its height presiding over the civic order of the progressive administrative state. Truman had no college degree, the last president to share this status, and was a machine politician and party man. He was born on a farm and was a failed haberdasher but distinguished himself in the First World War. Truman represented a midwestern and western agrarian tradition that is increasingly gone from the Democratic Party of today but represented its amazing geographical diversity yesterday that propelled it to command such heights over the country's politics. The social class differences reflected in Truman's life were split over two different orders and represent the antipathy of the class divisions of his time: "They [the Republicans] did not understand the worker, the farmer, the everyday person.... Most of them honestly believed that prosperity actually began at the top and would trickle down in due time to benefit all the people."[xxix]

But it was not as simple as Truman put it. The Dewey-Vandenberg ticket featured two popular, young, energetic, and progressive GOP governors from states (New York and California) that bookended the country.[xxx] A preview of the coastal elites derided today, the relative progressivism of the Dewey ticket against Truman's middle American roots and extreme campaigns to his right and left from his own party coalition allowed Truman a populist lane, which he took advantage of. The very populism of Truman's "Give 'em Hell Harry" campaign of '48 was very reminiscent of the final few weeks barnstorming from incumbent President Trump, which took him from a four hundred electoral vote landslide in the media's eyes to a vote count that took days to sort out and led to thirteen House seat pickups in the most trying of years for a presidential incumbent since 1932 and Herbert Hoover. In those days the press was considered Republican-dominated[xxxi] or at least dominated enough that Truman could campaign directly against them as FDR had done, and as Trump would later do.

1952

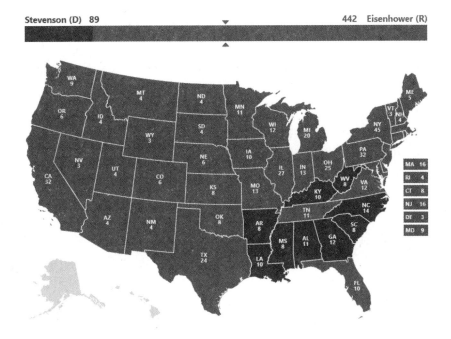

Stevenson (D) 89   ▼   442 Eisenhower (R)

Presidential landslide election victories, whether won by a dominant party in the civic order or the weaker one, are some of the most illustrative county-by-county and state-by-state maps to look at. They show you what the core of your party is no matter how popular the opponent or how weak your candidate. A look into the partisanship strength of both the Democratic Party of the Second Civic Order and the Third Civic Order until at least 1960, and even a couple of elections after that (1976, 1980), shows a party where strength is greatest in the South. This makes total sense given the outcome of the Civil War. It is both a vote against the Republican Party of Lincoln and the Union but also evidence of the more hierarchical and traditionalistic political culture. Eisenhower's 1952 victory shows a Democratic Party strongest in the South still, but it also shows a Republican Party making inroads there. Outside the South, the Democratic Party also has a few pockets around the country, with the biggest one being in the Iron Range of Minnesota.

41

Eisenhower's two wins in the 1950s represented a nostalgic era in American politics when the country had both high confidence and a booming economy whose broadly shared gains contributed to the pastoral and traditional family life when both birth rates and marriage rates were increasing. Socially, some of the greatest gains in the civil rights movement were made under Eisenhower, a story that gets glossed over today precisely because of the need for the Third Civic Order to protect its origin story and status as the only justifiable and legitimate steward of American life. On domestic matters generally, Eisenhower was genuinely conservative, far closer to Taft than to Truman.[xxxii]

Yet beyond broadly shared economics, a booming family life, and gains of social movements, the main drivers were matters of foreign policy and geopolitics in American politics after the initial years of the Third Civic Order, once the order had its first transfer of party power. It is these much-ignored and unimportant areas to many contemporary American voters, who by and large do not serve in the international arena, that came to dominate the first full generational alignment of the Third Civic Order, which we'll call the War Generation Alignment. For veterans of World Wars I and II, whether in government or on the battlefield, it was the accidental superpower nature and the need to rebuild much of the devastated economies of the world that thrust America into the role of international security guarantor and stable currency, creditor, and economy-of-last-resort. When the country was unified by a set of shared values, mandatory service, and a singular defying enemy, the Soviet Union to replace Nazi Germany and Imperial Japan, this was made much easier. The politics of the Cold War came to dominate American politics and put foreign policy and geopolitics at the forefront in ways they have not been in the previous three decades since.

CHAPTER 3

WAR GENERATION ALIGNMENT (1952 TO 1992)

Within a civic order, which can best be described as a section from American history class or as representing a long human lifespan, there are various alignments, usually two full alignments, driven by a dominant generation. The dominant generation upholds the civic order and institutions, and gives birth to another dominant generation. In this sense, dominant means larger, the large generational cohort of the postwar baby boomers being the most recognizable version of this. Other versions are the post–Civil War immigration waves that lasted for decades until the controversial at the time but ultimately wise immigration reforms and restrictions of the early 1920s allowed for a cooling period in American life that lasted for four and a half decades. This cooling period, presided over in its beginning stages by President Coolidge, who was like so many presidents, an embodiment of his namesake, helped bring about the country and people that sustained at home and fought abroad through the tumultuous decades of crisis (1930s, 1940s) and through whose shared experience in that crisis brought about a tragically misunderstood and too-ignored American High (postwar 1940s, 1950s, into the early 1960s). The shared experiences from this generation allowed for greater assimilation at home around the American civic creed and helped strengthen the institutions through the crisis.

No one had a greater stake in the new civic order than the American GIs who fought in the Second World War. The hard-fought peace was almost immediately threatened by the emerging Cold War rivalry and battle of systems between the liberal democratic West led by the United States and the communist bloc under the Soviet Union. While this Cold War never turned bright hot other than its downstream related and sometimes tragically, too, unrelated proxy wars, the threat of conflict and the dawn of the nuclear age ensured that foreign affairs and geopolitics would continue to dominate American politics and American political coalitions. While a relatively lean Democratic voting generation, the Greatest Generation, or GI Generation, or as we'll call them here the War Generation, was at once communitarian as well as traditional. The ranks of veterans' service organizations like the American Legion and Veterans of Foreign Wars (VFW) swelled in the pastoral 1950s, and despite lean Democratic voting habits established from the Depression and the war, this habit was not ideologically leftist nor even particularly liberal or progressive. When a young Jack Kennedy first campaigned for Congress in 1946, he campaigned as and was referred to as a "fighting-Irish conservative"[xxxiii] and went to American Legion halls to speak with Gold Star mothers, remarking how his mother was a Gold Star mother too, as his older brother Joe had been lost in the war. Kennedy's attempt to claim the mantle and verbiage of conservative[xxxiv] is similar to then-candidate Abraham Lincoln's attempt at the Cooper Union nearly four score and seven years earlier. To the extent this generation was conservative though, it found its highest expression in domestic matters of the home.[xxxv]

In these years Democrats and Republicans alike were far less ideological, and while the new "center" was many of the structures of the New Deal, it was also pre–Great Society, traditional and pastoral, and military service was a gold standard for elected office for both elites and the masses. Cold War politics and the political coalitions formed around them were the center of American politics. Within both parties, other ideological disagreements got sidelined, and party managers attempted to avoid them at all costs. In the 1950s, during the beginning of the War Generation Alignment, this worked wonders, and President Eisenhower made it look easy. Eisenhower's coalitions were held together by a demographically large and dominant generation whose unity of purpose was forged at young ages on European battlefields and Pacific island chains and on the home front in industrial factories. This was the time of G.I. Joe and Rosie the Riveter, of Truth, Justice, and the American Way.

Two other features are interesting and drive our rejection of both party systems and popular media and cultural notions of the often-referenced 1932, 1968, and 1980 years. One, the period of the War Generation Alignment is defined, almost without exception, by Democratic Congresses but Republican presidents who usually won in landslide elections by historical standards and certainly by today's standards. Two, every single president of the War Generation Alignment served in uniform. Their character and nature of this service differed greatly, from Eisenhower's command of the Allied Expeditionary Force during the war and his tour as the first commander of NATO to Ronald Reagan's stint as an actor in military training films. A picture of their service can be found. And since the War Generation Alignment's final president, George H. W. Bush, the precise opposite of both of these features has occurred.

These two features might sound coincidental and small, but they drive home the foreign policy- and geopolitics-first nature of the political alignments and coalitions of the first half of the Third Civic Order and the subsequent abandonment of it, along with so many features of traditional American life as the alignment got replaced by the next one, which we'll call the Boomer Alignment (chapter 4). You can see the impact of military service and the impact of the war on our politics during this period just as much as you can note its absence since, as major wars and even controversial draft-era American wars have given way to the professionalized all-volunteer force America has used since the 1970s. The civic and veterans' service organizations that are going strong but aging out rapidly, and with a seat at the table based on that institutional history, also provide a window into both where we've been and what may be restored in the decades to come. Consider the third pillar of the American Legion—"Americanism." Defined as the nation's cultural, moral, and patriotic values, the legion's pillar of Americanism embodies its devotion to law and order, the raising of wholesome youth, an educated and law-abiding citizenship, and respectful observance of patriotic holidays and remembrances.[xxxvi] Historian and author Thomas Frank once opined that "if it's 100 percent Americanism we're looking for, Kansas delivers 110 percent."[xxxvii] It was precisely this middle American and patriotically infused part of the country that powered past coalitions from mere winning to consensus governing, even if only for a time.

This alignment was international but a *constrained* internationalism that existed in a bipolar geopolitical paradigm between the United States and the West (NATO) and the Soviet Union and the Eastern Bloc (Warsaw Pact). On the home front this alignment straddles both a 1940-to-1952 early Third Civic Order, the first part of the American High, and also kicks off the second part and zenith of the American High, from 1952 to 1962. "Where Were You in '62?"

The tragically ignored 1952 election in particular kicks off so much about what can be understood about this era and is misunderstood today. Four years later, 1956 was almost literally a replay of that election. You can understand how people would get a little restless and bored with this reality, but many forget just how good America had it in those days. This War Generation Alignment kicked off a series of elections where reelections were incredibly similar to the first round if the incumbent was reelected, and like Hoover in 1932, tremendous Electoral College rejections occurred in the case of a loss (Carter in 1976, H. W. Bush in the final election of the War Generation Alignment, 1992).

Eisenhower's two landslide wins included slight increases in both the popular vote and electoral vote, but his moderate presidency that kept the midwestern Taft conservatives at bay also had little coattails after '52, losing both houses in '54, which Republicans would not win back until the

1980s for the Senate and the 1990s for the House, under an entirely new generation as the dominant voting cohort. Nixon's close loss in '60 was nearly repeated in '68, and as Kevin Phillips foretold in *The Emerging Republican Majority*, broke decisively for him in even larger numbers than his former boss in '72. Reagan's two landslide victories and the first successor electoral win since Truman in '48, Hoover in '28 for the Republicans, with H. W. Bush in '88 comprised six total landslide victories over the course of four decades and ten total elections. This is the backdrop to the supposed realignment or critical election of 1968, or the realignment or critical election of 1980. Yes, in both of those years the country overwhelmingly rejected the one-party rule of the Democratic Party, but those elections also represent outcomes more in line with the generational cohort consensus than most observers would admit.

Electoral landslides today just don't happen. No one has received over four hundred electoral votes nor above 53 percent of the popular vote since 1988. While Nixon was always strongly disliked by the media, he also was a ticket balancer with Eisenhower, in many ways a reset president of the Third Civic Order just as General U. S. Grant was a reset of the republic president of the Second Civic Order. Just as Eisenhower's landslide wins were lonely, with few coattails, so was Nixon's landslide win. Even Reagan's two landslide wins failed to have the coattails to flip the House for the Republicans. Democratic control of the House especially but Congress almost always is a central feature of the War Generation Alignment, and their failure to hold Congress for more than a single term since is a central feature of the one we're in now. While American society and culture were undergoing great turmoil after the high in the 1960s due to assassinations, civil rights, Vietnam, and rioting in the cities, this division failed to fundamentally alter the nature of power. By the 1960s, in the post-Eisenhower years, and especially after the Kennedy assassination, the cultural and media domination by the Democratic Party and those stakeholders' roles in upholding the civic order became apparent.

In this sense, they operate more like a royal court acting entitled to rule, governance, and stewardship over the country than a political perspective in a representative democracy and constitutional republic who views their opponents as legitimate operators within the system. This is the most important feature of civic orders. The legitimacy of rule versus the illegitimacy of the challengers to that rule, playing out in society and culture as much if not more than it plays out in the corridors of political power. While both Nixon in '68 and Reagan in '80 interrupted the "onward and upward" momentum of the liberal order and progressive administrative state, they did so as the beneficiaries of some truly dreadful domestic and foreign policy outcomes that were happening in the country at the time. But no analysis of the general rules of this alignment is complete without taking into account the exceptions, of which there is only one, 1964, the only landslide for a Democrat in this period, a mere eight years before one of the Republican landslide wins, which coincide in between what we'll call "the crossroads" elections of the War Generation Alignment.

Republican Presidential Vote during the War Generation Alignment

Year	Candidate	Popular Vote (%)	Electoral Vote
1952	Eisenhower	55.1	442
1956	Eisenhower	57.4	457
1960	Nixon	49.5	219
1964	Goldwater	38.5	52
1968	Nixon	43.5	301
1972	Nixon	60.5	520
1976	Ford	48.0	240
1980	Reagan	50.7	489
1984	Reagan	58.8	525
1988	W. Bush	53.4	426

The Case of 1964

In each of these exceptions what will differ from most accounts is de-emphasizing the importance most bring to these elections and emphasizing a narrative that has more statistical significance and coalitional consistency to it. In the case of 1964, the only landslide victory of the Democratic Party during the War Generation Alignment, and really the only landslide election victory period since the FDR victories, is LBJ's win over Barry Goldwater.

The 1964 to 1972 period gets a lot of attention because of the vast turmoil and changes that went on in American culture and society but tend to be overrated by both conservatives and liberals. Prior to this era, Republicans usually won the presidency, often in clear and landslide fashion, while Democrats won Congress. After this era, that was still the case. Goldwater's candidacy was in many ways a precursor to Reagan. But this does not mean that this tradition defines American conservativism as modern origin story. There was an Old Right before there was a New Right. But there is another origin story that many progressive activists and leftists today may find in the turbulent decade of the 1960s to an extent—that of a triumphant and righteous Democratic Party that passed the Civil Rights Act and Voting Rights Act in 1964 and 1965 respectively and completed the work of a slain president. And that this was passed by a southern president in Lyndon Johnson takes on additional significance. These achievements are considerable and should not be dismissed either, but it is a story that is a half-truth.

The full truth is that for the better part of nine decades the Republican Party was the party of civil rights and equality under the law for black Americans, and this continued for three decades after the Republican Party stopped receiving majority votes from black Americans and while very outnumbered in Congress in the mid-1960s, cast a higher percentage of their votes in both the House and the Senate than the Democrats did for both the Civil and Voting Rights Acts. The narrative emphasis on this historical achievement for modern politics also diminishes the

accomplishments during the American High of the civil rights movement, as well as the significant legislative progress that was made in the
Eisenhower administration with the 1957 Civil Rights Act, which is rarely
mentioned today, and his executive actions at Little Rock, repeated in the
early 1960s by Kennedy, whose civil rights record was arguably behind
Nixon's, as was Johnson's prior to 1960. But what Johnson did have was
political cunning, and he was also a legislative master of the Senate, which
was instrumental in passing his legislative programs prior to but especially
after the '64 election.

The fuller truth though is that the tragedy of Kennedy's assassination
on November 22, 1963, changed the course of America for the worse and
also began emboldening a 1960s left that has been romanticized by media
and culture beyond anything it deserves. Both the genuine accomplishments of the 1960s whether in politics or in society were the work of others, and the work of the 1960s activists was the beginning of so much that
has been broken in our culture and politics today. The first few years of
the 1960s could have fit easily in the American High of the late 1940s and
1950s still, yet as the brilliant television series *Mad Men* (2007–2015)
shows, the arc of the moral and cultural universe began bending toward
chaos for much of the rest of the decade and into the next. The decline and
fall of New York City and the deindustrializing northeast corridor begins
to particularly shine through. Before his assassination, Jack Kennedy, a
man who had served in the Senate with both Johnson (with whom he did
not get along) and Goldwater (with whom he did), had been planning an
entirely different campaign for his reelection that was about to kick off
in the late fall of 1963. He fully expected Goldwater to be the nominee
but not out of political calculus. The man who had written *Profiles in
Courage*, which showed moments of political courage, a showcase of US
senators, and the times when taking a then unpopular but correct stance
that stood the test of time, had planned an act of courage for his final
campaign: frequent and collaborative debates with Senator Goldwater
over the issues. Rather than the intensely negative and political campaign

we got from Lyndon Johnson in '64 that included the "Daisy" ad, which implied a nuclear holocaust if the civil libertarian–leaning Goldwater got elected, we could have gotten a much more positive, better for the country and the issues, and what would have been a closer campaign in '64. Kennedy would have certainly still won against a Goldwater candidacy that was run more to prove a point and take over the direction of a political party than it was intended to win. To the Goldwater enthusiasts downstream, conservative Americans first conceived of themselves as being the actual majority or at least the plurality in these years, yet the country just didn't know it yet.

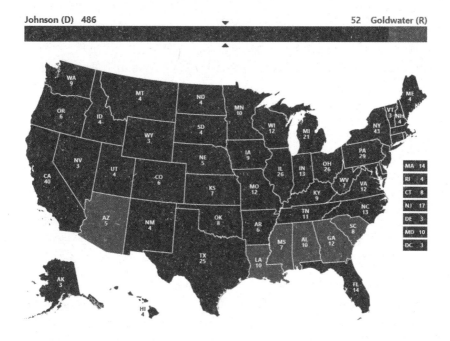

While a Kennedy-Goldwater campaign would have yielded a closer and more balanced result, it would've still been a Kennedy victory and likely a much bigger one than in 1960 but without that much variation. As Rick Perlstein pointed out, the slice of America that disdained Kennedy grew slimmer throughout, but it did grow more distinct, become better organized and more articulate[xxxviii] thanks to Goldwater, who got along with Kennedy just fine but instead had to face Johnson. Incumbent presidents for reelection tend to have very little variation across the Electoral College in their results because at least one-half of the choice is the same. The only exceptions are when incumbents lose in clear fashion after one term. A second important difference of this what-if scenario is the great "southern switch" narrative would be an even bigger stretch for modern-day Third Civic Order and successor ideology writers. Kennedy would have performed better in the South against Goldwater, and Goldwater would've performed better elsewhere. The anti-Republican streak in the South was still very strong throughout the 1960s, and for the most part both in office and at the voting booth, there was considerably less switching than the media lets on. It was not until the 1990s, an entirely different generational alignment later, that a majority of state legislative seats in the South became Republican, and it was not until the last decade that voter registration of Republicans surpassed that of Democrats in the South. Additionally, because an entirely different electorate was alive in 1964 compared to even 2014 when completely different issues were driving politics by then, it says more about the court jesters and journalists of the Third Civic Order than about what voters in the electorate were actually doing. That Kevin Phillips later pointed out what was already happening and possible in 1969 is just the convenient excuse. Nixon's 1972 and later Reagan's coalitions were not that different from Eisenhower's more moderate and nonpartisan coalitions, and all three of their coalitions were influenced by national security and foreign policy more than they were influenced by anything Democrats talk about. This is why it's most accurate to call the political alignments in America during these four decades the War Generation Alignment, as they represented the major voting years of World War II veterans and the driving foreign policy and geopolitical issue of the Cold War and its connected issues and framework.

And perhaps the fullest truth is that the Democrats simply lost control of the country during the 1960s, and much of what they lost control of was under their governing responsibility at the national, state, and local levels. And it was over a multitude of issues as historian Amity Shlaes documents in the *Great Society: A New History*.[xxxix] Whether it was the Democrat-escalated war in Vietnam, the rioting in the cities, or the excessive spending of the Great Society programs, which exceeded New Deal programs in 2002 and have been growing exponentially since, Nixon came into office because he seemed like the only person who could hold the country together at the time. Hubert Humphrey, a well-meaning Minnesotan and stalwart traditional liberal, had been too tainted by Vietnam, Wallace was a nonstarter and a regional candidate only, and Nixon set out to do the same thing his former boss had done: get out of a Democratic-initiated war. Unlike with Korea, Nixon had a much more difficult go of it in Vietnam, but it was the Democrats losing the country that ended any unilateral benefit of the doubt from the electorate on their rule. The Third Civic Order wasn't over, but the electorate had had enough of its "progress" by 1968 and certainly by 1972. In many ways the '68 campaign was the last gasp for old Labor's position within the Democratic coalition, at least outside of cities like New York and a few others. But a Republican emerging future was far from the only conclusion after the tumultuous year of 1968. From United Auto Workers' leader Walter Reuther's point of view, there were small consolations. The Nixon victory was narrow, and voters returned Democratic majorities to the House and the Senate.[xl] Michigan remained in the Democratic column even while other parts of the coalition began falling in the industrial Midwest: first, the Mayor Daley fiefdom in Chicago and Illinois, which became a precursor to what would befall the Democratic coalition as it tried to transfer from Labor-machine politics to an urban machine politics that had more in common with the party's immigrant and Tammany Hall history in fusion with the New Left's identity politics.

The Case of 1972

It was a mirror of 1964, with a close election in between. In '72 the activist and younger New Left Democrats got their man just as conservative activists got theirs eight years prior. It helped that McGovern was instrumental in the primary reforms after the disastrous '68 convention. McGovern's institutional advantage became the party's downfall as his dysfunctional campaign never took off and was written off easily as "acid, amnesty, and abortion." Yet like Goldwater, McGovern is cited frequently today as a harbinger for the future coalition of the Clinton era and onward. The trend of highly educated professional-class voters switching from Republican to Democrat, for instance, began with McGovern. Landslide elections are some of the most fascinating elections to look into for precisely this reason: What went the other way while nearly all the country went the prevailing way? What bucked the overall trend?

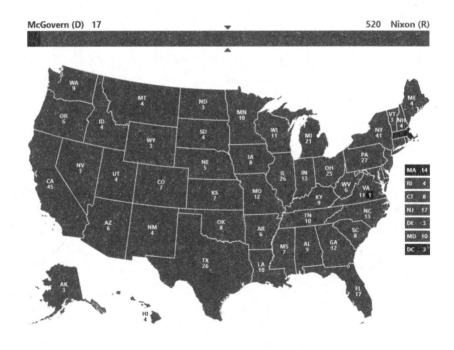

The so-called "revenge of George McGovern" coalition would not take shape until two decades later under a different generational alignment—the boomer generation. But perhaps because people like Bill Clinton cut their political teeth on that campaign in Texas and elsewhere, and began professionally running for office immediately after, the association and story run strong, just as it did with the Goldwater to Reagan coalition. Yet, like with Goldwater and the South, it's not that significant that McGovern did better with professional-class voters either. In both instances it's only been significant because writers from the *New York Times*, *Washington Post*, and various outlets said it was. It's passed into origin story myth and legend, and if you don't dive into more material, many newly energized voters in their particular party take it at face value until reality asserts itself otherwise.

For the professional-class realignment, to this very day there simply are not enough professional-class voters to form a reliable and durable coalition anywhere except for a few urban enclaves that because of their economic and cultural pull end up hurting the coalition in other geographical areas of the country. By the 2000s and the era where the Kevin Phillips *Emerging Republican Majority* had played out according to John Judis and Ruy Teixeira, upwardly mobile professionals of the "creative class" were critical of their *Emerging Democratic Majority* thesis. These voters were critical to the "coalition of the ascendant" but also were the very same voters who helped inform policy preferences that drove economic and cultural wedges between voters of the older coalition who were supposed to just get in line. This tradition of elite party manager arrogance at the flight from old voters is constant in every era of American politics. The dislike of populism from elites stretches back to the Populist Party itself in the nineteenth century.

In the end, even George McGovern's revenge proved to be a less than durable one. Going from one state in '72 to 43 percent of the vote twenty years later, the Democrats at the presidential level were not gaining voters and emerging at all—they were trading voters, and all too often the trades have worked out like the Herschel Walker trade did for the Minnesota Vikings, which helped set the stage for the Dallas Cowboys to win three out of four Super Bowls in the 1990s. Coalitions of everybody *rarely*, if ever, last longer than an election cycle or two, and we'll see that again and again as our narrative goes on. In the case of the white liberals, the only group of white voters ideologically who vote Democratic today, they frequently find themselves on the opposite side on vital issues from ethnic and racial minorities. And as we've seen in primary election after primary election, the vast majority of racial minorities in the Democratic Party have politics that are considerably more moderate than white liberals of both yesterday and today. If coalitions of everybody are to work, they often need an overriding issue or two binding the pieces of the coalition together.[xli]

Democratic Presidential Vote during the War Generation Alignment

Year	Candidate	Popular Vote (%)	Electoral Vote
1952	Stevenson	44.4 (-5.15)	89 (-214)
1956	Stevenson	41.97 (-2.4)	73 (-16)
1960	Kennedy	49.72 (+7.75)	303 (+230)
1964	Johnson	61.05 (+11.33)	486 (+183)
1968	Humphrey	42.7 (-18.35)	191 (-295)
1972	McGovern	37.5 (-5.2)	17 (-174)
1976	Carter	50.08 (+12.58)	297 (+280)
1980	Carter	41.01 (-9.07)	49 (-248)
1984	Mondale	40.56 (-0.55)	13 (-36)
1988	Dukakis	45.65 (+5.11)	111 (+98)

The Crossroads Elections of the War Generation Alignment

Woven throughout the intraparty struggles of 1964 (Republican) and 1972 (Democrat) were various crossroads elections. All these very close crossroads elections from 1960, 1968, and 1976 are much remembered but, as is the theme, misunderstood especially in comparison to the very close election era of 1876 to 1896 and the one we're slowly coming out of today (2000 to 2020). LBJ's landslide victory that exceeded every FDR victory in popular and electoral vote except for 1936 was a false sense of security for the ruling Democratic Party. The country was far closer to 1960 and 1968 than the mandate given to LBJ in '64. And this would have been seen but for the tragedy of Kennedy's assassination.

The major difference between the close elections of the tumultuous 1960s and '70s coming out of the American High and the others is the incredible amount of split-ticket voting that existed then that does not today. The lone Democratic landslide win in the War Generation Alignment had coattails that failed to materialize in Republican landslide wins for the presidency. This speaks to the Republicans winning the presidency, often in landslide wins, and Democrats winning Congress nature of the War Generation Alignment. This alignment existed because of the Cold War, because of the War Generation, and it was due for a shakeup once the Cold War was over, and foreign policy and geopolitical issues were no longer at the forefront. The cultural excesses of the left wing in American politics and their increasing pull on the Democratic Party began in the 1960s. Under this alignment, only twice did the electorate give a majority of the popular vote to the Democrats, compared to six times for the Republicans. By definition, a close election with any significant third-party vote will produce a situation where neither party gets a majority of the vote, even in America's two-party system. The only exception to this is if there is a significant popular and electoral vote misalignment. Even if there is such a misalignment, this mismatch does not last long, as any reasonable and self-preservation party within the system will make moves to correct the fact that it is having trouble getting

57

to 270 electoral votes. What's remarkable about 1960, 1968, and 1976 is how different the electoral coalitions were that propelled the Democrat into the White House to work with a heavily Democratic Congress. America's choice in all three elections was not, "Do we want a Republican or do we want a Democrat as president?" but, "Do we want a one-party Democratic federal government or a split federal government?"

Had the party elites and liberal intellectuals gotten their way in 1960, the candidate would have again been Adlai Stevenson, who would have most certainly lost to a Richard Nixon coming off eight years as vice president. None of the weaknesses of Nixon drawn out in contrast to the youthful and vigorous appearance of fellow navy veteran and Senate colleague Kennedy would have been present against Stevenson. Nixon's win would have been larger than Kennedy's but not as great as Eisenhower's two landslide wins. Stevenson would have joined the ranks of Democrat William Jennings Bryan as a three-time major party loser for the presidency. Had it not been for Kennedy competing directly in political primaries, a popular appeal to the voters meant to persuade the party managers and state delegates, he would not have been the candidate, and perhaps the McGovern primary reforms after 1968 would have been delayed a decade or two.

By 1968, another contested primary occurred in the ruling party, but this one suffered from another tragic assassination. However, it is genuinely a matter of dispute whether Robert Kennedy would have performed better than Hubert Humphrey of Minnesota did. In fact, the 1968 crossroads election was quite similar to 1960's. Republicans did not yet take the South, nor would they permanently take it in 1972 either. Not until the 1990s did the South become the most Republican-voting part of the country under the next generational alignment. Hatred of the party of Lincoln was still too strong in the South for a permanent realignment of the region to take hold (a permanent realignment means party loyalty up and down the ballot, to include registration). A partial realignment is what actually occurred, where split-ticket voting was common (as it was throughout the country), and party registration advantages did not change much.

War Generation Alignment (1952 to 1992)

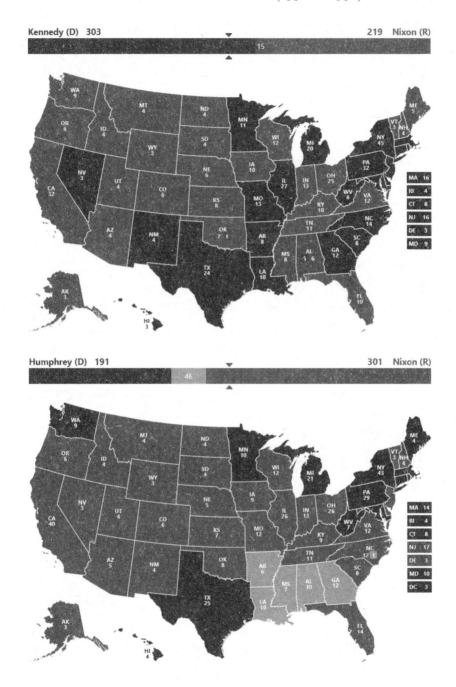

Kennedy (D)   303   219   Nixon (R)

15

WA 9 · MT 4 · ND 4 · MN 11 · ME 5 · OR 6 · ID 4 · SD 4 · WI 12 · VT 3 · NH 4 · NY 45 · WY 3 · IA 10 · MI 20 · PA 32 · NV 3 · CA 32 · UT 4 · CO 6 · NE 6 · IL 27 · IN 13 · OH 25 · WV 8 · VA 12 · KS 8 · MO 13 · KY 10 · NC 14 · AZ 4 · NM 4 · OK 7 1 · TN 11 · SC 8 · AR 8 · MS 8 · AL 5 6 · GA 12 · TX 24 · LA 10 · AK 3 · FL 10 · HI 3

MA 16 · RI 4 · CT 8 · NJ 16 · DE 3 · MD 9

Humphrey (D)   191   301   Nixon (R)

46

WA 9 · MT 4 · ND 4 · MN 10 · ME 4 · OR 6 · ID 4 · SD 4 · WI 12 · VT 3 · NH 4 · NY 43 · WY 3 · IA 9 · MI 21 · PA 29 · NV 3 · CA 40 · UT 4 · CO 6 · NE 5 · IL 26 · IN 13 · OH 26 · WV 7 · VA 12 · KS 7 · MO 12 · KY 9 · NC 12 1 · AZ 5 · NM 4 · OK 8 · TN 11 · SC 8 · AR 6 · MS 7 · AL 10 · GA 12 · TX 25 · LA 10 · AK 3 · FL 14 · HI 4

MA 14 · RI 4 · CT 8 · NJ 17 · DE 3 · MD 10 · DC 3

59

Also in 1968, Humphrey matched up with Kennedy quite well considering the presence of a third-party Democratic split in George Wallace, who would go on to run and win Democratic primaries into the 1970s. Indeed, Wallace was the major difference between 1960 and 1968. The 1960 election was a two-party crossroads and close election where nearly every state was fifty to fifty, with only greater variations at the rural county level (the Democratic South and the Republican Midwest and West) and major city level (eastern cities being Democratic, western cities being more Republican). It was quite remarkable really. If anything, Nixon suffered from being too overconfident in this election having been associated with the "I Like Ike" years of peace and prosperity that, while not perfect, come as close as any American period does in the twentieth century. Nixon promised and executed a barnstorm of every state in the union, the first candidate of either party to perform this feat. Even with disadvantages in the press, and at the dawn of the TV age of American politics, he still likely would have won had they tailored the strategy a bit more to thirty to thirty-five states.

The two-party crossroads in 1960 gave way to the three-party crossroads in 1968, with that third party essentially being the party-split that ruined a Republican coalition in 1912, coming from inside the party, and a third party was temporarily built around a personality, with little to no hope of any staying power after that personality was off the scene and no longer running. This same thing would happen years later at the beginning of the next generational alignment with Ross Perot. This feature represents genuine discontent with the civic order and political and generational alignment in some way. In America 1968 was such a tumultuous year that it has come to represent the political decade in many ways. There are many years where decades happen and many decades that seem to stretch on as indistinguishable from the prior decade.

Just after Nixon's political comeback of 1968, the Phillips book came out. *The Emerging Republican Majority* turned out to be spot-on for 1972 and another two decades after at the presidential level. This is the standard by which we measure the success of the second book in the next chapter. After the Phillips book, the only contradiction at the presidential level was the post-Watergate midterms of '74 and the strange case of the unlikely southern governor, Jimmy Carter.

The Disjunctive and Unrepeatable Political Coalition of Jimmy Carter in 1976

In some respects, Jimmy Carter's victory is merely the realization and fulfillment of a political rule that would last until Barack Obama. The Democratic Party after the Depression and World War II could only win the presidency with a Southerner at the top of the ticket. And for the entirety of the War Generation Alignment this was true, as well into the first decade of the Boomer Alignment.

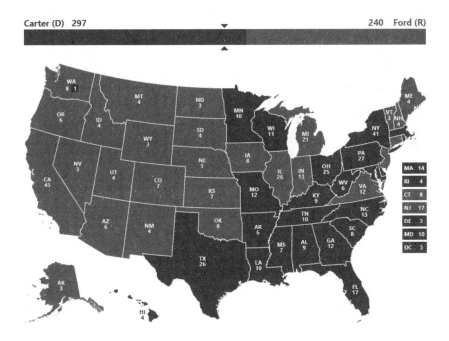

Carter's coalition at the time was referred to as the last dying gasp of the New Deal coalition, but in truth the New Deal coalition was already gone and what existed was the Third Civic Order. This was a country oscillating between Rooseveltian Democrats at the beginning of the order to Eisenhower institutionalists and managers as the order entered its fourth decade. Richard Nixon, sometimes called the "last liberal president," whatever that means, was willing to work with Democratic Congresses to pursue both universal health care and a form of universal basic income. He implemented civil rights far faster than Johnson before him did. Nixon's real focus was the same as Eisenhower's—foreign affairs. Until Reagan in 1980, the first true movement conservative president and first smaller government in theory president since Calvin Coolidge, the Republican Party lacked a coherent domestic vision. The emerging cultural battlegrounds that came out of the 1960s had yet to become truly partisan. Carter won a significant amount of support from Evangelical Christians for instance and was one himself. He also won significant support from African Americans as Democrats before him would, and ones after would in wins or in losses. Despite his narrow margins of victory, Carter won by appealing to everybody[xlii] in '76 and then four years later proved again how coalitions of everybody rarely last long, especially if policy outcomes are not trending in a preferable direction.

Whatever Carter's failings politically and in policy stewardship of the country, he should get credit for anticipating the conservative direction the country was about to take. This was a hint that liberal lions like Senator Ted Kennedy did not take. If you want to make your party's president a one-term president for sure, you run a viable primary challenge. In this case, Kennedy's cause was that of universal health care, or rather universal health insurance. Universal health care was passed under Nixon in the form of universal emergency room care, which accomplished the literal definition of the term but also has introduced all sorts of policy problems since. Five decades later, universal health care to the liberal and left American has become the white whale of the party. No matter how many times it is passed into law, it both already exists and is insufficient in its existence. This sidebar is critical to understanding a later contention that the Third Civic Order, or administrative state, is stressed, breaking apart, and winding down because it has nowhere else to go, much like the working-class Democrats supposedly had nowhere else to go in the 1990s and onward according to Bill Clinton and his political advisors.

Carter deserves some credit for understanding the country more than those before him and since, and for being the last Democratic president who had significant experience with smaller towns and rural America. This cultural gap has only widened since between urban American and smaller-town rural American counties. Despite their final electoral and popular vote tally, one consistent trend of the last four Democratic presidents is that their winning coalition was won with fewer counties out of the over three thousand counties in America than their predecessor. Carter understood at least what the *New York Times* and company did not—that a generational renewal was needed for the ruling Democratic civic order. And one was eventually found in the Boomer Alignment, just not the one that was needed to sustain a consistent winning coalition at the presidential level and now this time, the congressional level too.

House of Representatives Vote during
the War Generation Alignment

Year	Rep. Vote Share (%)	Dem. Vote Share (%)	Rep. Seats	Dem. Seats	Trend
1954 (Eisenhower)	47.0	52.5	203 (-18)	232 (+19)[7]	Lean Democratic
1956 (Eisenhower)	48.7	51.2	201 (-2)	234 (+2)	Toss-Up
1958 (Eisenhower)	43.6	56.0	153 (-48)	283 (+49)	Solid Democratic
1960 (JFK)	44.8	54.8	175 (+22)	262 (-21)	Toss-Up
1962 (JFK)	47.1	52.4	176 (+1)	258 (-4)	Toss-Up
1964 (LBJ)	42.4	57.1	140 (-36)	295 (+37)	Solid Democratic
1966 (LBJ)	48.2	50.9	187 (+47)	248 (-47)	Lean Republican
1968 (Nixon)	48.5	50.2	192 (+5)	243 (-5)	Toss-Up
1970 (Nixon)	44.9	53.6	180 (-12)	255 (+12)	Lean Democratic
1972 (Nixon)	46.5	52.1	192 (+12)	242 (-13)	Toss-Up
1974 (Ford)	40.7	57.5	144 (-48)	291 (+49)	Solid Democratic
1976 (Carter)	42.3	55.9	143 (-1)	292 (+1)	Lean Democratic
1978 (Carter)	44.8	53.7	157 (+14)	277 (-15)	Toss-Up
1980 (Reagan)	47.8	50.5	191 (+34)	242 (-33)	Toss-Up
1982 (Reagan)	43.4	55.2	165 (-26)	269 (+26)	Lean Democratic
1984 (Reagan)	47.0	52.1	181 (+16)	253 (-16)	Toss-Up
1986 (Reagan)	44.4	54.3	177 (-4)	258 (+5)	Lean Democratic
1988 (H. W. Bush)	45.6	53.3	175 (-2)	260 (+2)	Lean Democratic
1990 (H. W. Bush)	44.3	52.1	167 (-8)	267 (+7)	Lean Democratic

The 1980s were like the 1950s, an era of Republican high, but they are misunderstood. Eisenhower's wins had few coattails, just like Nixon in '72; Reagan's victories had an initial coattail that was the biggest since the

---

[7] Republicans picked up the Senate in 1952 along with the House in a landslide win for General Eisenhower. By 1954, despite peace and pulling out of Korea and economic prosperity, both chambers were lost.

1920s but relatively modest for a forty-nine-state landslide win in 1984. Therefore, the consistent trend in these years was that of Republican presidents, often winning in landslide victories that do not happen anymore, and Democratic Congresses. Only in 1966, a backlash election to the Great Society direction, did Republicans have a significant congressional victory, picking up forty-seven House seats, whereas Democrats had such elections in 1958, 1964, and 1974. Most important, never once did Republicans win the overall House vote in these years. In the years since 1992, this story is entirely flipped but without the landslides.

And the landslides in the Democratic direction are what the court of the Third Civic Order (the institutional culture and legacy media) desires most of all. Even though journalists tried to make the claim that 1992, 1996, and 2008 represented significant and emerging Democratic majorities, only one of those presidential elections was an above 50 percent majority of the popular vote, and none of those elections even exceeded the 1988 election of Reagan successor George H. W. Bush, the landslide that everyone forgets about today.

H. W. Bush, one of the more policy-successful one-term presidents, had no coattails in 1988 as well but also had no great backlash against him in 1990. Heading into the 1990s he was the odds-on favorite to win reelection for himself and win the fourth straight presidential term for his party. Instead, he became one of the rare incumbents that lost.

Incumbents usually win, and successors usually lose.

When Incumbents Lose

The incumbent political party splits or faces a viable primary challenge where the primary opponent wins a significant amount of the vote (which happened to Taft in 1912, Carter in 1980, and H. W. Bush in 1988). Notably, the 2020 Trump election is unique and analogous to Hoover in 1932 having neither of these features. But unlike Hoover, Trump was not turned away in a landslide that predates and eventually moves into a new paradigm; rather Trump had one of the more interesting showings for a presidential incumbent, who if they do lose, normally get turned away in a landslide, at least electorally.

When Successors Win

The electorate shows its clearest desire for the continuation of the status quo and direction the country is on when it elects a successor. In the Second Civic Order this successor transition happened frequently, as it did in the first as well. In the Third Civic Order it has never happened once except for from the out-party in the system. H. W. Bush won in 1988 as a successor. Truman in 1948 is the closest thing you can get to being a Democratic successor, but his impressive '48 come-from-behind win despite two party splits is an incumbent reelection victory as he was the sitting president, just never elected in his own right. Truman's position as belonging to the dominant party though is what Gerald Ford in 1976 lacked, opening the door for the unlikely presidency of Jimmy Carter.

If civic orders and generational alignments sound a bit like a monarchy, it's because it quasi is. The office of the presidency has become America's elected monarch for four years, with a media and culture that has been all too compliant in playing the role of the court, or court jester, and an academy as the clerisy.

This is why it's important to understand the dynamics of this civic order, the third, and why it is slowly but surely changing, in transition, and ultimately coming to an end. And how is it coming to an end? This story begins in 1992.

If the electorate genuinely likes the direction of the country, they should strongly consider not upsetting the apple cart. If the successor proves to be ineffective with too few of the strengths of what made them a successor and considerable weaknesses, or the outcomes are no longer going in a desired direction, that is the best time to go in another direction, as the rising boomer generation would choose to do in 1992. This was another three-way split election, not unlike 1912 and 1968, but also one that is entirely all its own that serves as our modern launching point to making sense of the emerging populist majority.

1980

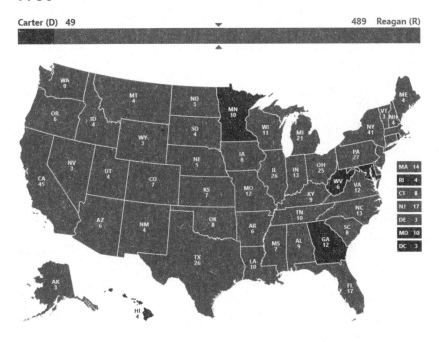

Carter (D) 49

489 Reagan (R)

1984

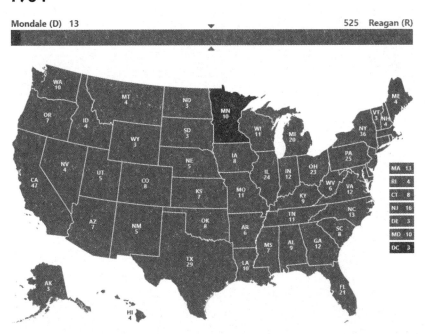

Mondale (D) 13

525 Reagan (R)

1988

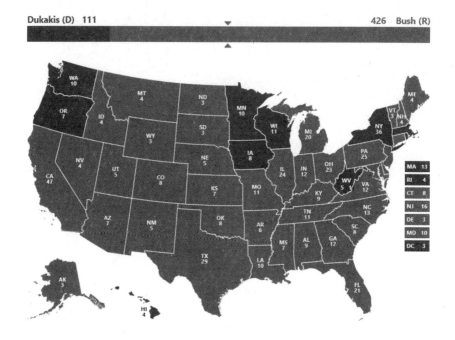

Dukakis (D) 111   426   Bush (R)

CHAPTER 4

BOOMER ALIGNMENT (1992 TO PRESENT)

The baby boomers may have come of age and been consumers and heavily influenced by the 1960s, but it's tremendously overstated how much they actually took part in those years of societal change, upheaval, and turmoil. On the positive end, those who marched with Dr. Martin Luther King were not boomers; they were of the silent generation, older than Joe Biden even, the first and only silent generation president. The oldest boomers were most definitely shaped by childhood in the American High of the 1950s and early '60s, and the prospect of being drafted during Vietnam shaped the generation and its subsequent politics in tremendous ways, and 1968 represents the first baby boomer presidential election (back then the voting age was twenty-one). Like Iraq and 2004 and Obama and 2008 are imprinted in the minds and memories of the elder millennials, so, too, was 1968 and 1972 on baby boomers. The origin story of each generational alignment generally coincides somewhere in the middle of the previous generational alignment. For a dominant generation like the GIs, boomers, and millennials, they will come to define the alignment more than the recessive (smaller) generations of the silents (sometimes called traditional), Gen X, and the rising Gen Z (sometimes referred to as zoomers).

Culturally speaking, the boomers have also been associated with liberalism and the New Left of the 1960s and 1970s. This is again, a mischaracterization of what this generation has accomplished and what their voting patterns actually are. It says more about the theory advanced in this text about civic orders (most seen and present in the court and gatekeeper role of the media and elite cultural institutions) than it does about how boomers actually voted. While the TV series *The Wonder Years* (1988–93) excellently showcased the coming of age years of the boomer generation, it also accurately depicted youth culture and support for George McGovern, a trend seen ever since the introduction of "the youths" and youth culture.

A young Kevin Arnold, enthusiastically supported the doomed '72 candidacy of McGovern with his TV girlfriend, Winnie Cooper. The real-life Bill Clinton similarly volunteered on the McGovern campaign down in Texas, sent there by campaign manager Gary Hart (who would later become a Colorado senator, the first "Atari" Democrat if you will) and finish runner-up to Walter Mondale in 1984. By those years boomers were not rallying around Hart or Mondale. Boomers in both 1980 and 1984 voted for Ronald Reagan. Like any large and dominant generation, boomer voting largely followed the winner in the years to come and became the ultimate swing vote. While it's fair to say boomers were more liberal, especially culturally, than both their GI parents and the silents, they were also less Democratic and more heterodox than reputation. Above all else, boomers loved politics and loved to argue about politics in a way their children have never warmed to.

In these twelve years in the presidential wilderness, Democrats still held the House throughout and the Senate through two-thirds of it, and while the Dukakis campaign self-destructed against what was thought to be a political opening against then Vice President George H. W. Bush, the Republican "lock" on the presidency was eventually picked by the opening salvo of the next alignment, the Boomer Alignment, who voted for Bill Clinton in a plurality just as they had for Reagan, before voting in the majority.

Consider the country in 1990 and 1991 and the political brilliance of Bill Clinton, despite his many personal and character flaws. So much of our politics and culture today can be understood by the 1992 election, both for good and for bad. And it is this alignment, the second full generational alignment of the Third Civic Order, that will also be the last one of it. In fact, we're in the final decade of it. And this transition out of both this alignment and the civic order forms the basis of the emerging populist majority. To find out what the emerging majority is today and in the future though, we must first understand what it is not and what it emerges in opposition to, just as most political developments and durable coalitions emerge from.

Above all else, the emerging political movements are propelled by a backlash and intense dislike of the processes of globalization and the political philosophy of globalism advanced by societal elites. This backlash did not emerge out of nowhere, and it existed before globalization even got going. Globalization and globalism are distinct from the twentieth-century internationalism that was vital to winning the Second World War and facing down the threat of the Soviet Union and navigating the Cold War that never turned bright hot. But the absence of the Cold War, the fall of the Berlin Wall, and breakup of the Soviet Union also did something else to US politics—it hastened the end of one political era and the coalitional alignment around it and brought about the beginning of another. The 1992 election perfectly illustrates this beginning.

Going into the '92 election cycle, George H. W. Bush looked like the incumbent that couldn't lose. Fresh off the quickest and cleanest land war in history, the liberation of Kuwait, which included Russia in the coalition, Bush the Elder topped out in the Gallup poll at 89 percent approval. He looked unbeatable. And if he was going to be beaten, a southern governor from a small state who bombed in his speech at the 1988 Democratic convention looked unlikely to be the victor. Whether the election was Bush versus Mario Cuomo (New York's then governor) or someone else, prognosticators had Bush as the easy reelection favorite. Eighteen months later, Bush had an approval at 29 percent in August heading into the fall election and looked like he was heading for massive defeat. The final result ended up being far closer than it could have been. So what happened?

Many could point to the economic downturn, but compared to past and later downturns, recessions, and depressions, that's not a convincing argument—especially considering the fact that the downturn coincided with those high approvals and was over by the time the election season heated up. While there was a sluggish recovery, considered a jobless recovery by some, that's not manifestly different from the economic conditions facing Barack Obama's reelection in 2012. Instead, I'll propose that it was success itself that undid the War Generation Alignment, held together by the presence of the Cold War. After four and a half decades, the public expected a victory dividend much in the same way the United States got one after the Second World War. Unlike the much-needed Marshall Plan with Germany and Japan, such a plan was less needed for Russia. The fall of communism in Russia and the Eastern Bloc need not be the economic equivalent of the war-torn and bombed-out cities from the 1940s. Americans and the Western world celebrated the end of the Cold War, and the fall of the Berlin wall and Reagan's famous words to Gorbachev gave him a plausible case to be remembered along the upper echelon of the American presidents.

While the old school liberals and new left progressives derided the idea of Ronald Reagan "winning the Cold War," and indeed that accomplishment should be shared in part by all the administrations from Truman to H. W. Bush, what both Reagan detractors and national security conservatives miss is that Reagan's legacy is just as much a rhetorical accomplishment as it is geopolitical or economic. Yes, the 1980s were, too, a decade of economic recovery and ushered in the last era of 4 percent and more growth in the country as far as GDP to this day, but above all what is remembered is the optimism and patriotism that made the 1980s and set up the 1990s as decades of relative renewal and prosperity after nearly two decades of upheaval and economic stagnation or decline against the backdrop of social and cultural change.

Above all else, the coalition that elected Republican presidents in landslides while electing Democrats to Congress overall from Eisenhower to Nixon to Reagan to H. W. Bush had been robbed of its reason to exist in the face of such success in the second half of the twentieth century's battle of systems: no Soviet Union, no Cold War, no Republican presidents winning landslides. But as we would soon find out throughout this alignment, there were no more Democrats running the show at the congressional level either. And when they did, it would not last for long.

Democratic Presidential Vote during the Boomer Alignment

Year	Candidate	Popular Vote (%)	Electoral Vote
1992	Clinton	43.0	370
1996	Clinton	49.2	*379*
2000	Gore	48.4	266
2004	Kerry	48.26	251
2008	Obama	*52.86*	365
2012	Obama	51.01	332
2016	Clinton	48.02	227
2020	Biden	51.26	306

Republican Presidential Vote during the Boomer Alignment

Year	Candidate	Popular Vote (%)	Electoral Vote
1992	H. W. Bush	37.45	168
1996	Dole	40.72	159
2000	W. Bush	47.87	271
2004	W. Bush	*50.73*	286
2008	McCain	45.60	173
2012	Romney	47.15	206
2016	Trump	45.93	*306*
2020	Trump	46.80	232

In 1992, Bill Clinton seemed to crack the code on the Republican lock on the presidency, but he also had a lot of help and good fortune. Perhaps his best good fortune was his own political instincts that led him to pass up what looked to be a favorable field for the Democratic nomination in 1988 while running in 1992 when most Democrats saw H. W. Bush as unbeatable. In many ways the very experienced at many areas of government President Bush was the ideal president to preside over the post–Cold War world. The only problem was voters no longer cared about the Cold War. The America facing 1992 wanted times of peace to soon be times of prosperity, no matter what the political configuration had been.

Incumbent President Bush made the typical Republican argument of less taxes and less government spending; challenger and Governor Bill Clinton made the typical Democratic argument more taxes (emphasis on the wealthy to avoid the reality that taxes go up for everyone usually) and more government spending, which he called "investments," but wisely avoided culture or played it safe there (for obvious reasons as we'd find out). While his political skills were considerable, he was also a political chameleon, which allowed him to be different things to different voters. But in the early '90s, both Bush and Clinton were for the fundamental opening salvo to the economic post–Cold War era that would usher in hyper-globalization and technological change—the North American Free Trade Agreement. What was most distinctive about 1992 was the third-candidate challenge of Ross Perot, who received a higher percentage of the vote of anyone going back to Theodore Roosevelt's Bull Moose run in 1912, also an election of generational change and also an election where a third-party candidate broke up a long-running Republican dominance of the White House. The 1992 election also featured, despite not winning any states, a viable primary challenge from within the incumbent party in the White House with Pat Buchanan's primary challenge, receiving nearly 40 percent of the vote, an impressive showing.

Both Buchanan and Perot failed to win a single state in 1992, but their showings have been highly influential and relevant in explaining what became the populist revolt to hyper-globalization that emerged in the 1990s, 2000s, and 2010s and that forms so much of the backdrop of our politics today. Buchanan brought forth a distinctive cultural and social conservative warning of losing traditional American values and morality in the wake of globalization, with Perot's focus being more on economics.

Buchanan also provided the model for political entrepreneurs to come, observed author and historian Thomas Frank, like Steve Bannon. Bannon may have worked at Goldman Sachs, but his working-class roots and experiences in the navy gave him a distinctive insight into what the political class had wrought on the common people and ordinary working families like the one he hailed from. "Class was central to the insurgency Bannon believed he summoned up as Trump's chief campaign executive," Frank observed.[xliii] While NAFTA, the 1992 election, and other generational trends may have been the boiling water of the 2016 election, the inciting incident lay slightly past its middle point in the financial crisis and bailouts that were done in a bipartisan fashion just like the Iraq War had been. And unlike other American populists, Bannon did not just seek to upturn globalism for America but for the globe itself. "For Steve Bannon, the financial crisis and the bailouts were the inciting incident for the global populist rebellion he wanted to lead."[xliv] A rebellion that probably becomes wholly unnecessary if the political class saw fit to cash in and broadly share a victory dividend post–Cold War, say no to NAFTA, and pump the breaks on the social and cultural onslaught to American traditions and families that were merely slowed down or slightly reversed in the 1980s and 1990s.

Perot was the only true critic of the three in the general on free trade; he warned of a "giant sucking sound" of jobs being sent to Mexico. Between Clinton and Bush, Clinton was more likely to request free and fair trade in deals with other countries, no doubt a nod to organized labor's pull on the Democrats. Organized labor was the original viable critique of the bipartisan free trade consensus of the Boomer Alignment. After winning the election, Clinton went on to sign NAFTA into law with bipartisan votes in

1993, and the rest is history—and the present. Perot also warned about the dangers of the federal deficit and national debt, which were held in check thanks to a good 1990s economy providing enough revenue, and the fiscal discipline of the Republicans in Congress, plus two-term President Bill Clinton's willingness and desire to cut any deal to stay in power, stay relevant, and have a legacy. And indeed he did have one. Despite having some genuine successes as president, he has become the president probably most associated with the Boomer Alignment and the generational policy consensus that alignment has represented. This consensus would come into full view after Clinton merely passed the American alternating monarchy back to the Bush family.

1992

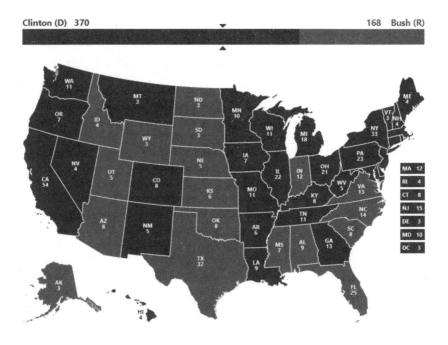

Above all else 1992 ushered in generational change and the beginning of a fifty-fifty gridlocked America, and it represents the actual "switch-era" in

American politics to the extent that one exists. Prior to '92 for four decades Republicans won the presidency usually during the War Generation Alignment, often in a landslide, while Democrats were stronger locally and held Congress nearly every year in both houses, holding the House of Representatives every year. After the '92 election, Democrats tended to either win the presidency or lose it while winning the popular vote. Since '92, only one election has been a clear margin for the winner in both popular and electoral votes (2008, which we'll end this chapter with), and like the War Generation Alignment (see 1964 and LBJ vs. Goldwater), there has been one exception election to this rule since, in 2004, when George W. Bush was reelected and also won the popular vote. Unlike the prior alignment, Republicans starting in 1994 have held Congress most of the time and have continued to grow in local and state strength, giving an unfair advantage in the minds of many partisan Democrats but also an advantage that actually is self-aware of the rules of the constitutional republican form of government and federalist system.

Another feature that gets to the heart of the dominant generational zeitgeist is military service. From 1945 to the '92 election, every single president served as commander in chief with at least some military service themselves, ranging from genuine war heroism in the case of John F. Kennedy, George H. W. Bush, and General Eisenhower to contributing to the war effort in uniform in some capacity even if stateside with Lyndon Johnson and Ronald Reagan. Since the election of Bill Clinton, whose avoidance of the draft under conspicuous events he was able to spin to his political benefit, a testament to his political skills, the boomer generation and alignment that came of age in the era of Vietnam featured no military veterans, and the only president and commander in chief of the last thirty years to serve in uniform in any capacity was again, for an exception, George W. Bush's service in the Air National Guard, which also was rather checkered during the 2000 campaign and again during the 2004 campaign. In fact, if anything, military service has been used against the presidential candidates who lost since '92.

1996

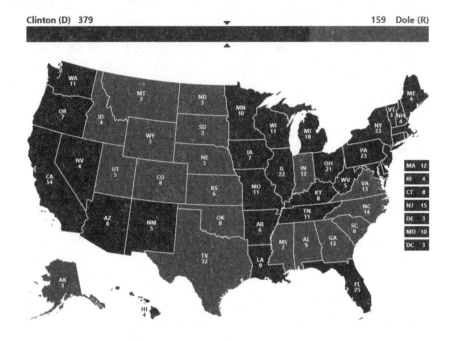

Clinton (D) 379   159 Dole (R)

From Bob Dole's attempt in 1996 to embark on "one last mission" for his generation to John Kerry in 2004, to John McCain in 2008. As the draft-era Vietnam generation continues to age and we move into the all-volunteer citizen and professional soldiers of the interwar years of the Persian Gulf and post-9/11 generation, it's entirely possible America does not see a military veteran as president ever again, when at one time it was a de facto qualification for the office that includes, among most important duties, roles, and responsibilities, the role of commander in chief of America's armed forces. The absence of the Cold War plus the all-volunteer age, plus the considerable and increasing influence of mass media in the pre-ubiquitous internet age, made the new boomer generation and consensus and transition from Reagan to Clinton relatively seamless, even if the experienced hands in Washington tended to view the incoming and relative youngster Clinton as deeply unserious and not deserving to be there. But before we move on, the question must be asked: Why in a generational alignment claimed to still be in function and form (despite three decades of subtle and not so subtle changes) are we devoting so much time to 1992?

Because 1992 is the window into the politics of today. It is the opening chapter. This is not to discount the American political and considerable cultural history prior to 1992 but only to elevate the importance of the current generation of voters and how important the narrative of American life and history is to this story and paradigm. Mentioned also are two people who did not win a single state—Pat Buchanan (who would run for president again) and Ross Perot (who also would). For their respective older generations, both of these figures are their generation's Cassandra to a large degree. In many ways the Trump coalition that would shock the political world in the biggest upset in American presidential politics since 1948 is a combination of Pat Buchanan's primary challenge and Ross Perot's candidacy and issues. The first vote for president that Donald Trump would ever receive was actually from Perot's political party that launched and then was unable to find any sort of successor—the Reform Party in California. Both Buchanan and Trump were possible candidates in 2000 for that nomination. All of this occurred before Trump switched his registration to Democratic in New York, among six other party switches in that closed primary state. Yet despite all those switches there remains a remarkable clarity and consistency on the actual issues and vision. The future anti-Trump coalition are those most committed to the globalization consensus that became established after the 1992 election, which was then brought into hyperdrive and defended by the party establishments of both the Democrats and the Republicans.

The Third Civic Order was articulated as needing to make the world safe for democracy, and in the twenty-first century, the more democracy would begin to slip into a recession after the first few years of the War on Terror, the harder it would become to maintain the consensus. Consider the 1992 election results but between only the two challengers to the incumbent (see the map below).

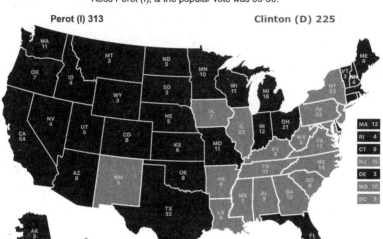

1992 US Presidential Election if the only two candidates were Bill Clinton (D) & Ross Perot (I), & the popular vote was 50-50.

What you see here is a remarkable consistency between the country that elected every Democratic president after Harry Truman, with Democrat Bill Clinton putting together a coalition at the county and state levels that is very similar to Jimmy Carter and to a lesser extent John F. Kennedy, and independent candidate Ross Perot, a full-on skeptic of free trade and the downstream effects of the new economy that would end up propping up the stability of the Boomer Alignment, and therefore the late Third Civic Order, performing incredibly well in what essentially is the old, old Republican coalition of Yankeedom (Northeast) and the Heartland (Midwest) all the way out west and to the coast. Of course in the three decades since, a lot of Clinton's strongest counties, especially in rural America, have gone away from the Democrats, which has made it incredibly difficult for their political results and outcomes to match their aspirations, and the cities have slipped further away as they had for many decades from the Republicans, that is…until the last eight years or so in many of the former industrialized areas.

First under Clinton and a Republican Congress, then under George W. Bush, who endured split, Republican, and Democratic Congresses, the uniparty consensus of liberal immigration bordering on a borderless vision of the world, of free trade and capital flowing throughout, and after 9/11, a foreign policy of undeclared, abstract, unwinnable, and forever wars made the Boomer Alignment and uniparty consensus harder and harder to swallow downstream.

And this is where the emerging populist majority, as a rejection of hyper-globalization, really begins to take shape.

2000

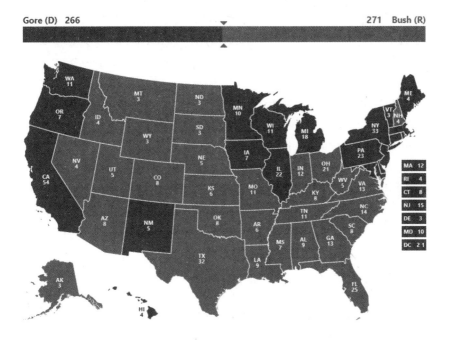

In 2002, thirty-three years after Kevin Phillips first published *The Emerging Republican Majority* and just off the heels of an underwhelming midterm that left the Democratic Party shut out of power at the presidency and Congress for the first time, Judis and Teixeira published *The Emerging*

Democratic Majority, which had tremendous political impact just as its predecessor had, even if the culmination of their thesis was a bit delayed in comparison, but it had even more cultural and media impact. Its influences on media and journalism, on academic theories and campus culture, especially after the 2008 election, cannot be overstated. Both of these books, while highly influential, thoroughly researched, and well-written, are also thoroughly misunderstood by many commentators and journalists. The rest of this book is about why that theory made sense for a brief time as the GOP of the Bush and boomer era became overwhelmed by neoconservatives, the religious right, and corporate influence but was also destined to fall apart the minute the GOP shed themselves of some of those influences and will only become more and more electable if it continues to. But regardless of what the GOP has done in the prior decade, and will do in the next decade, whether from establishment, conservatives, or populists, the crux of this thesis rests more on the Democratic Party, both on what they are doing and becoming, and also not doing and becoming. If you want to understand American politics today, you have to look more closely at the Democratic Party than the Republican Party. The Republican Party is the answering party of the civic order, searching for a new consensus after helping to shatter the old one, but that shattering, like all the great movements in American politics, came from the outside, not from within.

The Judis-Teixeira book is the heart and soul of the "demographic inevitability" thesis or the coalition of the ascendant, or the revenge of the George McGovern coalition if you will. And it was described both as a diverse coalition that includes the white working class, as well as an upwardly mobile professional-class coalition that would somehow continue to be in that same party. The next election of their book proved to be the opposite of an emerging coalition, and instead overly zealous Republicans envisioned a "forever majority." White House political advisors like Karl Rove, who had studied the McKinley coalition for years, made such claims. The 2000 election, much like the crossroads election of 1960—very, very close, with albeit much larger cultural divides than

in 1960—was supposed to be a fluke. The emerging coalition of demographic and cultural trends would eventually come to overwhelm a fading
coalition. The Bush coalition was but a temporary one holding a post-
9/11 "patriotic center," but soon the Clinton- (and later Obama-) forged
"progressive center" would come to dominate American politics in the
first half of the twenty-first century.

2004

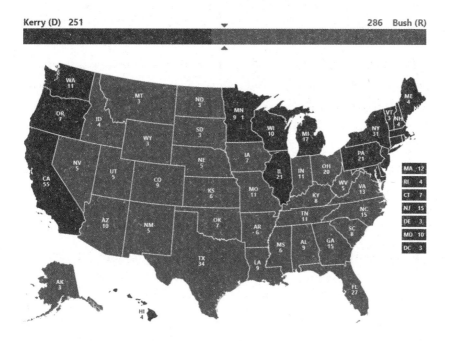

As this writing will show from here on out, the "progressive center" or
"coalition of the ascendent" predictions were both premature and unlikely
because coalitions of everyone rarely last very long. Political parties in
our two-party system reinforced by the electoral and constitutional system are coalitions of ideas, identities, and interests. And those coalitions
come under stress the longer they hold power, especially in a close to fifty-fifty nation as America largely has been since 1992. Unlike the pre-1992

alignment though, which also could be characterized as fifty-fifty (but in an entirely different way under Republican presidents and Democratic Congresses), the Democratic half of the alignment of the last few decades had higher and higher expectations that a generational consensus made up of younger, college-educated, and diverse voters was emerging around their party. The Republicans contributed to this mindset through their campaign tactics that mirrored this theory and bought into the narrative itself in many ways. This "doomer" fallacy has in many respects been proven premature and wrong too.

From 2006 to 2009 however, the Judis and Teixeira thesis seemed to be fulfilled, just a cycle after Phillips's had a generation earlier. Disapproval with the direction of the Iraq War, the Katrina response, and the failed reforms on Social Security and immigration because of misread mandates, and, frankly, because of narrow mandates led to the only significant and deep victories for the Democratic Party during the last thirty years. Ultimately, both Clinton's victories failed to achieve the modern "landslide" standard of the last actual landslide—1988. Clinton did not achieve a pure majority of the popular vote in either 1992 or 1996 (because of Ross Perot), and the 1996 clear electoral victory looked like the same lonely victory and nonexistent coattails that had long characterized the Republican landslide wins for four decades. The same limiting features of the professional class–led Republican coalition of yesterday were now becoming the same limiting features of the professional class–led Democratic coalition of today. While the 2006 midterm win was significant and stands out, it was not as deep as the Gingrich revolution of 1994, which won fifty-four seats in the House, or the later Republican midterm "Tea Party" wave of 2010, which won sixty-three seats in the House. The pure House vote that went Democratic every time for four decades now only barely went Democratic in 1996, despite having an easily reelected incumbent president at the top of the ticket, and could only muster the House vote they used to routinely have against one-party Republican governance in Washington. If this was an "emerging" Democratic majority at all, it sure was an evasive and peculiar one. However, if you freeze time after the 2006 midterms, or perhaps more accurately, after the 2008 election, one can understand how you would see it as fulfilled given the historical nature of that election of the nation's first black president.

What would give one pause though after that is to consider how dependent 2008 was on the timing of the financial crisis and subsequent Great Recession.

House of Representatives Vote during the Boomer Alignment

Year	Rep. Vote Share (%)	Dem. Vote Share (%)	Rep. Seats	Dem. Seats	Trend
1992 (Clinton)	45.1	50.1	176 (-9)	258 (+9)	Lean Democratic
1994 (Clinton)	51.5	44.7	230 (+54)	204 (-54)	Solid Republican
1996 (Clinton)	48.15	48.22	226 (-3)	207 (+2)	Toss-Up
1998 (Clinton)	48.4	47.3	223 (-4)	211 (+5)	Toss-Up
2000 (W. Bush)	47.6	47.1	221 (-2)	212 (+1)	Toss-Up
2002 (W. Bush)	50.0	45.2	229 (+8)	205 (-7)	Lean Republican
2004 (W. Bush)	49.4	46.8	232 (+3)	203 (-3)	Lean Republican
2006 (W. Bush)	44.3	52.3	202 (-30)	233 (+31)	Solid Democratic
2008 (Obama)	42.6	53.2	178 (-21)	257 (+21)	Solid Democratic
2010 (Obama)	51.7	44.9	242 (+63)	193 (-63)	Solid Republican
2012 (Obama)	47.7	48.8	234 (-8)	201 (+8)	Lean Democratic
2014 (Obama)	51.2	45.5	247 (+13)	188 (-13)	Solid Republican
2016 (Trump)	**49.1**	48.0	241 (-6)	194 (+6)	Lean Republican
2018 (Trump)	44.8	53.4	199 (-42)[8]	235 (+41)	Lean Democratic
2020 (Biden)[9]	47.7	50.8	213 (+14)	222 (-13)	Toss-Up
2022 (Biden)	50.6	47.8	222 (+9)	213 (-9)	Lean Republican

---

[8] Republicans picked up two seats in the US Senate.

[9] Biden's largely basement campaign was billed by the campaign and the media as a "return to normalcy" just as Harding and the Republican Party had sloganeered one hundred years prior, also during a pandemic and just after the Great War.

While *but for* analyses of presidential elections can go both ways, the reality is that the 2008 election was going to look much closer to what the 2012 result would be four years later. If the financial crisis had not occurred when it did, the Obama-Biden ticket would have still won, but it would have been far closer to the 3 or 4 percent steady lead and just over three hundred electoral votes that existed back in the day when polling science and actual election results were relatively in line with one another. And they would remain in line with one another for just one more cycle for reasons varied and complicated depending on the polling institution.

Nevertheless, more than any other election, 2008 and its precursor midterm success far more than the 2020 result represents the closest to the fulfillment of the Judis-Teixeira thesis that America will ever see, with the country's new political coalition emerging out of what they called "ideo-polises," postindustrial metropolitan areas where tolerance and creativity rule in their words at the time. But what is also notable, even in victory, is the seeds set, as all these maps show, of the counter-pivot somewhere else in the country and somewhere else in the coalition. There was never any doubt that unless substantial boom economic times and public outcomes were posted, a restlessness would set in to the Democratic coalition of post-2008 just as the post-2002 restlessness of Karl Rove's strategy of building a neo-McKinley coalition with George W. Bush set in across Republican-town. In part, because in many ways people felt that much of that town had been deindustrialized, too, and that maybe Ross Perot and Pat Buchanan had a point after all about trade, the family, and the eroding American culture. The temporary success of the Obama-led emerging demographics coalition and the downright failure of the neoconservative and globalization and corporate-centric Bush-Rove coalition set the stage for the events to come.

2008

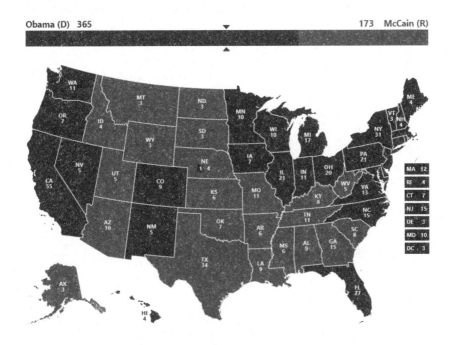

Obama (D) 365   173   McCain (R)

CHAPTER 5

THE DEMOCRATIC PARTY IN THE
LAST DECADE (2008 TO 2020)

B arack Obama was supposed to be the Democratic president of generational renewal. Whereas Bill Clinton cracked the code on the
Republican lock on the electoral college, Barack Obama was to be the
transformational figure that "changed Washington," fulfilled and ushered
in as prophetic—*The Emerging Democratic Majority*. In 2006 and 2008,
a few cycles after that book was published, it had "emerged." Or so the
media and journalistic response would have you believe, first after 2008,
and then again, inexplicably, after 2012. Additionally, this emerging coalition was referred to as the "coalition of the ascendant" by Ron Brownstein.
A coalition led by minorities, young voters, and college-educated whites,
particularly women, would prove to be durable and long-lasting. While
solid analysis has been done on how conservatives won the Heartland
of America, just as much can be attributed to the genuine preferences
and strategy of the official Democratic Party response, whether it was
the McGovern reforms post-1968 that removed organized labor from
their essential veto power role within party primaries to the Democratic
Leadership Council (DLC) and Clinton-era strategy to "forget blue collar
voters and concentrate instead on affluent, white collar professionals who
are liberal on social issues."[xlv] In a sense, as the coalitions crossed each

other in parts reminiscent of past party coalitional crossroads, in tandem with the increasing but still minority share of the population obtaining a college education, both parties increasingly became vehicles for the upper-middle class throughout the 1990s, 2000s, and 2010s.

What was seen first in the McGovern campaign of '72, the losing primary campaign of Senator Gary Hart and the "Atari Democrats" of 1984, on to the Ivy League–educated presidencies of Bill Clinton and Barack Obama, the Democrats positioned themselves toward the new economy and the so-called "learning class." This cohort was to be made up of individuals who were "better educated, more affluent, more mobile, and more self-reliant" than others, and both of America's political parties would be required—on pain of utter destruction—to compete single-mindedly for their votes.[xlvi] The prescient analysis delivered by Thomas Frank in *Listen, Liberal*—almost anticipating the result of 2016—detailed Democrats' betrayal of working-class interests in their dogged pursuit of white collar professional-class voters and showed that this courting and upper-bracket excess could only go so far before it triggered a populist backlash…and that America had reached that point.

That was in 1990. Sixteen years later a cottage industry of articles, books, and analysis sprang up in Democratic circles around whether the Trumpian populist backlash was cultural or more economic. And in general, old school Democrats of the New Deal variety who wanted a return to the party's twentieth-century roots on economics tended to cite it as economics, and the lean-in, get and stay "woke" gender, race, and identity cohort tended to cite culture. In reality, it was both. Another cottage industry of ostensibly civic-oriented and discouraged moderates and independents grew frustrated over the political divide and began to propose dozens of iterations of a new or third party that always seemed to sound like the same relative social liberal, economically "pragmatic" as the party elites of the major parties already were. This, too, mistakes what party coalitions actually are.

To reiterate, political coalitions in two-party systems are made up of ideas, interests, and identities. Winning coalitions, whether they last or not, can be broad (overall number), deep (commitment to the cause itself), or both. In the wake of such pronouncements, that a new generation led by a younger boomer who represented America's future as a multiracial and multicultural democracy in Barack Obama had defeated an older coalition that was less diverse and too white, proved irresistible for a media so deeply invested in this narrative and so deeply invested in the court role to the Third Civic Order. As this chapter will show though, all these media narratives have gone up in smoke, and had they never existed in the first place, had people just tried to strive for objective and honest journalism that acts closer to referees rather than reducing politics and coverage down to team sports and entertainment, we probably would have some different history. According to the court and clerisy (academia) narrative, Republicans were supposed to never win another election because of changing demographics, and a prolonged period of Democratic dominance was taking over for a more Republican-leaning one. There was only one problem with all these narratives. None of them were true, and all of them have contributed to a confused and frustrated citizenry.

Had a new era dawned in 2008, whether ones calls it a realignment election, a critical election, or a new and/or continued era where "progressive centrism" of *The Emerging Democratic Majority* reigns actually happened, Democrats would not have lost the House of Representatives in the 2010 midterms, the Senate in the 2014 midterms, the presidency in 2016, and a lasting majority of the fifty states along the way. Instead the second book and related theories of the "emerging" genre have aged poorly, to the extent that the authors denounce them today (at least the fair-minded ones). This was similarly true at the geographic level up and down the electoral map. Consider the electoral map that was promised and projected, with notes and annotations below for Solid and Lean Dem and GOP.

Electoral Map of the once Emerging Democratic Majority
320 Dem (light gray), 218 Rep (dark gray)

Just like with coalitions of everybody from a demographic standpoint do not last more than a few elections, geographies of everywhere cannot last either. Somehow, the political culture of Missouri, West Virginia, and Ohio would mix just fine with the upwardly mobile and ascendant coalition along tech corridors, finance capitals, and other beneficiaries and winners of globalization. It's notable that not only did the geography miss greatly on the Democratic to Republican side but also in reverse from Republican to Democratic. There are two notable statewide wins and permanent realignments associated with Barack Obama's win—Colorado and Virginia. And while it's tempting to chalk those realignments up to demographic change and the emerging professional class–led coalition prophesied, the HR department that was promised if you will, the reality is even its proponents missed the realignments where that was true. Virginia, which has gone Republican at the gubernatorial level two times since 2008, will now only go Republican at the presidential level in a landslide year; and Colorado has become an even tougher lift for the Republicans, having gone Democratic every year since 2008, and only once at the statewide level for Senate has it gone Republican. Even these realignments are not permanent, but they look tough for the foreseeable future. Every election, trend, swing, and "realignment" is relative to one another. In this sense, it is relative to the national trend and national number where one exists. This is why the focus throughout has been not just on national presidential elections (even though presidential elections are also, for good reason, a series of state elections), but also on the national popular vote in the House of Representatives. Unlike Senate and gubernatorial elections, these are the only two measures that can accurately assess the national party strength in an "everywhere votes at once" type of way.

Going the other way, since 2008, many of the Judis-Teixeira projected Democratic states, whether leaning that way at the time or Republican at the time, have failed to materialize or moved steadily away from the Democrats. This wasn't just true in 2016; it was visible in 2012 as well. By 2012 it was apparent that West Virginia was long gone at the presidential level, and this should have been apparent as early as 2004 when George W. Bush expanded his five to six point win in 2000 and more than doubled it to thirteen. This makes Bill Clinton's '92 and '96 wins there the last you'll see for some time in what is now one of the most Republican states in the country. West Virginia, as you saw in earlier chapters and maps, was once the most Democratic state in the country, along with Minnesota. Dating back to the beginning of FDR's four straight wins, both of these states in the last few decades have trended heavily away from the Democrats: Minnesota to the point of being the most Democratic state in 1984 to being only a few points more Democratic than the nation in 2020 (and even much earlier than that, idling there since around the millennium), while West Virginia went from being one of the few states to stick with Jimmy Carter in 1980 to voting Republican by over 40 percent four decades later. This marks just the beginning of how off the Emerging Democratic Majority map was. In addition to West Virginia, Missouri, Ohio, and Iowa have trended so far away from the Democrats that they could be characterized as strong Republican states now. This is similarly true of Florida. In the lean or toss-up and not looking category, the once-projected strong Democratic states of Wisconsin, Pennsylvania, and Michigan are no more.

While in good Democratic years these states may go blue, in any election where the two-party popular vote is split fifty-fifty, Republicans can be expected to win all three, winning the Badger and Keystone states with clear margins.

What should have been more obvious in 2012, that the Obama coalition was no realignment at all nor any lock on the Electoral College or America's political future with "demographic inevitability," was missed by most observers. One reason it was missed is that the electoral lock and supposed "blue wall" was in place to such an extent that a fifty-fifty election would have resulted in a Democratic win, even with a loss in the popular vote. This was also true in 2004 when John Kerry was a win in Ohio away from losing the popular vote while winning the only election that counts—the race to 270 in the electoral college. The gravitation to who wins the Electoral College in fifty-fifty scenarios has fluctuated throughout American history, only coincidentally affecting the Democrats, first in the nineteenth century, then again in the twenty-first century. However, there is no doubt that had Nixon failed to reach 270 electoral votes in both 1960 (when he did) and 1968 (when he did not), Democratic delegations in the House would have proceeded to perform their constitutional duty in selecting the president, which would have gone along partisan lines: Kennedy in 1960 and Humphrey in 1968. What is today a Democratic weakness in the Electoral College as it compares to the popular vote was once more often a Republican one. The simple fact is the Democrats have concentrated too many of their voters in too few areas. In a sense, even if the Democratic coalition of everybody is demographically diverse and rich, it is not wide enough geographically, nor is it deep enough in difficult years. But none of this mattered at all in the wake of the 2008 historic victory, where just like in 2004 and 2012, a fifty-fifty election year or slight Republican popular vote win would have resulted in a Democratic presidential victory (see table below).

2008 State Voting Relative to the National Trend (7.3 - D)

States	Electoral Votes	Relative to National Trend	In a Fifty-Fifty National Situation
Colorado	9	2.6 more Democratic than the nation	
Virginia	13	1 more Republican than the nation	Goes Republican
Indiana	11	6.3 more Republican than the nation	Goes Republican
Missouri	11	7.4 more Republican than the nation	
Nebraska Second Congressional District	1	3 more Republican than the nation	Goes Republican
Pennsylvania	21	3 more Republican than the nation	
North Carolina	15	7 more Republican than the nation	Goes Republican
Georgia	15	12.5 more Republican than the nation	
Florida	27	4.5 more Republican than the nation	Goes Republican
Arizona	10	16.4 more Republican than the nation	
Nevada	5	5.2 more Democratic than the nation	
Texas	34	19.1 more Republican than the nation	
Michigan	17	9.1 more Democratic than the nation	
Iowa	7	2.2 more Democratic than the nation	
Ohio	20	2.7 more Republican than the nation	Goes Republican
Wisconsin	10	6.6 more Democratic than the nation	
Minnesota	10	3.1 more Democratic than the nation	

Results if the Nation Voted Fifty-Fifty: Obama 277, McCain 259

This same exercise would have yielded a slightly narrower 272 to 266 victory for Obama's reelection over Mitt Romney rather than the 332 to 206 electoral vote margin of the actual result. This underscores the reason the Electoral College exists in the first place. The founders were distrustful of direct democracy and noted, correctly, that every total democracy had cannibalized itself within a generation. The Electoral College, like other compromises, was put into place both to distance the passion of the voters from the responsible governance of the country and also to ensure that no one geographic area of the country could dominate it. Keep in mind that at the time of ratification there were no truly large metropolitan areas in the country. The country was largely rural and smaller towns and villages. To the extent the country industrialized, that larger-scale industrialization was more associated with first the Whigs and then the Republicans early on rather than the Democrats. But this is not the reason for progressive activist hostility and desire to move beyond the Electoral College and much of the Constitution writ large. That reason is they have come to believe they cannot win often enough to enact the agenda they desire with the rules as they currently exist. And this reality is both why the Republicans have a sense of urgency today and have changed their strategy and approach in the past decade and also why the Democrats have become more and more frustrated with their inability to win large majorities.

Simply put, the "emerging" Democratic, next-generation coalition might have appeared deep, but it was not wide, not nearly wide enough. In contrast, the FDR coalition from the New Deal, which commanded support from both large cities and the small towns and farms, was able to be far more durable than any Democratic coalition dating back to the beginning of the party system itself and certainly since. Much to their frustration—as seen in first West Virginia, then Missouri, Ohio, and Iowa; and then through the "blue wall" itself—it has become the Republicans that are far closer to putting together that coalition than the Democrats. This large gap between aspirations and expected, if not entitled, rule, reminds one of "You're the Top" from Cole Porter in 1934: nostalgia for the Coolidge dollar and all, and presumption of the nominee of the GOP "on top." The first half of the decade trend away from the Democrats and the emerging or ascendant coalition should have been the warning for 2016, but it was not. As the bubbles of media and academy served as cultural blinders, reinforcing an arrogant and ill-advised strategy where large swaths of the country were written off in advance, none of this would have happened if it weren't for the underlying outcomes themselves tied to the era of globalization and in many ways back to the 1970s.

For a moment after the 2012 election, these trends were again set aside as President Barack Obama won what is in retrospect a fairly impressive reelection victory given the sluggish economic recovery. Obama's considerable political skills made him a fundamentally better candidate than Mitt Romney, who lacked the necessary counterpunch to win. Writing in *Our Divided Political Heart*,[xlvii] E. J. Dionne Jr. of the *Washington Post* summed up the 2012 election as a "vindication for the Long Consensus, Obama and the next generation of progressives need to prove that its ideas and approaches are capable of renovation, and can restore the living standards of Americans, particularly those who rallied to the president in the nation's industrial Heartland and the inner cities, but also voters in suburban and rural areas who had opposed him. What both sides shared was a desire to put an end to fears of American decline and to inaugurate a New Prosperity that would prove to be durable, and widely shared."

2012

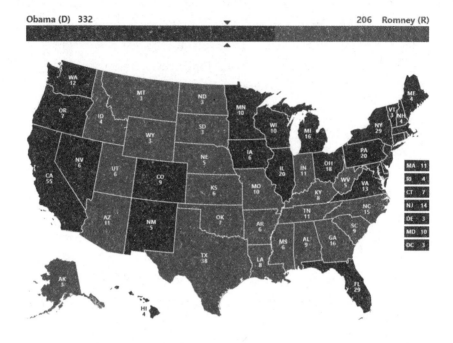

In 2008 even in the midst of the largest popular vote percentage and a convincing electoral vote win, there was already a significant urban and rural divide that was somewhat present in the previous decades, but not to the extent of the past fifteen to twenty years, where it's been growing. Clinton, a son of the South and, more importantly, from a smaller community, was able to stem this long-term trend of small towns and rural communities drifting away from the Democratic Party, but after, the trend resumed in earnest. In 2008, winning candidate Barack Obama won 879 counties. In his reelection, which still was a wide enough coalition to win the electoral vote even if he had narrowly lost the popular vote, he won 689 counties, nearly 200 fewer. And in 2016, Hillary Clinton won 200 fewer exactly for 489.

In 2020, Joe Biden made presidential election history by capturing the presidency with the fewest won counties—509, winning only twenty more than Hillary Clinton. Of course, this was immediately written off by the media as unimportant. But it underscores the urban-rural divide, one that is actually going to close in the coming years if other trends continue. While it looks unlikely that rural counties will begin supporting Democrats again en masse, there are other trends that are closing the urban-rural gap the other way. The 509 or so number is important because there are limits to how many states can be won among the fifty states simply by spiking urban turnout. And this matters because the less rural and more urban and suburban the makeup of the Democratic coalition becomes, the more they'll lean into a culture-first (over economics and foreign policy) strategy that will alienate rural America more and more, thus making a comeback there even more unlikely.

In the 2019 book *Why Cities Lose: The Deep Roots of the Urban-Rural Political Divide*, Jonathan Rodden noted that the urban-rural divide has been most responsible for political polarization but also added the caveat that the most interesting battles to come will likely come within parties rather than between the parties.[xlviii] In this sense, analyzing the makeup of the parties themselves from a geography (the Electoral College, representation, and state-by-state control itself), demography (race and gender, but especially education, age, and parentage), and ideology (whether the coalition can unite around shared values, vision, and principles enough or whether there is too much tension within) standpoint. As much as our politics seems hopelessly divided today, a much more accurate analysis is looking at the battles within the parties themselves, as the UK group More in Common did both in the United States and parts of Europe with their *Hidden Tribes* report. Regardless of specific characterization, a growing consensus away from the traditional discussion of left and right continues to animate the most astute analysis of American politics. And while the urban-rural divide is far more accidental than anything else and it is closing, there is no doubt that the left versus right divide of the twentieth century becomes less and less helpful with the party of the left in the United States now strongly allied with the forces of well-compensated urban professionals and venture capitalists who benefit from global free trade, and the party of the right increasingly critical of free trade and global capitalism[xlix] or globalism.

In 2008 the country was more polarized than in 1992, which seemed more polarized than in 1978. Much of this "polarization" is merely the work of media and culture and turning politics into a version of "team sports" or the celebrity-fication of politics that started a bit with John Kennedy at the dawn of the TV age and took another step forward in 2008 with Barack Obama and, to some extent, Sarah Palin on the Republican side. Both figures were ratings draws that aspects of the corporate media fawned over. The same was true of a literal celebrity and reality TV figure in Donald Trump in 2016, and the lightning rod and stand-in for the millennial progressive activists in Alexandria Ocasio-Cortez in 2018. But AOC, as she is now known, in an attempt to cosplay past glory years of FDR and LBJ, lacks any popular reach outside of urban enclaves, much like the progressive activist political tribe itself.

The *Hidden Tribes* report from 2018, updated in subsequent articles since, broke down the American electorate as comprising no more than 8 percent as "progressive activists," which made up one "wing," while another "wing" was composed of 25 percent between "traditional conservatives" and "devoted conservatives," which the report and survey did not distinguish well. Two other features are why "traditional liberals" comprising 11 percent, along with "passive liberals" comprising 15 percent, "disengaged" voters comprising 26 percent, and "moderates" comprising 15 percent were included in the "exhausted majority" thesis in one group. Later on in this text, absent an update of these American political tribes, we'll speculate on what has happened since and where these groups could end up and the role they will play in an emerging majority coalition that is trending in the opposite direction from what psychologist Jonathan Haidt hoped for (by his own admission, seeking to figure out how to bring about an emerging liberal majority through his work), political messaging figures like George Lakoff tried to coach for (*Don't Think of an Elephant*), or the trend analysis of two decades ago that foretold an emerging Democratic majority from prior trends that the media and our culture picked up and arrogantly ran with, causing much confusion and frustration on both sides of the aisle ever since.

Since that time, the Democratic Party has switched or become on the other side of the Republican Party on two key issues, both of which on the less popular side. On economics, voters now see the Republican Party as better stewards of the economy, including the middle class; and on foreign policy, then as now, Republicans have opened up an advantage even though the party is moving to very different positions than the neo-con-heavy party of the post-9/11 era. For purposes of what drives voters to the polls usually, it's the economics and the Democratic Party's coalitional changes, dependencies, and the fundamental policy outcomes that drive an increasing reliance on social identity and culture issues to hold together its ossifying and fraying coalition.

None of this appeared so in 2008 though. Candidate Barack Obama campaigned on one hand in a very patriotic and post-partisan way yet also held out the possibility of a "fundamental transformation" of Washington, DC, politics as usual. The vagueness of "hope" and "change" was as politically brilliant as Biden's basement campaign twelve years later, as voters, frustrated with the war in Iraq and the financial crisis, were able to read into the message and the man whatever they wanted to see. For progressive left activists, and many traditional liberals, what they wanted to see was generational change for the party and an FDR for the twenty-first century. They were expecting the "prince (and princess) that was promised"—the emerging Democratic majority.

As Obama governed, the contradictions in him, much like those of Bill Clinton in the 1990s, were not necessarily confined to personal traits but rather the pulling demands of the aspiring Democratic coalition itself, which grew to have less and less in common with one another, held together only by being *against* Republicans, which in 2016 and in many ways 2020, when Democrats lost thirteen House seats, proved to be insufficient. On one hand the Obama of 2004's patriotic convention speech held where he charted a post-partisan vision of an America that was "not a collection of blue states and red states, but the United States of America," and on the other hand those who were not down with globalization, free trade, and the new America were merely "clinging to guns and religion," and four years later there was—"You didn't build that." Between all this and a media and dominant progressive monoculture that asserted without scruples that the biggest scandal of the Obama years was wearing a tan suit, the stage was set for a true celebrity president but also a genuine outsider to the political system to get elected by running against the establishments of both parties.

If you recall, Obama got elected as an Iraq War critic; in fact, it was the defining issue of separation between him and Hillary Clinton in the primary, and by the time he was leaving office, America's two undeclared wars (from Congress) had increased to five under the auspices of the war on terror. He got elected promising to roll back the civil liberties abuses of the Bush administration but in power continued and expanded them, turning aspects of the administrative state into investigatory and scrutinizing agents of political opponents in ways that make Richard Nixon look tame, a trend that was continued and dramatically expanded in the Biden years. The economic recession that was inherited, while not his fault, also saw great continuity between Bush and a bipartisan Congress with its financial bailouts (Troubled Assets Relief Program) and the economic stimulus, which kicked off the first of five trillion-dollar bills funded mostly by money printing from 2009 to the present.

There were also disappointments for those to his progressive left. The economic growth that did occur was continually uneven, and the wealth inequality gap widened, setting the stage for the Bernie Sanders campaign against heir apparent, Hillary Clinton, and the lofty rhetoric of lowering the water of the oceans in combating climate change was reduced to an awkward nondecision on a major pipeline in North Dakota (DAPL) in the closing months of his second term. Above both of these was the aloofness that stemmed from a fundamental confidence that he could persuade anyone through sheer will of personality. America's middling economic outcomes with only a few brief interruptions has formed the backdrop of prior working- and middle-class-backed Republican coalitions within the margins. Gone for decades are the days where Democrats presided over a strong economy, and the one president associated with a strong economy, Bill Clinton, did so with a Republican Congress in the 1990s. The war economy could not possibly last forever, and postdraft, post–Vietnam War and Great Society, it was certain not to. Prior to the 1970s, most American economists were strict Keynesians. The general notion fiscally was that when prices started rising too fast, you slowed down the economy via an interest rate hike. And if growth looked to be cooling, you heated up the economy with a tax cut or spending or both. Inflation and economic growth were believed to be inversely proportional.[1] First under Nixon and a Democratic Congress in 1974, and then under a Democratic President Carter and Congress in 1978 though, this thesis was debunked, and by the early 2020s it operates as a near baseline with propagandists changing definitions of recessions, growth, and rate of inflation at a pace that even Orwell underestimated. The markers of 8 percent inflation and growth projections of less than 3 percent, *stagflation*, have now become America's new baseline under Biden. The near Goldilocks economy of around 3 percent growth, low inflation and costs, and low unemployment of the Trump, pre-COVID years, has given way to high inflation, sluggish growth eaten out by costs and overly dependent on government spending, and unemployment remaining low around incentives to stay at home and drop out of the labor force entirely.

If Donald Trump ended up being a deeply flawed and disliked man who produced solid policy outcomes, his predecessor, Barack Obama, was and is still a popular man whose immense likability never translated to support for his policies or good policy outcomes. Obama was also more popular than his party, who lost over one thousand state legislative seats throughout the decade, a position that was barely clawed back from during a good midterm in 2018. Much ignored in the wake of all of America's societal, cultural, and spiritual battles is that a lot of this can be explained through the Democrats' insistence that they are "America's Natural Governing Party," especially during a time of economic crisis, but have failed to post good economic outcomes when in power for many, many decades now. Since the Ford administration in the mid-1970s, using government-provided economic data, and while not a perfect analysis, using the three major data points of *growth*, *jobs*, and *costs*, the American economy has increasingly fared better under Republican political control or split political control rather than Democratic political control (see the forty-five-year sample size below).

Alignment	Growth (GDP)	Unemployment (Jobs)	Inflation (Costs)
Under DEM President + Congress	2.49%	7.10%	6.39%
Under DEM President + GOP/ Split Congress	3.08%	5.53%	2.08%
Under GOP President + Congress	3.03%	4.73%	2.52%
Under GOP President + DEM/ Split Congress	2.58%	6.90%	4.59%

**(Data sources: official government statistics
from the Labor Department, 1974–2019.)**

The most significant correlation point in the past four and a half decades was Republican control of the House of Representatives, which makes sense as this is where spending bills start. While the Republican Party has frequently erred on fiscal discipline in the post-9/11 era, its record in Congress during the 1990s helped generate a solid economy that Bill Clinton was smart enough to take political credit for, shared or otherwise. What is secondarily clear is that giving Democrats a trifecta is bad for the American economy. It was bad in the late '70s under Jimmy Carter, it was bad in the early '90s under Bill Clinton prior to the Gingrich Revolution of '94, it was bad during the sluggish recovery after the financial crisis under Barack Obama, and it is bad today under a bare Democratic majority in Congress that existed under Joe Biden prior to the '22 midterms, before giving way to a slim Republican-held House and a split Congress. The American economy has become a hollowed-out empty shell that's trending in the wrong direction in the long run and also the short run. This data doesn't just exist on paper; it translates to voter perceptions and sentiments as well and has created upward pressure the longer it goes on. While George W. Bush became the first American president to not preside over a single year of 4 percent growth, and Barack Obama then became the first American president to not preside over a single year of even 3 percent growth, this trend line looked like it was slowly reversing itself from 2017 to 2019, when nearly perfect economic conditions were presenting themselves (full employment, 2 to 3 percent growth but more growth in the bottom four quintiles than the top, and low costs for households), but now our economic era is reaching the under end of its bracket with high costs and inflation.

An economic era with high inflation at the ends and increasing globalization in between characterizes both the decline of the American middle class and the economic inability to produce and try to spend our way out of problems that are ultimately more social, cultural, and spiritual deeply undermines a Democratic Party whose ambitions in governance far outweigh what it's able to achieve. Prior to the trio of trillion-dollar bills signed by President Biden that no one will be able to recall in a decade or so, President Obama with greater margins signed the first trillion-dollar bill that was supposed to rescue the economy from the depths of recession but disproportionately rewarded Democratic special interests. Not only was the economy not rescued, it never recovered.[li]

Party and media arrogance, poor political strategy, and less than ideal outcomes, especially for those most loyal to the Democratic Party in the black community, equal the lost opportunity and lost majority of the Democratic Party in the 2010s. By the end of the decade, even in victory and narrow trifecta, they do not appear like a confident party but rather look like a ruling monarch deeply insecure on the throne and with no heir apparent.

This conflict within was already showing itself throughout the 2016 Democratic primary, where attempts to crown Hillary Clinton early were met with significant resistance by Bernie Sanders, a self-proclaimed Democratic Socialist. Prior to Sanders's viability and growing support in the primary, there were five candidates in the early race, compared to an eventual seventeen in the Republican primary. In addition to Clinton and Sanders (who both represented voters at one time or another in the Northeast), Martin O'Malley, Lincoln Chafee, and Jim Webb all hailed from either the Northeast or the Beltway itself. Of those five, only Jim Webb would've been recognizable in, say, a 1984 Democratic primary, with the politics of John Glenn if you will. But in the early debate of the 2016 Democratic primary, he did not get the memo and was mocked off the stage by Twitter and pundits—not culturally elite or right-think enough for the media and professional activist class, and a symbol of the party's past, not its emerging majority future. Chafee, a former Republican (of the New England liberal Republican variety), also went nowhere. Maryland Governor Martin O'Malley lasted only a few moments more. Sanders, becoming the one voice for those who preferred a non-establishment, and non-Clinton candidate, was the beneficiary of a primary that was going to be between just two candidates. Sanders nearly won Iowa, won New Hampshire with ease, and gave Clinton a much greater challenge than any had expected—totaling twenty-three state wins in the end, 43.1 percent of the primary vote, and over thirteen million votes total. Indeed the Sanders to Trump voter was a frequent article in the days after Clinton lost the "can't lose" election, but these characterizations fail to grasp this voter.

Going into the 2016 cycle many Americans strongly disliked the idea that America's two parties were seemingly owned by two political families, the Clinton and the Bush dynasties. Americans have always had an anti-dynastic streak in their politics and voting habits dating back to the American Revolution itself. While many articles, books, and analyses have endlessly pored over trying to explain away 2016 as a fluke on one hand, or argue that it was the moral failings of ordinary people if you're, say, *The Atlantic* or the *New York Times* or some other increasingly elitist publication, the simplest explanation is that one party rejected their dynasty as having produced middling or worse outcomes, and the other party embraced their dynasty, opening the door for an outsider candidate to run against both political establishments. Donald Trump ran not just against Hillary Clinton but arguably the entire Boomer Alignment of the Third Civic Order as this book characterizes it. For every time candidate Clinton brought up experience, it only reinforced the central theme and narrative the Trump campaign was trying to convey in 2016, and every time the campaign brought up Trump's uncouthness and unfitness for the job, it was balanced against statements like "deplorables." Despite much talk about who was punching up and who was punching down, Citizen Trump saved his biggest insults for Washington, DC, itself and career politicians, while Secretary Clinton coined an enduring symbol that many ordinary people ended up wearing as a badge of honor.

Of all of the many postelection postmortems, only a probing journalist who simply drove across the vast and mostly deindustrialized Midwest and Heartland like Salena Zito in her book with Brad Todd, *The Great Revolt: Inside the Populist Coalition Reshaping American Politics*, seemed to get to the signal rather than embrace the noise by asking questions free of judgment.

Zito's book talks about economics, about the wars, about trade, about immigration, and indeed all of these issues Trump put himself on the more popular side of with the electorate, but a unifying theme throughout all of the travels seemed to be a Heartland and midwestern culture that was fundamentally worried about managed, real and relative, American decline—a decline that has been felt not just in Iowa, Ohio, Wisconsin, Michigan, and Pennsylvania, but also, as 2020 would begin to show us, within the tall building urban enclaves of America's culturally diverse but economically unequal cities.

This is why Hillary Clinton's retort to Make America Great Again being, "America is already great," fell on deaf ears with so many, as did the aftermath of, "We won all of the areas that are growing, that are dynamic," and so forth. Increasingly, the Democratic coalition was proving itself incapable of showing that it was still the party of the common person and common sense, and showing the weakness of reducing "diversity is our strength" and "unity is our power" down to mere slogans without any underlying reality to them. Consider the increasingly high cost of elections.

Total Cost of Elections (Inflation Adjusted)

Year	Democrats	Republicans
2020	8.4 Billion	4.8 Billion
2016	3.4 Billion	3.3 Billion
2012	3.1 Billion	3.7 Billion
2008	3.6 Billion	2.7 Billion
2004	2.7 Billion	2.9 Billion
2000	2.0 Billion	2.5 Billion

Source: Center for Responsive Politics

If the last decade of last century and the first decade of our own century is when the parties were "crossing over" via social class, the last decade was when the Democratic Party went all in on moving on from both campaign finance reform and credible claims of representing working- and middle-class Americans. To date, neither party represents working- and middle-class Americans very well, but the Republican Party for a decade now is much closer, even if by default.

The beginning of moving past campaign finance came in 2008 when candidate Obama rejected and opted out of the public campaign finance system itself. Since then, only with candidate Mitt Romney, a man whose profession before politics was in private equity, did America's campaign donations flow through the Republican Party more than the Democrats. But this is only the first feature in understanding what has happened in the last decade. There are other ways, by geography, and by other sociocultural stand-ins that we can get a fuller picture still of this long realignment.

2016

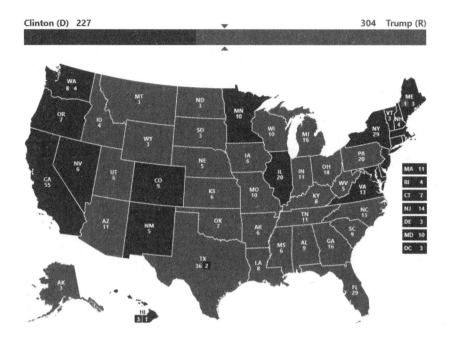

Clinton (D) 227   304   Trump (R)

In 2016, 206 counties "pivoted" (see Ballotpedia's Pivot Counties project) from long-term voting Democratic to voting Republican. Only six counties "reverse" or "counter"-pivoted. In 2020, of those 206 pivot counties from 2016, 181 of them stayed Republican. One of the themes of both this book and the American constitutional republic itself is the importance of geography in determining political culture, history, and the balance of power itself. To the extent that "critical election" or "realignment" theory exists at all, one has to admit that 2016, shown again in 2020, shows a far greater realignment than 2008 and 2012 did. And while this realignment goes both ways, the trade-offs are not the same. Senator Chuck Schumer's quote, "For every voter we lose in Western Pennsylvania, we'll pick up three in the suburbs," does not hold true at all—both as a mathematical fact and a political reality.

109

The "new" voters that Democrats are getting are from smaller groups than the voters they are losing. And the "new" voters that Republicans are getting are not just from larger groups, but many are from groups once assumed to be key pillars to any emerging Democratic majority. Considering that voter coalitions are both influenced by party decisions on key issues and events and then come to shape policy preferences on issues, the Democrats will find themselves having a harder time holding their disparate coalition together and an even harder time returning to their old FDR foundational civic order messaging. Consider socioeconomic class and political control of the wealthiest congressional districts by real GDP in the country.

Political Control of the Wealthiest Congressional Districts by Real GDP

	Wealthiest 10	Wealthiest 25	Wealthiest 50
In 2008	8 of 10 Democratic	18 of 25 Democratic	31 of 50 Democratic
By 2018	All 10 Democratic	All 25 Democratic	45 of 50 Democratic

Now balance this reality against how much support was lost from 2008 to 2016 in middle-class communities.

Democrats Lost Support in Middle-Class Communities

	Obama 08 (%)	Clinton 16 (%)	Dem diff.	Share middle income
National	53	48	-5	51
Johnstown, PA	50	30	-20	56
Muskegon, MI	64	48	-16	56
Wausau, WI	54	38	-15	67
Monroe, MI	51	36	-15	58
Scranton, PA	57	43	-14	56
Youngstown, OH	59	45	-14	60
Jackson, MI	50	37	-13	56
Utica-Rome, NY	48	35	-13	57
Eau Claire, WI	58	46	-12	61
Canton, OH	50	38	-12	59
Janesville-Beloit, WI	64	52	-12	65
Reading, PA	54	43	-11	57
Kankakee, IL	52	41	-11	62
Joplin, MO	32	21	-11	57
Fort Wayne, IN	46	35	-11	59
Sheboygan, WI	49	39	-10	63
Glens Falls, NY	49	39	-10	58
Lebanon, PA	40	30	-10	63

Sources: Middle-class data from Pew Research Center analysis of the 2014 American Community Survey (IPUMS). Election data from Pew Research Center analysis of 2008 and 2016 county-level election returns.

And then one more indicator of socioeconomic changes to both of the parties: the presidential vote in one hundred counties with the highest median income, using 2019 data.

Presidential Vote in One Hundred Counties with Highest 2019 Median Income

Year	Democrats	Republicans
1980	9	91
1984	7	93
1988	17	83
1992	36	64
1996	43	57
2000	32	68
2004	34	66
2008	51	49
2012	46	54
2016	49	51
2020	57	43

This is not to say that rich people are now Democratic, and non-rich people are not. That's a simplistic analysis. But such simplicity is also how much of political rhetoric is delivered by both high and low culture, rightly or wrongly. The fact remains that over the past decade and change, the Democratic Party has become more and more of an upstairs-downstairs coalition of rich and professional class, and especially "aspiring" professional-class voters, while the Republicans have been adding working-class voters of all demographic backgrounds onto their historical strength with the middle class and small businesses on Main Street. The changes and new voters affecting the Democratic Party are going to make it harder still to hold a governing coalition that delivers outcomes to the people while the changes and new voters affecting the Republican Party are literally pointing the way toward an emerging coalition that could be both deep and wide, and last much longer. Whereas the "deep" part refers to demographics and numerical voters, the "wide" part refers to literal space and geography. Consider the recent 2020 presidential election relative to the national trend if the election was exactly fifty-fifty, as many pre-COVID surveys were suggesting and many surveys now are suggesting at a minimum (if not Republican-leaning).

2020 State Voting Relative to the National Trend (4% D)

States	Electoral Votes	Relative to National Trend	In a Fifty-Fifty National Situation
Nebraska Second Congressional District	1	2.2 more Democratic than the nation	Barely remains Democratic
Maine Second Congressional District	1	11.4 more Republican than the nation	Easily goes Republican
Pennsylvania	20	3.3 more Republican than the nation	Goes Republican
North Carolina	15	5.9 more Republican than the nation	Easily goes Republican
Georgia	16	4.3 more Republican than the nation	Goes Republican
Florida	29	7.8 more Republican than the nation	Easily goes Republican
Arizona	11	4.2 more Republican than the nation	Goes Republican
Nevada	6	2.1 more Republican than the nation	Goes Republican
Texas	38	10.1 more Republican than the nation	Easily goes Republican
Michigan	16	1.7 more Republican than the nation	Goes Republican
Iowa	6	12.7 more Republican than the nation	Easily goes Republican
Ohio	18	12.5 more Republican than the nation	Easily goes Republican
Wisconsin	10	3.8 more Republican than the nation	Goes Republican
Minnesota	10	2.7 more Democratic than the nation (down from 16 in 1984)	Barely remains Democratic

Result *If* the Nation Voted Fifty-Fifty: Trump 311, Biden 227

The above graph and the underlying demographic realities that Trump did better with Hispanic voters, Asian voters, and black voters, both men and women, while doing worse with college-educated white women, and holding about even with white men while 2016 third-party voting white men rallied to Biden in 2020 overall, sets up two potential futures for the Republican coalition, but two futures that can only be understood by first looking at the same last decade (2008 to 2020) within the Republican Party itself. One major reason the Republican Party stands to benefit from the emergence of a populist revolt against globalization and elite failure is that it is largely finished with intraparty battles. The Republican Party "civil war" if you will, began in earnest after 2008 and saw many primary defeats in the 2010 Tea Party wave. And the consistent energy and momentum was on the populist side of the party, whereas on the Democratic side as Thomas Frank points out in *The People, No*,[lii] the establishment and elite forces continually repulse all attempts to upset the status quo, preferring a revolution from within and on the streets only when convenient. Regardless of definitional differences and scope, Frank observed that "populist uprisings occur all the time in American life, always with the same enemies—monopolies, banks, and corruption—and always with the same salt-of-the-earth heroes."[liii] And this same elite distaste for populist uprisings wherever they reside often stems from elite and political class mismanagement: weapons of mass destruction in Iraq, globalization as a weather pattern rather than a policy choice, deindustrialization, the financial crisis, the opioid crisis, COVID-19 and institutional cover-up, the botched withdrawal from Afghanistan, the list goes on. And when anti-populists do mention their failures, they dismiss them as inevitable and unpredictable and turn to lashing out at the masses for getting angry. Thus the story becomes the anger of the common people[liv] rather than elite mismanagement and managed decline of the country.

But for all of his eloquent writing about the changes in the Democratic Party from the party of FDR to the party of HR the last fifty years, and his realization that populism works and has worked throughout that time from Nixon to Reagan to Trump, where Frank gets it wrong is that the so-called populism and movements on the left are influenced more by Karl Marx than by Henry George, and more by contemporary post-liberal and post-national movement progressivism than the agrarian populism of the People's Party of the nineteenth century.

What he also misses is that the 1960s represent the true launching point of most politics on the left today—culture and identity first, economics and foreign policy an increasingly distant second. And to the extent economics does get discussed, it, too, often revolves around the upstairs and downstairs, with little room left for middle America or the American middle and working class. Despite some of the earliest critiques of globalization coming from labor and from the left,[lv] even within its own world, the establishment was caught flat-footed and still does not get it. Today, the most astute and objective geopolitical thinkers have declared the era of globalization over,[lvi] just as globalization's most identifiable president, Bill Clinton, once declared the era of big government to be over, before big government got its groove back shortly after. Even from within their own ranks, in *The World Is Flat*, Thomas Friedman cautioned against mistaking technological determinism for historical determinism,[lvii] and in his updated *Hot, Flat, and Crowded*, he argued for more nation-building at home.[lviii] This is a movement that clearly needed a neoconservative and interventionist Republican Party to face up against. And the modern Democratic coalition and ruling establishment still wants this part back.

This is why, if anything, the Democratic Party is about to go through a civil war of its own that can only be deterred or slowed down by scaring their base and people through ratcheting up rhetoric toward Republicans—a strategy that even when nominally successful, could and should be interrupted and intercepted by a Republican Party that comes to grasp and understands the movement that lay beneath its feet and the possibilities that could transpire.

CHAPTER 6

THE REPUBLICAN PARTY IN THE LAST DECADE (2008 TO 2020)

In his book *The Lost Majority*, Sean Trende wrote about the nature of coalitions being not unlike the wedding tradition of something old, something new, something borrowed, something blue. This metaphor was used in reference to the Eisenhower coalition that began building in the midterm backlash election of 1938 to FDR and had its last successful presidential coalitional win in 1988, the last election of the Cold War. According to Trende, what pundits and academics call the "Reagan coalition" was in truth the *Eisenhower coalition*. This argument is very convincing, as was the argument that the New Deal era was a so-called era. The '38 midterms reveal a GOP that was already beginning to regain its footing, and over the next decade and a half Congress went through one of the more unstable periods in its history in terms of switching hands. Additionally, the confluence of events in the Cold War era, the real era that splits the New Deal from its liberal intellectual class origin story, gave the GOP from Eisenhower to Reagan a multigenerational lock on the Electoral College that only sees one exception.[lix]

For Eisenhower, something old was the beginning of the southern exit from the Democratic Party, relevant because the Democratic South had been so solid since the Civil War. While Eisenhower only made slight inroads in the upper South, that he won any states in the region at all was notable. Something new was the suburbs, growing rapidly with new home construction from Long Island to the Pacific coast. Much of this new building was propelled by the GI Bill and returning veterans from the war who were catching up on home life and expanding their families. The something borrowed refers to the weakest part of the opposition coalition being borrowed, wedded, and added to your own. For Eisenhower, and later for Clinton, this was the white working class. Finally, under Eisenhower the Democratic coalition of urban workers and minority voters was enough to hold down Congress still, even while split-ticket voters often voted for Eisenhower, Nixon, and later Reagan at the top of the ticket. This was something borrowed as part of the coalition that went back to Clinton in 1992...or did it?

There is a case to be made that while Bill Clinton did win back parts of the New Deal coalition that voted for Roosevelt, Truman, and Johnson, and that the Carter and Kennedy coalitions represent those coalitions, too, in smaller margins, it's perhaps more accurate to say that Clinton represents a transitional era where the Democratic Party began its professional-class supplantation of its working-class roots.

Why the focus on Clinton in the chapter on the Republicans? Because Clinton's election in 1992 set the stage for the Gingrich Revolution of 1994 and the dueling "centrism" and monoparty culture wars of the Boomer Alignment—dueling centrism in its progressive (Democrats of the emerging Democratic majority) and patriotic (Karl Rove's attempt to turn George W. Bush into a McKinley-type figure) forms.

Parties in Power during the Second Half of the War Generation and Boomer Generation Alignments

	Senate Majority		House Majority		
Year	Dem.	Rep.	Dem.	Rep.	President
1969	14		51		Nixon
1971	10		75		
1973	14		51		
1975	24		147		Ford
1977	23		149		Carter
1979	17		121		
1981		7	51		Reagan
1983		10	103		
1985		6	73		
1987	10		81		
1989	10		85		H. W. Bush
1991	12		100		
1993	14		82		Clinton
1995		4		26	
1997		10		19	
1999		10		12	
2001	0	0		7	W. Bush
2003		3		24	
2005		11		32	
2007	0	0	31		
2009	16		79		Obama
2011	4			49	
2013	8			33	
2015		10		59	
2017		4		47	Trump
2019		8	36		
2021	0	0	10		Biden
2023	2			10	

Note: War Generation Alignment in gray,
Boomer Alignment in white.

The Boomer Alignment across the presidencies of Clinton, W. Bush, Obama, Trump, and the lonely and only late silent generation presidency of Biden has dominated our politics since 1992 but dominated our culture since the 1960s: on one hand, the Vietnam War, a war that broke American society and trust with government that has only slightly recovered at times from its long-term downward trajectory, and on the other hand, a jovial and jousting generation that, while polarized, genuinely loved the battle and game of politics as the late conservatarian humorist P. J. O'Rourke often said. As much as we come to think of the 1990s as a boomer battle between a Democratic President Clinton and a Republican Congress headed by Newt Gingrich, the resulting policy consensus of the 1990s made it appear at the time as the second decade in a row of renewal (along with the 1980s) after a long 1960s of turbulence and the malaise of the 1970s. The globalization-escalating 1990s and neoliberal policy consensus prior to 9/11 made urban rebound, fiscal discipline, the appearance of a post–Cold War victory dividend, and eventually, greater cultural harmony seem possible.

It was this "divided" but relatively peaceful America of 2000 that made the controversy of that close election roll off the American shoulder just like the close election of 1960 had. After the tragedy of 9/11, President George W. Bush's top political advisor, Karl Rove, foresaw an emerging majority of his own in Bush. A majority of the "patriotic center" rather than the "progressive center." And in a sense these two zeitgeists are a fair, if crude, stand-in for our rhetorical battles to this day, but at a policy level they are very far apart from where, especially, the Republican Party would be by the end of the next decade. The Republican Party from at least Goldwater to Gingrich would stand for less government and lower taxes and regulation, and at least in its foreign policy wing would be the more hawkish party on the Cold War and military defense spending. The end of the Cold War would disrupt this coalition, proving an unfortunate adage about political coalitions to be true. Solving a problem and meeting a challenge can end a current coalition faster than maintaining or endlessly working on the problem. In this sense, the Democratic Party has often had the advantage around its abstract utopian notions of "more fairness" and "more equality." Its fuel has become righteousness in not just a progressive direction but increasingly in the cultural direction, with economics and a coherent vision for America's role in the world in the rearview mirror. Meanwhile, the fuel then and now for the Republican Party has become patriotism. The politicization of the American flag itself is not just an anti-American message for the progressive left but, more importantly, an anti-Republican message. Today, beyond any sense of righteousness, the Democratic Party is increasingly held together in a coalition of everybody that's getting smaller and smaller by an intense dislike of Republicans, while the Republicans are increasingly held together not just by a dislike or sense that the Democrats' vision for the country is fundamentally wrong and unwise, but also by a sense of fear and dread that the country has long been in real and relative decline culturally, economically, and in international prestige.

Rove's bid to turn George Bush the younger into a turn-of-the-century William McKinley figure, in reconfiguring and updating the prior coalition for a new age, went up in smoke in the 2006 midterms and 2008 presidential election. Bush left office with approvals mired in the low 30s, and the relative stability of the late 1990s and unity of the early 2000s turned out to be the exception to the rule of our time rather than a societal renewal and unity of purpose on the level of the American High of the postwar era.

For the post-Bush Republican Party, rather than try a fundamentally new direction that listened to and followed the voters, the 2008 and 2012 candidacies turned out to be a "last dance" of the moderates, who were called more extreme than the prior Republican candidate by Democrats and the media. After the 2012 election, much was written about the "emergence" of the lasting progressive center to center-left Obama coalition, and much was written about the "center holding" and the need for a Republican autopsy. And that autopsy was written. The major theme was the need for the party to diversify itself, especially with regard to the Hispanic population, which was at the time America's fastest-growing minority group (now it is Asian). There was a more lonely autopsy though from writers like Sean Trende who argued that the strength of the Clinton and Obama coalitions was overrated. Something borrowed, something new. Something old, something blue. And it is this articulation of political coalitions and their fragile nature, especially in an era of low and lowering trust in institutions, in politicians, and in the two political parties, that makes far more sense and holds more statistical and narrative validity rather than the grand narrative of realignments, critical elections, and the baked-in media, cultural, and political class assumption that America's demographics and history pull inevitably to the left.

Mavericks, Rogues, and the Last Dance of the Moderates

In 2008, the Republican primary went with a media darling, a so-called maverick who also had a voting record that aligned with outgoing President George W. Bush, who had approvals in the low-30s throughout the campaign. Karl Rove's dream of a McKinley-esque patriotic center-right coalition around Bush went up in flames as the Republicans lost Congress in 2006, then the presidency in 2008. Above all else, the party leaders and enough of the primary voters lacked the confidence and convictions to go in a fundamentally new direction. In retrospect, McCain was more moderate than Bush in both 2000 and in 2008, and represented bargaining with the country to try and hold on to power. What may have helped with independents failed to ignite the base, breaking one of Rove's few rules that has held throughout this time—that of a base-turnout strategy. But what 2008 did provide was a small preview of things to come from a little known Alaska governor, Sarah Palin, a rogue to McCain's maverick.

While the result was the worst Democratic versus Republican performance in twelve years, the early weeks of the Palin pick, prior to the scrutiny and her own flaws becoming more magnified, the country and political world saw the potential power of a conservative and populist fusion coalition. Not Rove's "patriotic center or center-right" but something more akin to how coalitions actually work and prove to be lasting. This misunderstanding of not just the country's direction but their own voting base became the theme of the last decade in the Republican Party and, to a lesser extent, the Democratic Party. But this all changed in 2010 as the party leaders and managers could not stop the desire for change derived from the frustration with the direction of the country.

The last dance of the moderates continued when a much larger Republican primary, the first in a string of larger primaries in terms of the size of the field for first the Republican then the Democratic Party, resulted in the most viable moderate choice being nominated, Mitt Romney, who again fit the familiar political legacy that had marked the increasingly stale political class of the country. Romney had been the governor of Massachusetts and campaigned to the right of McCain and in some ways to the right of early front-runner Rudy Giuliani in 2008, and was nearly the front to back poll leader in 2012, except this time he was the most moderate candidate of the viable part of the field. Like McCain, such moderation was quickly forgotten by an increasingly liberal and progressive-oriented media culture who failed to cover such slander from then Vice President Joe Biden who claimed to an audience during the campaign that if Romney wins, he is going to put "y'all back in chains," referring to black Americans. Had this slanderous remark been covered with the same gusto as Romney's factually correct but optically and politically incorrect 47 percent remark, a relatively close 2012 result may have turned out differently.

The optimistic campaign Barack Obama ran in 2008 was out the window four years later. After four years of stagnant economic recovery outcomes at home but a few successes abroad amid mixed results, his 2012 campaign turned decidedly cynical. Turning up the temperature on identity appeals, the Democrats, too, began to believe their own emerging Democratic majority. In many ways, 2012 was the precursor to the trend lines that broke the blue wall in 2016; the trend to that point was just not quite enough.

For both the doomed McCain and Romney campaigns, what the press called a fractured and fracturing Republican Party at the time had in reality turned out to be the last dance of the moderates, with its replacement taking its cues not so much from the Reagan or Gingrich revolutions but rather the American Revolution and spirit of 1776 itself.

The Tea Party Wave of 2010

Had the Democrats been more aware of the nature of their 2008 victory, perhaps a majority of the emerging Democratic kind that Judis and Teixeira wrote about a handful of years earlier could have emerged. But not only did the Democrats overplay their hand in governing in a partisan manner, with few exceptions, they also fell victim to their own state media and theory of the case for what America's electoral future would be. A coalitional theory that kept West Virginia in the same party as culturally progressive but economically unequal San Francisco, Los Angeles, and New York City was bound to show its cracks. And increasingly those cracks would take on a populist bent from both the left and the right.

From the left came Occupy Wall Street, driven in part by anger over the bailouts but made possible through a slow and sluggish recovery. The Occupy movement had figures that would go one of three ways in the years following. One, the grassroots followers would be drawn to the aspiring populism of the Sanders campaign, perhaps best represented by the liberal argument that populism from writers like Thomas Frank belongs exclusively to the left wing and in the American sense takes its historical roots from the Jeffersonian rural and agrarian traditions. While the Sanders campaign had a strong base of support in rural areas, this argument is getting harder and harder to defend today. Two, Occupy became a stalwart defender of a party that increasingly became more pro-war than the Republicans and more pro–Wall Street and big business as the decade wore on, as represented by the incredibly fact-challenged Occupy

Democrats account on social media. And three, where some of the most authentic voices of the Occupy movement ended up—the heterodoxy represented by grassroots and independent journalists like Tim Pool—they realigned and after a flirtation with the Sanders campaign, became either Republicans or more closely aligned with Republican populism. It is this third group that represents so much of not just what has happened in the last decade to the Republicans but also the opportunity an increasingly out-of-touch Democratic Party elite and political class has granted their opponents, if only the opportunity is seized.

Unlike the failings of the anti-war left in the Bush years, and the fecklessness and selling out of Occupy in the Obama years, the populist movement known as the Tea Party benefited from the same decentralization and outsider grassroots status that powers populism in most instances but also benefited from the fact that the conservative Republican establishment wanted nothing to do with it for the most part. Like most of what fuels conservatism or a good Republican-aligned movement in America, its fuel was patriotism. The Tea Party on one hand had the same central concern of Reagan classic conservatism in the size and scope of government, high taxes, and regulation. The TEA in the Tea Party stood for "taxed enough already," for instance. But the mainstream's response to it added an additional cultural layer. The movement almost immediately was described— just as Sanders-style professional-class, left-populism would be—as racist and xenophobic by a corporate media more interested in propping up the bottom line and the approval of their affiliated politicians. A Republican Party once far more associated with business was now failing to see the tea leaves in front of them at the establishment and party leader level. Prior to the Tea Party wave of 2010, the third-ranking Republican in the House, Eric Cantor of Virginia, was defeated in a primary. Other primary successes and surprises also happened, which made the media declare that the Republicans were blowing their chances of being an electable party any time soon by nominating so-called extremists in place of Chamber of Commerce-approved candidates and incumbents.

In truth however, this trade-off benefited the Republican Party all decade whether or not one knew it or liked it. Prior to 2008, Republicans were almost always the better-funded party, especially by the business class and wealthiest Americans. After 2008, only in 2012 with Mitt Romney out-raising and outspending President Obama by a narrow margin have they been. In 2008, 2016, and 2020 corporate America went all-in and hedged their bets on not just the Democratic Party but the emerging Democratic majority where demographic inevitability would propel the party to an FDR era–like dominance. Instead, what has happened is the continued erosion of the Democratic position in seats at every level of government overall, with only about one-fifth of the country trending Democratic over that time.

In short, by accepting, even if against their will, the populist and grassroots energy through the Republican Party, the party has ended up in a much stronger position with a chance at a much higher ceiling but also occasionally a lower floor than before. In contrast, by rejecting and co-opting the populist and grassroots movements on the left, and countering them with activist-infused, or worse corporate-infused, and government-sanctioned identitarianism, the Democratic Party has weakened their position nearly across the board. Whether the Republican Party can fully take advantage of this historic opportunity or wants to is the X factor of the next decade, but in the prior decade the gains and favorable trade-offs of voters and coalitions are clear.

While the Tea Party wave brought the Republicans the House and significant gains in the states, the Senate results proved to be disappointing and just out of reach. This mismatch of 2010 and later 2018 results in the midterm congressional elections is one reason why this writing does not consider Senate elections in determining political power, as they have their own individualized and state-level factors. Despite the prevalence of the decentralized Tea Party a decade ago, their influence over the party, even at the grassroots level, has waned significantly today. In part, this is because a candidate closer to their choosing won both the primary in '16 and then scored the upset of the century in the general election in the out-sider candidacy of Donald Trump. But also, the issues that drove the Tea Party grass roots fit in with the classic Reagan conservative Republicanism a lot more than what propelled Trump in the primaries and general. The Reagan revolution was also a revolution inspired by the spirit of 1776 and by patriotism and love of country. It was concerned with the size and scope of government and high taxation and excess regulation. Only the absence of the Cold War differed. In this sense the movement served as a bridge between the party of old and the party that is emerging today, a party where its populists are no longer the red-headed stepchild and can no longer be ignored by party elites.

Still, there remains a disconnect between elected Republicans and party officials and the grass roots that is much larger than the one within the Democratic Party. Even some Tea Party–infused candidates of 2010 are today viewed suspiciously by the populist grass roots (Florida Senator Marco Rubio) or downright derided as sellouts to the cause (Illinois Representative Adam Kinzinger, who voted for Trump's second impeach-ment, and along with Liz Cheney came to represent the continued sidelin-ing of the former Republican Party of the Bush-Cheney years).

The Real Origins of 2016

Some wrote off the 2016 election as a fluke, as a temporary setback on the road to Democratic generational renewal. Hillary Clinton was a flawed candidate, too experienced, too tied to the Washington establishment in a "change" election year. So much has been written about 2016 from both the Democratic and Republican establishments, almost all of them missing the forest for the trees. In a way the clearest voice on this mat-ter is the simplest voice. The very same architect of the emerging theory (version Democrat), John Judis wrote after 2016, *The Nationalist Revival: Trade, Immigration, and the Revolt Against Globalization*. The word "revolt" was similarly used in the road warrior political travelogue: *The Great Revolt: Inside the Populist Coalition Reshaping American Politics* by

Salena Zito and Brad Todd. One from the left perspective, another from the right. Put simply, 2016 was a backlash to globalization and Hillary Clinton, through both Barack Obama's and Bill Clinton's presidencies, and became synonymous with the Washington, DC, consensus of neoliberal and cosmopolitan-driven globalization. That neoconservative military intervention and adventurism, the "democracy wars," was added to the mix reflected poorly on the Republican Party and set it back far more than the era of Donald Trump. On the contrary, it was the Bill Kristols of the world, whose father, Irving, was dubbed the "godfather of neoconservatism," who nearly ruined the "patriotic center to center-right" McKinley attempt around the turn of the century.

This legacy was never really fought over in either the 2008 or 2012 primaries, allowing the Republicans to incorrectly still be characterized as a country club and robust military intervention party. While much of their base was ready to move on beneath them, on key issues of trade and globalization the Republican Party had not developed a coherent alternative.[ix] Only occasionally with figures like Ron Paul in 2008 and to a lesser extent in 2012 were the endless wars of the post-9/11 era questioned in GOP orthodoxy. This all changed in the Republican primary of 2016, when Donald Trump skewered Jeb Bush and the Bush legacy over the Iraq War and accused much of the Republican establishment of selling out the country along with the Democrats over trade, immigration, and ill-conceived wars. This internal battle that played out over seventeen candidates in 2016 ended up strengthening the Republican Party in the end, against its establishment leaders' wishes and to their surprise. Part of their opposition throughout was an embarrassment of being exposed, and only later did sincere ideological differences come in where any existed. It was personal and professional, not political and ideological.

In the midst of professional liberal media meltdowns on the night of the '16 upset, former Carter administration official turned commentator Chris Matthews slipped in a moment of honest reflection that could only come from a Democrat who had grown up or spent a good amount of time in Pennsylvania, Ohio, Iowa, Wisconsin, Michigan, or even as far west as Minnesota, where Democrats only won by 1 percent, or even Upstate New York, where the historically reliable Republican counties outside of a few midsized cities ended their 1990s and 2000s flirtation with the Democratic Party and began trending back toward the Republicans. After Rachel Maddow reached peak-no-self-awareness, Matthews chimed in with:

> Let me give you the other version of that notion, there was three issues that he [Trump] tapped into, trade, immigration, and wars, that I think he was on the popular side of, I think the country hates all these wars, the establishment of both parties have been supporting these wars including Hillary, the fact that we don't have an immigration system that we enforce because business wants the cheap labor, and Democrats want the votes, no one has gotten it together, and in terms of trade, the fact is…a good part of the states we're looking at tonight, just drive through Michigan, drive through Wisconsin, and you'll see places that are hollowed out….[lxi]

Elsewhere, author and now US Senator J. D. Vance's book *Hillbilly Elegy* became required reading for the same coastal commentators and status-seekers who thought American history operated along the onward and upward linear lines of the professed ideology of the moral betters. For them, J. D. Vance from Middletown, Ohio, who went to Yale Law School, was their new and chosen oracle that validated their sense of superiority over the middle. Donald Trump won because people in rural America were too poor, too dumb, too opioid addicted, and too desperate to see that the establishment knew what was best for them. But then something funny happened. Not only did Vance refuse to join their club, but he also refused to play along anymore on their cable television shows. The celebrated *New York Times* bestselling author had refused the offer that few could refuse and chose instead to cast his lot in with the deplorables, the irredeemables, and the uncouth hillbillies he wrote about. Vance's book, the elite establishment's hysterical rejection of him when he revealed himself to be a populist-conservative instead of joining their secret elite club in Manhattan, Brooklyn, San Francisco, or Los Angeles was yet another revelatory chapter for the dukes and earls of Our Democracy. But in the new paperback afterword to *Elegy*, Vance offered some solid advice for the would-be populist-conservative fusion attempt:

> To the degree I've commented on politics in the past five years, I've usually argued that my own party has to abandon the dogmas of the 1990s and actually offer something of substance to working- and middle-class Americans. And despite all of my reservations about Donald Trump (I ended up voting third party), there were parts of his candidacy that really spoke to me: from his disdain for the "elites" and criticism of foreign policy blunders in Iraq and Afghanistan to his recognition that the Republican Party had done too little for its increasingly working- and middle-class base. For so many years, I and a few of my intellectual fellow travelers in the Republican Party were telling politicians to make precisely those sorts of arguments. Yet the populist rhetoric of the campaign hasn't informed the party's approach to governing. Unless that changes, I suspect Republicans will pay a heavy political price.[lxii]

A few years later, J. D. Vance of Middletown became Senator Vance.

What Ronald Reagan was to smoothing over Barry Goldwater's movement conservative takeover of the Republican Party Donald Trump now is to the populist infusion and revolt animating and running through the Republican Party today. And this will be seen in both those who are his most loyal supporters in 2016 and 2020 and those who started off as extremely skeptical like Vance yet agreed that his arguments were essentially correct or closer to being correct than the left or the establishment's diagnosis.

The more the media goes against it, the more they're powerless to truly stop it, because its power lies in the grass roots, like all populist movements. Its secondary power lies in its observational and lived experience and commonsense tendencies rather than ideological ones. While few would agree with this, the fact is that lifelong businessman and the brand that is Donald Trump is significantly less ideological than Ronald Reagan or Barry Goldwater was. But like Reagan, Trump spent significant parts of his life as a Democrat and brings in elements of that tradition. In Reagan's case, while his early political hero may have been FDR, on policy and philosophy it ended up being far closer to JFK. In many respects, Reagan, like Kennedy before him, stood for economic growth, limited government, and peace through strength, and both presidents cut taxes. Since the time of Kennedy and Nixon, the two parties flip-flopped on these traditions in a relative sense, and Reagan seized on this while Democrats mostly rejected it[lxiii] and drove it out of their party.

In 2016, in addition to being the first Republican to win Wisconsin since 1984, the first to win Pennsylvania and Michigan since 1988, and the first to win the Maine Second Congressional District since that state began awarding electoral votes by congressional district. The conservative-populist fusion also nearly won Maine at the statewide level; New Hampshire, Nevada, and even Virginia showed signs that it is not permanently lost to the Republicans. Meanwhile, the much talked about future Democratic states of the emerging majority of Arizona, Georgia, North Carolina, and the Democrat's white whale, Texas, all went Republican by clear margins. The Electoral College trade-off, where elections are actually held through the states, showed a clear advantage emerging for the Republican Party under this new fusion coalition. And while the coalition would have growing pains in power, the zoomed-out larger arc of American life still reveals trade-offs that hint toward an emerging Republican majority, not a Democratic one, and more accurately, this majority is populist, powered by a backlash to an era that had not delivered what was promised. This populist revolt first ran through the Republican primary and was snuffed out in the Democratic primary. In the end the Trende theory of electoral coalitions proved more accurate in 2016 and in 2020 as well.

The "coalition of the ascendant" described by journalist Ron Brownstein of *The Atlantic*[lxiv] that became an alternative way to describe the demographic or coalition of everyone theory was precisely the precursor dialogue to how utterly shocked the mainstream media and establishment political institutions of both parties were. But those outside of this world in the outside data and electoral analysis world had been on to something as early as the 2012 postmortem. Just days after the election, Sean Trende calculated that the Romney-Obama election might have included fewer than ninety-one million white voters, down seven million from 2008, and further argued that the Democrats' insistence on the inevitable rising power of minority voters was premature and an insufficient explanation for Romney's loss.[lxv] Calling out this was not necessarily some refutation of the Democrats even, but rather the media and cultural characterization of what was going on in American political life and the prevailing assumptions of the establishments of both major political parties. It was in these days after 2012 that the winning campaign of 2016, which represented the biggest political upset in decades, was first articulated, notably, by another outsider. And rather than have an honest discussion about what had occurred, the postmortems of 2016 began to double down on these inaccuracies,[lxvi] proscribing motives out of data and exit polls while continuing the increasing disrespect the coasts have shown to swaths of the country. To their great credit, journalists Salena Zito and Brad Todd did no such thing and provided a nuanced picture of the various realignments and subtleties of the emerging coalition reshaping American politics.

The path of least resistance is the best electoral strategy; borrowing and ideally realigning the weakest aligned voters from the opposing party is that path. In 2016 this meant many of the same Reagan Democrats or their heirs in the working classes. Whether it was winning a clear majority of union households in Ohio, or even in a loss, the realigned Iron Range of northern Minnesota, 186 of the 206 pivot counties (counties that voted two times for Obama before voting for Trump in 2016) held in 2020, as did all six of the counter or reverse-pivot counties that voted for McCain, Romney, and then Hillary Clinton and Biden. Biden won a historically low number of counties for a winning candidate, and his relative gains in the suburbs, while enough to narrowly win the presidency, are also the same electoral theory just in reverse—borrowing and attaching to your coalition the weakest and most tenuous parts of your opponents' coalition. While the 20 (out of 206) pivot counties that narrowly went back to Biden in 2020 (the "boomerang" counties) are very winnable going forward for a conservative-populist (and then some) fusion candidate, the six counter or reverse-pivot counties from 2016 are gone for good, and Republicans should embrace this fact. Six counties, three of them in Georgia, do not mean that the suburbs are lost for good. The suburbs will remain presidential and other campaign battlegrounds for the foreseeable future. However, the party would do well to look closely at the suburbs and recent electoral history to understand the deeper nature of what is very much a social class realignment, rather than the old economic and interest battles or the racially obsessed demographic conversations that characterize the legacy media and Democratic politicians.

2020

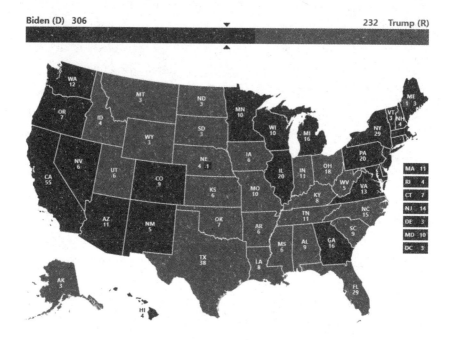

Biden (D) 306   232   Trump (R)

In so many ways, even in a loss, the 2020 demographic profile of the Trump-led Republican conservative and populist coalition was even more encouraging. As he outperformed his 2016 margins with black, Hispanic, and Asian voters, which subsequent 2021 elections and the 2022 midterms show were but a prologue to border working- and middle-class realignment of conservative Hispanics. Historically, since the 1960s, white Americans were polarized along ideological lines and that would motivate their voting pattern to a degree, but the same was not true for anyone else. However, conservative ideology holds relatively consistent across all racial demographics. Much of the 2020 growth in the Hispanic vote for Republicans was driven by this, and this realignment has a much higher chance of holding because it is held together by real issues and philosophy rather than the relatively small number of suburban and professional-class socially liberal, economically and fiscally conservative voters who are leaving the Republican Party for the Democratic Party or for the political wilderness.

More on the growing diversity and demography of this emerging coalition will be discussed in chapter 10, but the larger point is how much 2020's vote gains by the Republicans undermine the Democratic "theory of the case" of any emerging and longstanding advantage held. Only the deepest of partisans would still hold to this theory now, and if they do, they would do well to read this book, if only to gain additional context and reasons for their frustrations. Such a deep dive would be far healthier for the country rather than simply chalking up Republican gains to the simplistic analysis that is often given from a media that ought to be tuned out not just for divisiveness, but because it is increasingly hard to be accurate or hit the target if one does.

Another striking misunderstanding about the future of America's politics and coalitions is the millennial conversation. While it is true this generation was the difference in electing Barack Obama not just in the primary over Hillary Clinton, and then providing key 66 percent to 32 percent margins over John McCain in 2008, it's also a generation that is talked about as if it's locked in to a straight-line analysis going forward. This is not surprising from a cultural place, as millennials are the children of baby boomers, another dominant generation whose early political experiences in American life and the promotion of early cohort liberal members to the corridors of political, media, and cultural power influenced greatly the inaccurate perceptions of a boomer generation that has since most often voted Republican. Another possible reflection of early voting patterns has been the pattern of generational development itself noted early on in *Fourth Turning* by Strauss and Howe, foremost observers of generational subcultures. "Parents are slowing down the developmental clock, letting millennials linger longer in childhood, reversing what Richard Riley terms the 'hurry-hustle' of the Awakening."[lxvii]

Millennials, too, like their parents, will eventually vote Republican, just as every prior generation has at least once. But it's most important to talk about the last decade of analysis. Millennials, along with America's growing diversity, were talked about as twin political challenges for the Republican Party, when in fact they were the same challenge because of those challenges operating under the same subset of the population. The millennial generation, along with emerging Gen Z, is significantly more diverse than Gen X, boomers, and the silent generation of McCain and Biden. Just as when Republicans were struggling with the youth vote, as they often have for decades, this did not represent a straight-line analysis from a point in time, so, too, does a diversifying Republican Party capturing the support of more Hispanic, Asian, and black Americans mean that it is also capturing more support from millennials. In fact, just twelve years later, and in an incumbent reelection year rather than an open election versus a party eight years in the White House, the same millennial cohort that voted 66 to 32 for Barack Obama voted just 52 to 46 for Joe Biden, Obama's vice president. This 14 percent erosion of support, and 28 percent closing of the gap, represents a fundamental truth about American politics. Just because the media is locked in ideologically and talks about politics this way, it does not mean the country they cover and talk about is. Precisely the opposite.

In chapter 7, where we'll look at the next decade of the Democratic Party, and in chapter 8, where we'll look at the next decade of the Republican Party, we'll discuss the realigning millennial trend even more. It's important to note younger generations, especially those raising families and searching for greater job opportunities, are far more transient. As crime and a second wave of urban decline and dysfunction have weighed on America's cities in the COVID and post-COVID era, new arrivals and leavers are a key component of the geography of American politics and elections, as this is ultimately the final determinant of the balance of power.

It's tempting to reduce so much of our nationalized era of American politics to the presidency and midterm congressional battles in between presidential elections. And it is far too easy to forget that even those elections are a series of state elections. However, when one looks at the

American republic itself through the rules of our electoral and political system, one can sometimes see the future. Looking at the states themselves and the state legislatures, which for a long time lagged behind presidential realignment especially in the South, you can see a new picture emerging.

In the emerging Democratic majority of 2006 and 2008, party control of the state legislatures accounted for 284 electoral votes in today's configuration for the Democrats, 164 for the Republicans, and 90 were toss-ups or had split legislatures. Just prior to the 2022 midterms, the next time a new Democratic president was ushered into office with Joe Biden, you can see most clearly through the legislatures themselves just how much the emerging Democratic majority has failed to emerge at all. It has *eroded*.

2009 Party Control of State Legislatures

State Legislatures in 2009

Republican (Dark Gray): 164
Democrat (Gray): 284
Split Legislature (Light Gray): 90

The as-of-2022 party control of the legislatures comes to 310 electoral votes now for the Republicans, 205 for the Democrats, with just 23 electoral votes as toss-ups (Minnesota and Virginia). When you take it a step further and compare the number of seats in 2009 to 2022 and where each state has trended in seats regardless of party control at the moment, a picture emerges: 324 electoral votes for Republicans through the trends in the states, 176 electoral votes for Democrats through the trends in the states, and 38 toss-up electoral votes (Delaware, Florida, and Nebraska have been unchanged since 2009). While with those trends Democrats have bright spots in Virginia and Colorado, and Arizona and Georgia, whether those trends are truly permanent is an open question. At the state level, only Colorado is in Democratic political control, while Arizona and Georgia remain Republican, and Virginia is split with a newly elected Republican governor in Glenn Youngkin. Much has been made about Biden's narrow margins in Arizona and Georgia, but the fact remains that Bill Clinton won both of those states one time in the 1990s.

2022 Party Control of State Legislatures

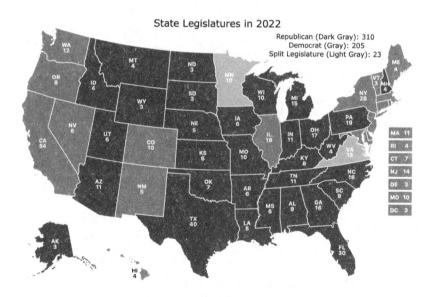

State Legislatures in 2022

Republican (Dark Gray): 310
Democrat (Gray): 205
Split Legislature (Light Gray): 23

The Trend from 2009 to 2022

Trend in State Legislatures from 2009 to 2022

Republican (Dark Gray): 324
Democrat (Gray): 176
No Significant Change (Light Gray): 38

Similar arguments were made in 2009 that trends in party affiliation were evidence for an emerging Democratic majority, but party affiliation and especially registration in total lag behind actual votes and realignment decisions. A late 2008 Gallup poll of affiliation showed states as Republican today as Arkansas, Tennessee, and Kentucky as solid Democratic for instance and only showed Utah, Wyoming, Idaho, Alaska, and Nebraska as solid Republican or Republican-leaning. The rest were either shown as competitive or lean and solid Democratic.

A presidential two-term cycle later, these self-affiliated trends had closed considerably. Despite Obama's personal popularity with his own party and with the country in some ways, his policies had never followed his personal appeal, and holding the presidency for eight years had done considerable damage to his party. In *The Great Revolt*, Salena Zito and Brad Todd interviewed scores of voters across Wisconsin, Iowa, Ohio, Michigan, and Pennsylvania, and one of the unifying themes, even among those who were not "pivot voters" (like pivot counties, voters who had voted twice for Barack Obama, then for Donald Trump), was a disappointment with the Obama years and the managed decline that had set in across the country, especially the Heartland regions and deindustrialized Midwest. In many ways, 2016 was Obama's personal likability and ability to hold his fragile coalition together removed, leaving just the policies that Americans had never really warmed to over that period of time.

By 2016 the same affiliation by state showed America's competitive regions emerging in the Sun Belt, along the Eastern Seaboard, and in the pivotal Midwest that would ultimately be the tipping point for both 2016 and 2020. Unlike the first two competitive areas though, the Midwest has trended Republican more than other areas of the country the past decade-plus. And indeed, there is a historical antecedent for this too. The Republican Party was born in Wisconsin, and it was in *The Emerging Republican Majority* that Kevin Phillips laid out a post–Great Society alignment of a united Heartland that powered Nixon, then Reagan, to landslide victories. Meanwhile, the Sun Belt and Eastern Seaboard remain competitive and up for grabs six years later. If anything is locked in at all, it is the state of Florida under Governor Ron DeSantis. More on this will be covered in chapter 9.

Phillips further noted the importance of a united Heartland in powering electoral landslides of either party: "The Harding, Coolidge, Hoover, and Eisenhower Heartland sweeps accompanied well-nigh unanimous GOP electoral-vote triumphs in the traditionally Republican Northeast, while the Roosevelt landslides were cemented by the full support of the South."

While Bill Clinton, and to a lesser extent Barack Obama, broke up the GOP's united Heartland that powered the Nixon and Reagan victories, one can see the trend since 2008 as being a Heartland rejection of the Democratic Party outside of large midwestern cities, and it's not merely a minor rejection of a vision of the future and the outcomes and results of the present but the strongest trend in the country outside of the southwest Texas border. While the border realignment is an indicator of the heart of the 2020 and onward based Hispanic realignment into the

Republican Party, the Heartland, one of the most egalitarian in outcome regions of the country, is an indicator of the social class realignment where working classes are becoming Republican and to a lesser extent college degree-holding professional classes are trending Democratic.

Taking this to the state level in those same presidential elections, since 2008, thirty-four states have trended Republican at the presidential level for a total of 306 electoral votes via the 2020 census, and just ten states have trended Democratic for a total of 174 electoral votes. Of the six states for a total of 58 electoral votes that show no strong trend toward either party in those twelve years, three of them are Democratic for a total of 34 electoral votes, and three are Republican for a total of 24 electoral votes. Of the trending Republican states that have already realigned, Missouri and Indiana with 21 electoral votes, which were more or less tied in 2008, are now firmly in the Republican column, as are Ohio and Iowa with 23 more electoral votes, which were Democratic. While Wisconsin and Pennsylvania narrowly voted for Joe Biden, the trend lines in those two states are clear. Wisconsin elected a Republican governor statewide a few times since, and more voters in Pennsylvania have changed their registration to Republican than almost in any other state. True independents, who often break against the party in the White House, are also breaking against the Democrats nearly everywhere, which should be enough to win the Midwest again in 2022 and '24.

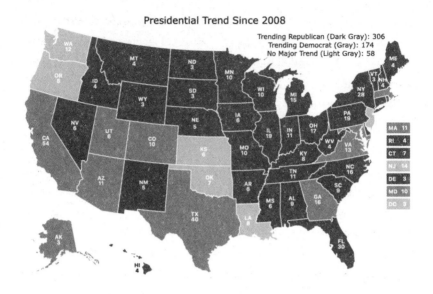

Presidential Trend Since 2008

Trending Republican (Dark Gray): 306
Trending Democrat (Gray): 174
No Major Trend (Light Gray): 58

While older Republicans act like the Reagan years were the glory years, the reality is that an even stronger coalition could be emerging that trades White House landslides for greater balance and political power throughout the states and Congress.

The classical Republican coalition of movement conservatism was in many respects powered by lower taxes, deregulation, and a strong military, but overall an ideological desire for a smaller government. Whereas the populist coalition is less concerned with the size of government and more concerned with the elites who have mismanaged the government and have run the country into the ground. While united in a desire to deconstruct, reform, and rein in the administrative state, the populist second wave of this emerging majority coalition is powered by the issues of globalization and a rejection of elite-driven globalism. Trade, immigration, and the wars—the issues that powered Trump to victory and near reelection in '20—are the issues of the populists of old. But there is an emerging group of issues associated not with a philosophy toward government like Republican-classic, not by the effects and issues around globalization like the populists, but by the creeping notion and fear that civilization itself is under assault. Rhetoric that has weaved in and out of the first two waves is now manifesting in the issues of technology, families, and the increasing realization of the need to build alternative and parallel institutions and infrastructure.

This is why in so many ways the 2020 narrow loss is more important for setting the stage for America's political future than the 2016 win. If a populist-conservative fusion of old and new, a diversified and diversifying coalition that is patriotic and understands the need to build new institutions and infrastructure because the old ones have lost their way and lost the confidence of the American people, and that confidence is not being restored or coming back, then we have something else entirely than 52 or 54 senators, 235 seats in the House, a majority of governors and state legislatures, and between 300 and 320 electoral votes at best. What we could be seeing instead in America's future is a slow but steady breaking of our long national nightmare and crisis. The country is in the metaphorical trenches of political warfare at the 50-yard line with two factions dependent on winning with long field goals, but what if it can instead be broken and reforged into a new social consensus and civic order as has been done in previous eras of crisis and crossroads?

A long journey out of the Third Civic Order of the progressive administrative state and into the institutions and coalitions that will make up the fourth.

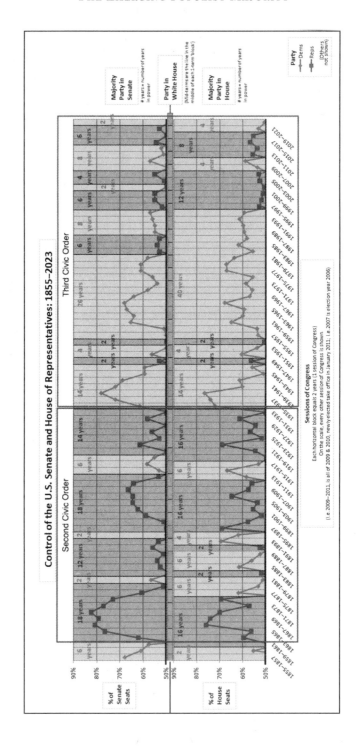

Control of the U.S. Senate and House of Representatives: 1855–2023

CHAPTER 7

THE DEMOCRATIC PARTY IN THE NEXT DECADE (2021 TO 2030)

In so many ways the 2020 presidential election was worse news for the Democratic Party than the 2016 presidential election was. Buoyed by a blue wave in 2018, powered by progressives far more than the more moderate-led waves of 2006 and 2008, driven by conditions localized to that time, the 2020 election was a Pyrrhic victory that destroyed the Democrats' idea of themselves, and the smartest members of that party know it. They also know they're largely powerless to stop it this next decade. They've cast their lot in with the millennial and progressive activists and are dependent on that support and enthusiasm going forward but increasingly lack even that.

The story of the Democratic Party in the next decade is ultimately a story of the last decade of the Third Civic Order, a key thesis of this book. Gone are the days where "demographics are destiny" and Democratic victory is "inevitable." Even its most ardent proponents discount that and instead are more likely to issue a caution and a warning. This chapter will lay out just how deep of a hole Democrats are about to be in and that if the party does not moderate its rhetoric, tone, and policies, and, most importantly, communicate a coherent vision for a shared American future rather than a global one, the party's position will go from bad to worse. Not only is Nancy Pelosi's "diversity is our strength" proving to be a slogan rather than an inevitability, it's also a current source of weakness, and only the second part of that slogan, "unity is our purpose," is keeping the current coalition of the Democrats in its relatively competitive position it's held since the Clinton administration.

The Democrats are a diverse coalition held together by an increasing need to be anti-Republican. And it is true generally that ideological polarization plus negative partisanship is a hallmark of the political age. What is also true though, and why we're starting with the Democrats first, is that even in pre-democratic societies, defining the ruling party or power and what keeps them in power is the first step, and only after is a compelling alternative vision going to rise and emerge until ultimately, a ruling civic order is slowly (or rapidly) toppled, and a new ruling civic order replaces it. This chapter covers the former; the next will cover the latter.

The 2020 presidential election needed to not just be a win for the Democrats (which they got, even while losing thirteen House seats), it needed to be a landslide victory. Why? Because 2020 was a census redistricting year. Back in 2010, the midterm election where the Tea Party movement brought about a conservative grassroots wave, was another census redistricting year. The one prior to that, 2000, wasn't particularly strong for the Democrats either. Bit by bit, the long arc of structural power, especially at the most local levels, has brought about a Democratic Party that has only risen in the cities the past few decades and is situationally and selectively successful in wealthier suburban areas while it has dramatically receded in power and control elsewhere. And it would be one thing if the Democrats' struggles in rural and small-town America were strategic and tactical, but their struggles are primarily cultural, which encompasses and includes economics as well. The Democratic brand in large swaths of the country has become toxic, and it will not recover in our lifetimes. This is our starting point.

While by historical standards no party has had a true landslide at the presidential level in the last three decades and only inside-straight midterm waves against parties in power have occurred, no party was in greater need of the landslide the legacy media was promising would happen than the Democrats in 2020. Even in a narrow victory, the margins and coalition of the victory was a significantly weaker one than Obama's in 2008, which was in many respects weaker than the Clinton coalition of the 1990s once you account for the Perot vote and make it a two-party vote only. The tenuous nature of the Biden coalition was built on gains with suburban white women and third-party and independent white men who broke against the incumbent that will likely not continue after Trump and may not continue even in the final Trump possible election of '24. The Pyrrhic victory was such that according to Edison Research/NEP, Democrats lost 3 percent with black men, 4 percent with black women, 4 percent with Hispanic men, and 3 percent with Asians and other ethnicities. Meanwhile, Democratic gains and victory were driven by incredibly modest gains with white women and the rallying of Johnson- and Stein-voting men.

For a media culture and country that continually racializes American politics in the direction of the progressive worldview, this is an incredibly risky strategy for Democrats to be doubling down on, and a strategy that is complemented by Republicans achieving both the Sean Trende strategy (doubling down and winning a higher share of the white vote that didn't turn out for Romney) of 2016 and the GOP "growth and opportunity" autopsy strategy of the 2012 postmortem in '20. Republicans under Trump have diversified the party, just not in the way that the autopsy had figured they would. How does this happen? Because the increasingly radical cultural progressivism is what is leading the way. The Democratic establishment continually makes deals on culture and identity while refusing to put forth a serious program and vision on America's economic future or a grand strategy in foreign policy and national security. But of course what made Trende right was not so much anything particular about our contemporary events but a far more common sense–driven argument about the nature of political coalitions themselves. For Trende, the critical problem with "straight-line analyses" of coalitions is when they are a "coalition of everyone." Coalitions are more like water balloons: if you press on one portion, other parts get stretched.[lxviii] This is what happened to FDR, and it has happened to the Republican coalition of Reagan as well, which was at the end of something rather than at the beginning, as most party systems and critical election theorists would posit.

Edition Research/NEP 2020 Exit Poll Data (and Change from 2016)

Demographic	Biden	Trump
White men	38% (+7)	61% (-1)
White women	44% (+1)	55% (+3)
Black men	79% (-3)	19% (+6)
Black women	90% (-4)	9% (+5)
Hispanic men	59% (-4)	36% (+4)
Hispanic women	69% (no change)	30% (+5)
Asian & other ethnicities	58% (-3)	38% (+7)

The Democratic Party has become wedded to the Davos elites and the neoliberal consensus on globalization. A party that has over 85 percent of the richest fifty congressional districts in America is not soon going to change its tune on these matters, nor does it really want to. In this sense, to figure out what is going on with American politics today, you have to look to the ruling party—the Democrats.

As of this writing, Joe Biden has rebounded slightly in his approvals thanks to going scorched-earth rhetoric against Republicans and getting some rebound support from the millennial and Gen Z progressive left who would rather see a Queen AOC than a President Biden. However, this, too, will prove to be a short-term gain and mid- and long-term loss. Another Pyrrhic victory for a party and company man who are increasingly realizing they have no true successor or plan in place. Ideologically, the more progressive the Democrats become and the more authentically populist the Republicans become, the closer the Republican Party will be to not just winning through the Electoral College and the Senate but also regularly winning the popular vote and House vote too.

This is another reason why 2020 represented the last chance for the Democrats to assert their position and achieve the generational renewal of America's natural governing party status. Had the Democrats achieved the sort of landslide its propaganda media was promoting, of 7 or 8 percent in the popular vote more akin to 2008, and an Electoral College rout that exceeded Clinton's 1996 peak to perhaps achieve the first modern-day landslide (standard being 1988), then more than fifty seats in the Senate and pickups in the House would have followed instead of being dependent on outgoing Majority Leader Mitch McConnell's foolishness and other GOP dysfunction in the days and weeks leading up to the Georgia runoffs. The fifty-fifty vice president–breaking ties may have seemed like a victory, and indeed more large trillion-dollar bills have gotten through this Congress than could have ever been imagined even when Democrats briefly had sixty senators over a decade ago, but it still lacked what was hoped for. A US Senate not dependent on West Virginia Senator Joe Manchin and Arizona Senator Kyrsten Sinema could have ended the filibuster, and not just for judicial nominations either but for everything. Fifty-two or fifty-three senators could have packed the Supreme Court, brought about statehood for Washington, DC, and Puerto Rico, and added four more Democratic senators in the process. In other words, in 2020 Democrats needed a relative landslide to stop what was coming and is happening the next decade. The fact that they won by forty thousand votes over three states, an Electoral College result closer than 2016 and 2000, and lost thirteen House seats and are dependent on the vice president to break ties, underscores the weakness of the party's position.

The Senate Problem and Battlegrounds of the 2020s

Democrats will come to fully understand just how 2020 represented the last chance after the '22 midterm elections and '24 Senate elections. The '22 senatorial class of elections only moderately favored the Republicans, even in a red wave year. It can be expected that Republicans will be able to defend the states that are increasingly realigned over the past half decade or so, in Florida and Ohio *for sure* and *most likely* be annually competitive in 2016 states Wisconsin and Pennsylvania. While set up perfectly to flip the Senate in the '22 midterms and representing a tremendous disappointment, Democrats focused their energy and out-funded Republicans in all of the closest seats like Georgia, Arizona, Nevada, and New Hampshire. In most years, winning the popular vote by 3 percent is going to do this, but not in the very bizarre and uneven '22 midterms. Democrats defended what they had to do and maximized their base turnout and used their money advantage. Yet, in many respects '22 simply delayed the inevitable.

In 2024 things get truly rough as the 2018 blue wave year gets fully exposed in a presidential year. There are almost no viable pickup attempts for the Democrats and as many as eight vulnerable seats in the Senate. West Virginia, Montana, and Ohio will stand to easily flip, while Arizona's other Senate seat, the one in which progressives will attempt to primary Senator Sinema anyway, will likely flip as well. In addition, Nevada, a likely '24 flip at the presidential level that has been trending away from the Democrats for many cycles in a row as the Harry Reid machine gives way to the Democratic Socialists of America takeover of local party organization, brings the potential total of Republican Senate seats to fifty-eight. Finally, there are three more seats that could be vulnerable in Wisconsin, Michigan, and Pennsylvania. While a Republican victory in '24 would bring about a favorable year for the Democrats in '26 by most historical trends, there are not enough opportunities to turn the tide, and certainly not if the number of Republican-held seats is fifty-eight or more. In '26 the most likely Democratic targets become Texas, North Carolina, and Maine, while the best Republican targets are Georgia's other seat, Michigan, Minnesota (Senator Tina Smith), and possibly New Mexico if the trends of Hispanic realignment continue. If '28 brings about more neutral territory where neither party has a particularly large advantage, somewhere in between the 2012 and 2004 cycles for instance, in such an environment only Pennsylvania (one-term senator for reelection), Wisconsin, and possibly New Hampshire look like viable targets for either party. Even if the '26 and '28 targets expand a bit, it'll be very hard to break the lock on the Senate. In other words, when, not if, Democrats lose the Senate by 2024, they may not get it back not just for years and cycles but for decades. By the 2030s if progressives are still oriented toward their current disposition and positions, there will be calls to abolish the Senate entirely. Indeed, there are already calls at the fringes for precisely that, citing its "un-democratic" nature.

Year	Democratic Senate Seats	Republican Senate Seats	Viable Pickup Opportunities (D)	Viable Pickup Opportunities (R)
2024	47	53	n/a	8 (WV, MT, OH, NV, AZ, WI, MI, PA)
2026	39	61	3 (TX, NC, ME)	4 (GA, MI, MN, NM)
2028	42	58	PA, WI, or NH	PA, WI, or NH
2030	43	57	TX?	NY?

Beyond even these trends, along the more creative and outsider area, let us briefly imagine the Democrats' dream of a blue Texas by 2030. Out of our four large states, California is locked in for the Democrats, but increasingly Florida is going to be locked in for the Republicans over the next decade. While Texas has trended blue in a relative sense, however, since mid-decade, New York has also trended relatively red. While still a long way to go, New York has voted Republican statewide more recently than the last time Texas has voted Democratic statewide. While majority leader, and soon to be minority leader, Schumer is locked in until he wants to retire, the same cannot be said for New York's junior senator, Kirsten Gillibrand. Senator Gillibrand exhibited an almost AOC-like parody level to the nation in her presidential run, between the finger waving at mythical white suburban women who lack sufficient wokeness on matters of race and identity. In many ways Gillibrand is the epitome of the new stock Democrat character that is some combination of blue and purple hair activism, a corporate HR department, and the latest idea from the faculty lounge. A good barometer of the direction of the Democratic Party can be seen in the county trends of the blue wave. In that election, despite being compared to a more neutral year of 2012, Senator Gillibrand saw sixty of New York's sixty-two counties trend against her and the Democratic brand at the senatorial level. Now part of this could be revision to the mean, but it's not like Republicans have been running competitive and active statewide campaigns recently—at least not until Congressman Lee Zeldin's campaign of '22 was much of a fight put up. What were the two counties that trended more in Gillibrand's direction? New York County (Manhattan) and Tompkins County. These are the two counties that house Columbia, NYU, and Cornell. In a sense this is a metaphor for who is becoming more Democratic today: the wealthy and the professional class and the enclaves of academia.

On the flip side, Senator Ted Cruz received a genuine scare from now-perennial candidate Robert Francis "Beto" O'Rourke in 2018. While it is very unlikely that Cruz receives such a contest in '24 or even '30 if he continues to run for his seat, the 2–3 percent margin in 2018, a good Democratic year, has become the stand-in example for "blue Texas."

If the trends of 2020 spelled *secret* good news for Republicans and bad news for the Democrats, the trends in the first two years of the Biden administration have accelerated this into overdrive. Democrats with complete electoral power, with only the Supreme Court and the states to check them, have endorsed increasingly their growing authoritarian tendencies upstream and the totalitarian tendencies emanating downstream in millennial and zoomer progressive culture. The problem with both of these tendencies is it's leading to more and more defections from their party. Absent preferable and good societal outcomes (which despite our division and polarization, reasonable people can generally still agree on), the

Democrats have been backed into a political corner and are increasingly acting how power acts when it is cornered: by lashing out.

The years 2021 and 2022 have brought about a narrowing of voter registration gaps and registration advances across battleground states and growing registration advances in favor of Republicans in red states. Even in many deep-blue states, registration advantages are closing in all but a handful of states. Voter registration is one thing, as it often lags behind actual vote decisions and ballots cast. Hispanic realignment has continued and accelerated the past two years, and there is clear evidence that it is not just limited to the border areas or Miami-Dade County in Florida. In places as deeply blue as New York City, Asian Americans are also deserting the Democratic Party and trended heavily toward Republican candidate for mayor, Curtis Sliwa. On one hand, Asian Americans are trending back to their historical party from the 1990s and prior, but it is decidedly modern issues and developments driving this realignment. A desire for public safety and curbing increasing crime rates, hate crimes targeting Asians, and differences on education and merit-based screening systems are driving this realignment in major cities like New York City and San Francisco. Driving this wedge further are the cultural and ideological preferences of millennial and Gen Z social progressives. The increasingly leftward pull and influence they have on the Democratic Party is driving a wedge between the old and new, and this is most particularly felt and will be felt increasingly in the 2020s in urban and diverse cosmopolitan America, the base of the Democratic Party.

Electorally, a state that Biden won in 2020 by 10 percent became a loss by a couple of points in the state of Virginia and now Governor Glenn Youngkin overcoming Clinton acolyte and former Virginia governor himself Terry McAuliffe. In New Jersey, an even more shocking result occurred when little-funded and much-ignored Republican candidate Jack Ciattarelli came within a few points of defeating incumbent Governor Phil Murphy, an alum of Goldman Sachs. New Jersey was a state that had long voted well into the double digits for Democrats at the presidential level. Considering that a year after Obama's 2008 victory supposedly ushered in the emerging Democratic majority, Republican Chris Christie won the state and was reelected in '13, New Jersey represents part of at least forty states that will still vote for a Republican candidate right now whereas Democrats have this same phenomenon in about thirty states right now. If the micro and macro trends continue throughout this decade, and millennial social and cultural progressives replace retiring silent and boomer Democrats, it's not a stretch to see this equilibrium of competitiveness reach a ratio of forty-five states that a decent Republican candidate can win, while the Democratic number goes as low as twenty-five. This generational divide underscores another emerging problem for the Democratic Party in the next decade—*there is no bench.*

Contrary to popular belief, in office and overall the Republicans have gotten younger as a party, and the Democrats, especially in leadership positions, increasingly are older. Consider the age of Democratic leadership today. Joe Biden is eighty years old, Nancy Pelosi is eighty-two, and Chuck Schumer is seventy-one, the youthful member of the bunch and older than Ronald Reagan when he took office.

The Democrats have also failed to make serious candidates out of any of their younger politicians. Vice President Kamala Harris currently polls, and has consistently polled, lower than Joe Biden, who has been underwater since August 2021. Transportation Secretary Pete Buttigieg, the millennial version of Bill Clinton in the sense that he's been preparing to be president ever since the Ivy League, and perhaps the most talked about Democratic figure that is youngest of all, Representative Alexandria Ocasio-Cortez comes off like an infantilized parody of the millennial internet comments. That scores of progressive activists genuinely want a future where someone like her is president of the United States, or someone even further along the radical rabbit hole, says a lot more about an increasingly lost but loud segment of a generation and corner of the internet that Big Tech has helped to mainstream in the Trump era than it does about anything else. With a weak to nonexistent Democratic bench, and losing ground with nearly every demographic except, in a relative sense, college-educated Americans, says more about the current state of academia than it does about newfound voters that Democrats are attracting. To the extent Democrats are making gains there, this is again a bad mathematical trade-off. Like the bad math of Majority Leader Schumer, who posited that for every western Pennsylvania voter lost, "we're picking up two or three in the Philadelphia suburbs," there are simply more Americans with no or limited college education than there are Americans with college degrees, and the Americans who are college educated are disproportionately clumped into the knowledge economy major cities and urban areas that already vote for the party. But these are trends that have happened in the past decade and are continuing. What are the newer trends?

Increasingly, while the polarizations around urban vs. rural; the identity politics trinity of race, gender, and sexuality; and college educated versus noncollege educated are yesterday's trends, today, tomorrow, and the next decade will feature two increasing trends. One, mentioned briefly, is the relative closing of nearly all those polarizations, which is a good thing for this country but a bad thing electorally for the Democratic Party, and two, parents with children are increasingly leaving the Democratic Party for the Republican Party. While there has long been literature on how having children makes you more conservative, and there is also a significant gap by party self-ID on who wants to have children, people who previously have voted Democratic or leaned liberal are also becoming more Republican once they have children. In a statistic that should alarm every Democratic partisan, one recent poll showed that of those with children under eighteen in the household, Republicans hold an identification advantage of two to one (62 percent to 31 percent). This trend has already shown up in actual election results and changed the nature of messaging. Despite media reporting, the school board and education issues pushing back on trans ideology and critical race theory was driven by organic and often first time political involvement from self-described moderates or disengaged people who became politicized over education issues. In addition, the COVID-era policies associated with teachers unions like the United Federation of Teachers and union leaders like Randi Weingarten have all but wiped out what was historically a Democratic issue—education. Today, there is either no advantage or a slight Republican advantage on this issue. Education and schools are going to increasingly be an issue as the next decade develops, and Democrats will need to come up with a better answer on this. After the Virginia gubernatorial result in 2021, one Democratic consultant was quoted as saying that "Democrats need to make sure the Republicans don't become the 'party of parents.'" Too late. The Republican Party already has become the party of parents and will become more of one tomorrow with the policies to match if they're smart, while the Democratic Party will become the party of single and childless people. The reason for this goes beyond just mere public policy; it goes to the root of modern progressive ideology that stems from millennials and younger—on abortion, on the climate, and on the future.

On abortion, progressives have driven the zeitgeist of the Democratic Party from the 1990s era of "safe, legal, and rare" to "shout your abortion." The Lena Dunhams of the Democratic Party are numerous. Not only do they want to have abortion as a right up until the moment of birth for any reason whatsoever, they expect society to approve or at least stay silent about the matter. Now in a post-Roe America, there are two problems with this continuing approach. One, progressives are mostly bubbled within coastal urban enclaves where the abortion law is precisely that. And two, their continued advocacy and radicalization on the issue is out of step with at least seven out of ten Americans and portrays a general disrespect for the value of life that makes much of the rest of progressive moralizing difficult to accept as sincere and genuine for ordinary common sense–driven Americans.

On the climate, AOC at an event not too long after she shocked (and frightened) the Democratic political world by upsetting a top-ranking House member, Joe Crowley, said that "the world is going to end in twelve years if we don't do something about climate change." Never mind the fact that even this is a total distortion of what the UN climate report said, and never mind the fact that there is no viable way to actually meet any climate goals or targets with current technology. The millennial left does not deal in logic; it deals emotionally and ideologically. But the real point is that if enough people truly believed her or any one of the countless other climate alarmists on this issue, the world isn't over in twelve years—it is over right now. This is because the present is very much driven by the fact that there is a future.

On the future broadly, a consistent theme that shows up is a lack of faith in a viable one. This is the actual anti-science, anti-humanity, anti-civilization, and anti-life approach. Positions on abortion and climate notwithstanding, the actual vision of the future communicated by the progressive and postliberal left is not a compelling future at all. Considering how long the will to live has powered the human spirit at both the individual and societal level, it's highly unlikely that when boomer and silent retirees are replaced by millennial and Gen Z progressives that the Democratic Party will be able to bring about generational change and renewal; instead, it will reach party's end the closer we get to that full transition. More on this in chapter 10 on demography.

The Institutional Confidence and Trust Problem

Beyond the Hispanic and Asian realignment away from the Democrats' once and future demographic inevitability coalition and the lack of tangible outcomes delivered to ordinary Americans in the first two years of the Biden administration, a larger problem looms for "America's Natural Governing Party." This is the crisis of confidence and trust in American institutions, both governmental and private themselves. Once institutional trust breaks down to the level it is at today, you're not going to get it back. What was broken in the 1960s and idling through the malaise of the 1970s saw some renewal in the decades of the 1980s and 1990s, but the last two decades have been rough in this area. The yearly Gallup research on this question polls Americans' trust and confidence across many different institutions: the public schools, the medical system, small business, church or organized religion, banks, the military, the US Supreme Court,

Congress, the presidency, big business, and the like. By 2021, the end of the first year of the Biden administration, only half or more of the country expressed "a great deal" or "quite a lot" of confidence in the following institutions: small business (at 70 percent), the military (at 69 percent), and the police (at 51 percent, up from a historic low of 48 percent in 2020). Institutions of the administrative state, of culture and society, and confidence in them are perhaps the most critical component in whether a civic and social order can remain legitimate or not.

Confidence in Institutions, 2019–2021 (Gallup)
% Who have "a great deal" or "quite a lot" of confidence

	2019 (%)	2020 (%)	2021 (%)	Change, 2021 vs. 2020 (pct. Pts)
The public schools	29	41	32	-9
The medical system	36	51	44	-7
Small business	68	75	*70*	-5
The church or organized religion	36	42	37	-5
Banks	30	38	33	-5
The U.S. Supreme Court	38	40	36	-4
The criminal justice system	24	24	20	-4
The military	73	72	69	-3
Technology companies	--	32	29	-3
Organized labor	29	31	28	-3
Newspapers	23	24	21	-3
Television news	18	18	16	-2
The presidency	38	39	38	-1
Big business	23	19	18	-1
Congress	11	13	12	-1
The police	53	48	*51*	+3

Italicized indicating institutions with majority public confidence

Breaking this down by party and party-leaners you get an even further window into the lack of institutional confidence. Only for small business and the military do both Democrats and Republicans cross the majority threshold. Additionally on the Democratic side, the medical system, perhaps left over from Covid, barely achieves it at 50 percent trust and confidence, while just 36 percent of Republican and leaners say the same, with 62 percent trust and confidence in the presidency, no doubt a circumstance limited to a Democrat being president. A few years back in the *Hidden Tribes* report the opposite was found. Where Democratic-leaning political tribes and cohorts cited the lack of "leadership" as a concern, Republican-leaning political tribes and cohorts did not. The report was from 2018, and any updates along these same lines would most likely yield opposite results. Current Republican confidence in the presidency is at just 13 percent. This is no way to run a country at this point, and with these institutions, and regardless of who and why the institutions are being propped up, their poor marks hurt the dominant party in the governing regime, the Democrats, not the oppositional one. Republican partisans' confidence in the sixteen US institutions ironically shows at least a way forward if followed. In addition to the military and small business, which also receive majority support from Democrats, the police receive 76 percent Republican confidence, and the church or organized religion receives 51 percent. The religion and science split between parties is much talked about, but the trust and confidence in either, even by "the religion party" and "the science party," barely achieves 50 percent.

Partisans' Confidence in 16. U.S. Institutions
(Gallup, June 1–July 5, 2021)
% Who have "a great deal" or "quite a lot" of confidence

	Republicans/ Leaners (%)	Democrats/ Leaners (%)	Rep-Dem difference (pct. Pts)
The police	*76*	31	+45
The church or organized religion	*51*	26	+25
The military	*78*	*62*	+16
Small business	*76*	*64*	+12
The U.S. Supreme Court	39	35	+4
Big business	19	17	+2
Banks	35	33	+2
The criminal justice system	20	19	+1
Congress	7	17	-10
Large technology companies	22	34	-12
The medical system	36	*50*	-14
Television news	6	25	-19
Organized labor	16	39	-23
The public schools	20	43	-23
Newspapers	8	*35*	-27
The presidency	*13*	*62*	-49

*Italicized indicating institutions with majority
public confidence within partisan affiliation*

What partisans and leaners on both sides also agree on is a distrust in the television news and newspapers. While Democrats show much more confidence in the media, no doubt in part explained by a significant, well-documented, and accelerated during the Trump years bias in the Democrats' favor, the Democrats themselves get nowhere near a majority support for the news media. But what is most significant in this arena is just how low Republican trust and confidence is in the news media: 8 percent for newspapers and 6 percent for television news. Along with a 7 percent rating for Congress, these numbers are so low that it is unrecoverable at this point.

Americans' Trust in Mass Media by Political Party; 1997-2022 (Gallup)

Year	Republicans	Independents	Democrats
1997	41	53	64
2002	49	52	59
2007	28	41	66
2012	26	31	58
2017	14	37	72
2022	14	27	70

The trend over the past two decades has been an American electorate that was about fifty-fifty on trust and confidence with mass media to a country where Republicans and Independents/unaligned alike are trending downward in trust in the mass media and where Republican support has utterly plummeted. Meanwhile, Democrats have gone from a near 50 percent low when Trump was elected to basically being in lockstep with the mass media ever since. Increasingly, Democrats and the media are synonymous with one another in the Trump and post-Trump era. This phenomenon is again a function of civic order theory, where the media, especially at the top levels, functions similar to a court while the academic world functions as a secular clerisy. The court and clerisy are two fundamental pillars to holding up the late Third Civic Order, characterized structurally and in coalition by the Boomer Alignment.

Many in the media defend themselves by saying the advent of the internet, social media, smart phones, and so on has fundamentally changed the delivery and consumption of news. While this is true enough, it is not a sufficient explanation for this collapse in trust and confidence in not just the news media but most of our public and public-facing institutions. Nonetheless, the role and timing of technological change, just as it had during the turn of the last century, cannot be overlooked or overstated. Chronicler of this in an exhaustive analysis was geopolitical analyst Martin Gurri in *The Revolt of the Public and the Crisis of Authority in the New Millennium*. Was Gurri's macro-technological analysis the long crisis foretold by the Strauss and Howe generational theory, or was it literally the crisis of 2020—which turned out to be the COVID-19 global pandemic? Or is it purely as Gurri had put it in speculation at the end of the Cold War: "The millennial triumph of democracy, appears in hindsight to have been the high-water mark for the prestige and legitimacy of this system. Once the external pressure applied by communism was removed, democratic countries lost their internal cohesion, and began the slow descent into negation."[lxix]

More critically, once the problem with public authority is a lack of trust and confidence in it, the burden of proof and work to restore that trust, confidence, and legitimacy lies not with the broader public but the institutions and authorities themselves. Public authority can simply not survive the twin assaults of this erosion of public trust in its authority and the erosion of the meaningfulness of citizenship that Dr. Victor Davis Hanson details greatly in his most recent work.[lxx]

For those in authority to retain the public's trust and rebuild that confidence, the way to do that is to distort nothing, to lie about nothing, to put the best face on nothing, and to try and manipulate no one. This is how President Lincoln handled the crisis of his times; this is how a crisis is best dealt with, and a leader must make whatever horror stemming from that crisis that exists concrete. Only then will people be able to break it apart.[lxxi] For the burgeoning populist conservative coalition, the challenge does not lie in the next election or even the next decade. The project of restoring institutional trust will take years, and the real lesson from COVID is on the need to restore an eternal skepticism and avoid succumbing to fear and manipulation. As journalist and writer David Marcus said in *Charade: The Covid Lies That Crushed a Nation*, "The defense of American liberty by those not enthralled by the all-consuming fear of death will be the work of at least a generation, and signs don't look fantastic that it will be successful. …if a new conservatism is to protect and defend the traditional values of America, it must do so not by catering to the whims of the elite, but by tapping into the power of the unheard millions who support liberty without a corporate megaphone, but nonetheless support it."[lxxii]

The Challenge from the Successor Ideology and the Democrats' Corrupt Bargain and Misplaced Trust on the Streets

Democrats have become a party today reminiscent of the easy to discredit "acid, amnesty, and abortion" of the doomed 1972 McGovern campaign. Today, the slogan could just as well be "loose morals in the sheets and chaos on the streets." Yet, Democrats upstream are convinced, at least in their performance, that they are not just preferable to the Republican Party but also morally better than it, and that all opposition to their proposals whether coming from the Republicans or elsewhere is simply illegitimate. In 2020 a considerable amount of attention was first focused on COVID and then later the summer of rioting that led to over forty people dead. Had the election been fought on even terrain without these issues, the Democrats' problems would have manifested clearly, but instead a narrow victory that really needed to be a landslide to avoid what is coming in the next decade transpired. As we transition out of a boomer-dominated political America and into a Gen X candidacy and millennial and Gen Z political culture–dominated one, the Boomer Alignment and story in American politics is coming full circle. The '72 McGovern campaign that became the "revenge of George McGovern" coalition is again succumbing to cultural excess and social decay, and a backlash continues to brew by the day even with people who recently described themselves as liberal. This is because liberals have lost control of the Democratic Party while moderates have been defeated or sidelined nearly everywhere. Today, there are still many well-meaning over-forty-five-year-old Democrats who vote with the party but are totally baffled by the chaos and downstream cultural and social mores on the streets. Just like "a coalition of everybody" and "diversity is our strength" are more slogans than reality, and just like a geographical party that included both the Northeast and Midwest was not going to last for long, a progressive activist push from the younger generations that asserts the world is ending because of the climate, that there are over forty genders, and that we'd like a student loan bailout where carpenters and electricians pay for the liberal arts and numerous studies degrees of urban professionals and the aspiring professional class (what passes as the populist left) is not going to last much longer. And this is the reason why Democrats and the media need to turn Republicans into evil villains who are out to destroy America, the same America that younger progressive activists have been asserting for years is hopelessly and irredeemably evil as well. Democrats are a party in greater need of unity through the use of an enemy because they are too divided to unite otherwise, and their coalition is now too clumped into bubbles. But what these same progressive activists do have going for them is a tacit agreement with the Third Civic Order through the late institutions of it. In this sense, a successor ideology in America is still theoretically possible, even if a traditional Democratic electoral victory like the ones they used to have is not. This cultural dominance that progressive activists enjoy leads to more and more electoral problems for the party benefactor though, and in this sense Democrats have made a corrupt and ultimately bad bargain that only yielded short-term gains at the expense of mid- and long-term viability.

Propelling the need for a successor ideology into overdrive throughout the Trump years, Democrats made the bargain, and progressives got more emboldened by the year. While achieving a short-term victory themselves and finding defeat inconceivable still, even if there is a growing awareness of their unpopularity with the broader public, what has been lost in America itself is something that cannot be recovered through the current civic order whose origins lie in the Roosevelt years. For the mainstream and upstairs Democrat, the year is always 1933 and 1965. And for the progressive activists, the expectation is articulated utopia around the corner, only to experience underwhelming outcomes, creating a heartbreaking cycle where politics and science have proven to be a poor substitute for religion, faith, family, and tradition.

Today, America has no agreed-upon consensus story and therefore no grand strategy. Yet the United States of America is still very much a legal state and polity, one that claims legitimacy and is attempting to reach for more and more power over the people. This contradiction between the successor ideology, the ruling order caught in between who believe they are using the successors but really are signing up for their own extinction, the court and clerisy that props it up, and the countercultural and emerging populist coalitional majority will form the backdrop to our battles in the 2020s—America's next and current decade.

Just as the foundations of the Third Civic Order were in part articulated by the populists' third-party challenge of the 1880s and '90s, especially out west and later by the Progressive Era, especially as a challenge to the establishment of the East, we can trace a six-decade journey from Port Huron, when it was the counterculture, to today, when it has become the dominant culture. The new counterculture increasingly articulated today is one that is populist, patriotic, conservative, and nationalistic against the failures of globalization and the internationalism of the past three decades.

Despite its seeming institutional and significant fundraising advantages, the ruling Democratic coalition cannot seem to bring about a knock-out blow. And the developments of the past two decades where the party has seemingly only improved its prospects in college towns and professional class–heavy areas of the corporate world are part of the reason why it's been robbed of the power of its historic story. Today's coalition increasingly resembles both the naive worldview of the university student and the more cynical worldview of the corporation seeking to put as much distance between the end user and consumer and the product as possible like the Dutch East India Company of old.

Civic Order	Generational Alignment	Presidential	Congress
Mid-Third Civic Order	War Generation Alignment	Republicans won in landslides usually.	Democrats held Congress.
Late-Third Civic Order	Boomer Alignment	Democrats win the popular vote.	Republicans held Congress.
In transition to…	The next decade	Democrats start losing the popular vote and become less diverse, Republicans more diverse around a shared set of national values.	Republicans lock in a Senate advantage to add to the House and states advantage, and usually win the presidency.
Fourth Civic Order	Republicans dominate US politics with an emerging populist coalitional majority.	The dominant rural-urban coalition's power is checked by the suburbs and Moderates (the New Conservatives).	Alternate possibilities: successor ideology enforced top-down, fifty-fifty stalemate continues, eliminated possibilities: *The Emerging Democratic Majority.*

CHAPTER 8

THE REPUBLICAN PARTY IN THE NEXT DECADE (2021 TO 2030)

After 2008, books by Sam Tanenhaus and others predicted the death of the Republican Party. Not unlike after the 1964 landslide win by LBJ, the last true Democratic landslide win at the presidential level, these projections were premature. There was no "permanent progressive majority," and as the *Hidden Tribes* report shows, progressives comprise no more than 8 percent of the country. However, the writings by Judis and Teixeira and others did get the growing ideology of the Democratic coalition right, as Sean Trende noted in *The Lost Majority*. That book detailed just how the Democrats' broad coalition came apart and, more importantly, gave convincing reasons why the faith that such a coalition existed was dubious at best. In the days after 2008, with 2010 on a distant horizon, and even well into the early summer of 2009 when the Democrats were able to hold a congressional seat in historically Republican Upstate New York, the death pronouncements of the Republican Party and exuberance of the Democratic Party got louder. Backing this were two trend lines that pundits always foolishly drew as a straight line forward into the future, a symptom of the progressive worldview itself and how history is viewed (as an onward and upward linear trajectory where we move forward, and that is good, and anything behind is backward and bad). Trende's book makes two broad claims beyond the many useful metaphors about the nature of coalitions and historical data throughout. First, that the 2010 midterm elections were made possible by a Democratic Party that failed to appreciate the fragile nature of its coalition.[lxxiii] This broadly tracks with conditions on the ground and the Obama campaign's decision to cannibalize its organization until re-election rather than rolling it into the DNC itself for midterms. The second claim is that broad demographic shifts that "many Democratic theorists believe are making them invincible are ephemeral and will not bring about their hoped-for realignment."[lxxiv] The irony of this second claim is that the theorists were largely an echo in the media of a few "oracles" that today largely admit their clairvoyance was temporary, and in those days Republicans largely believed them as well and responded accordingly. The Trende book offered no sexy prediction about what will happen next in American politics, declaring no inevitability, casting aspersion on such theories from political oracles, and posited the future of American politics remains wholly up for grabs.[lxxv] Ten years on, the "up for grabs" still feels true in the abstract, but updating it in the wake of a new round of post-2020 similar articles and a much-changed political culture in America and the western world broadly feels wholly necessary.

Back then, but not quite to the same extent today, Republicans had both a youth voter problem and a diverse voter problem, they said. The problem again with that truth is that the voter problem was in fact the *same* problem. The diversity of Obama's coalition was not markedly different from the diversity of Bill Clinton's coalition or even John Kerry's coalition, nor was it surprising that young voters voted in large numbers for Democrats. With few exceptions, this had been true for a while. However, young voters were simply more diverse than older voters and generations. Pundits were claiming two separate beneficial trends for the Democrats that were actually just one trend, and they still are doing so with few exceptions. In addition, a secondary mistake of drawing that straight-line analysis forward into the future followed without any pause toward what history tells us. History shows that all generations eventually vote for both parties throughout their voting lifetime. Therefore, the "emerging Democratic majority" that pundits were claiming would actually have to set new historical precedents to emerge at all in the permanence many were claiming had arrived. Heading into the 2022 midterm elections the math and balance of power revealed a nation with two coalitions of many unhappy Americans still competing to win games via long field goals, but on close examination one can see which party coalition has the stronger leg.

US Political Party Strength Heading into the 2022 Midterms

Presidency	US Senate	US House	Governors	State Senate Majorities	State House Majorities
Democratic	Democratic (VP breaking ties)	Democratic	Republican	Republican	Republican
306–232	50–50	222–213	28–22	32–18	30–18–1

Instead, what has happened is the Republican Party has both grown more diverse and attracted the support of more millennials. Again, this is not two separate trends; it is the same trend. Millennials realigning and changing their voting patterns from Democratic to Republican are also going to diversify the Republican Party as well along the margins. And this trend of the next decade rather than the previous decade is the final emerging wave of what makes up a political future in America that is no longer played out in between the 40-yard lines. Indeed, since the 1960s, and even back to the beginning of the civic order with significant Republican pushback in '38 and '42 midterms, and holding a plurality of the states from the war until Eisenhower's first midterm, there has been a consistent and enduring pushback against the ruling Democratic Party, and in the next decade, the Republican Party, by becoming more effectively populist in policy to add to its rhetoric, has the opportunity to become the de facto ruling party in America as we transition out of the final years of the Third

Civic Order where institutional decay has set in to a point beyond recovery of trust and confidence.

Consider the downstream trends of state house and state senate majorities and how much they have proven to be a precursor for the electoral futures within states at the congressional and statewide levels, with states only breaking their trends as a bulwark against one-party rule like in Louisiana, Kentucky, and Kansas. A state like North Dakota for instance, is the Republican equivalent in one-party dominance of a state like New York, yet North Dakota continues to trend away from Democrats while New York has not shown in the past decade the equivalent trend the other way.

If anything, most blue states have shown a trend back toward a more competitive posture in the last decade, and the question for the next decade for the Republican Party is where these trends can continue and where should efforts be most focused. In other words, while it may seem like a long shot for either to occur at the moment, it is far more likely that a state like New York, Rhode Island, or Connecticut votes statewide for a Republican in the next decade than a state like North Dakota or Wyoming votes statewide for a Democrat in the next decade. And in states as Republican as Wyoming and Idaho is one of our best examples of the socioeconomic class realignment in America. The most Democratic and only blue counties in each state are also the wealthiest. Between that and the congressional makeup by median income, and online progressive activist and elitist rhetoric of "maker" states versus "taker" states, the Democratic Party trends further and further from any claim to representing America's working and middle classes. The truth is, blue urban progressive bastions have significant conservative and populist elements developing in them as well, even if the trends are more minor than what we've seen elsewhere in the past decade.

For Republicans, the trend that is most striking in the next decade and the one it should organize the vast majority of domestic policy around is the fact that parents with children under eighteen in the household are now self-identifying as Republican at a ratio of two to one. And this is a trend that holds across geographic and demographic boundaries. Like the education gap of college versus noncollege, it's become a crude but helpful stand-in for social class. And nowhere do both of these emerging 2020s issues manifest themselves as much as in K–12 education and issues related to COVID-era policies, masking and mandates, losing essentially two years of child development and learning, and in other issue areas like the teaching of critical race theory and gender ideology, pushing into classrooms as young as elementary school. These are the matters that helped politicize a new cohort of parents who had not been involved in politics before.

The early signals of the potential potency of this coalition cannot be seen by analyzing any presidential campaign or even midterm congressionals but by looking at state elections for governor and legislature and local school board elections where across the country from Loudoun County, Virginia, to San Francisco, California, moderate or "anti-woke" candidates for school board were ushered into office. Like on many economic issues, the education gap may be larger and switched at the national level voting patterns, but there is a new education gap closing and emerging around which party is trusted more on education. What used to be a Democratic issue by double digits is now either even or a mere margin of error lead. The election of Glenn Youngkin to governor of Virginia against the epitome of the globalization-friendly, Clinton political world in former Virginia Governor Terry McAuliffe, only crystalized what had been brewing downstream even further. If Republican Youngkin can win in one of Barack Obama's two realigned states (and yes, there were only two), then Republicans can win and compete in a lot more states than Democrats can.

Adding parental moderates, who had previously been disengaged, or politicized parents generally is a recipe for success in building a solid and lasting majority party by popular vote as well as electoral vote through the 2020s for the Republican Party. This impulse is again a populist one: going to the doorstep of what people actually care about and meeting them where they're at rather than dictating policy from on high and from ivory towers. What was started on the universities and claimed by the naive that it would stay there and be outgrown is now seeping into all of society. Within education policy lies the heart of America's civic future and shared destiny. A Republican Party that backs activists and citizens who both push back within current institutions and build out alternative and parallel institutions is a party putting down payments on a future where the humble constitutional republic can be preserved and the progressive administrative state quelled and set aside for good. At the college level this could take the form of a de facto "conservative" or "patriotic" Ivy League modeled after Hillsdale College in Michigan, which dates its founding back to before the Civil War and fought to preserve the Union in its earliest decades. Hillsdale notably does not take any government funding. At least three more Hillsdales will be needed that are also free of government funding and that achieve the quality or close to it. At the policy level, in Congress and in the states, Republicans would be wise to move toward taxing university endowments and going after tax-exempt status with the same gusto that progressives have at religious institutions and churches. There is also a socioeconomic component to the grift that has become America's most prestigious universities in the form of expansion that has pushed out middle- and working-class housing. In the case of both Harvard and MIT, a payment in lieu of taxes (PILOT) program has started as a compromise between calls for taxation. Considering the vast amounts of government spending that goes to higher education and has driven a generation or two to the tune of 1.5 and counting trillion-dollar higher education debt, this is a runaway bottomless pit of money that needs to be checked from many different angles at this point.

This continued backlash that started at the higher education levels is now moving downward all the way to the elementary school level, which will continue to accelerate school and parental choice efforts. The more public bureaucrats and leadership, who at a rate of 100 percent fill the campaign coffers of the Democratic Party, resist what is organically brewing from the populace and from parents, chastising them as "extremists" in public forums, the worse the downfall will be for yet another American institution that the public has lost trust and confidence in. Stemming also from Hillsdale College is the Blarney Charter School Initiative that connects us to the capacity issue and supply side of school and parental choice. Charter schools, Catholic schools, Christian classical education (CCE), and homeschooling options and innovations such as pod parenting, a twenty-first-century schoolmarm tutoring not unlike what was done in rural America a century ago, all form the alternative and choice core of what a future beyond public education monopoly could look like. Additionally, policy options between tax credits and vouchers, with a preference for the tax credit option, could be passed at the state levels, perhaps eventually expanded later on at the federal level. Just as the states proved to be "laboratories of democracy" nearly one hundred years ago for the New Deal, so, too, could they be "laboratories for the republic" this century. Traditional alternatives to public schools have taken the image of the wealthy private and prep schools, but many of those schools are more all-in on wokeness and cultural progressivism because they serve as a pipeline to the Ivy League, which are also all-in on it. To the extent that the country seems to be bifurcating across institutions, geography, and ideology, it's the public monopoly and private-prep against the emerging alternatives of the home and the three Cs of charters, classical, and Catholic schools. This alternative is in addition to a pushback from within. The school choice movement should consider an educational equivalent of the Federalist Society to ensure a consistent pipeline of both quality educators and a pipeline and option for frustrated and trapped schoolteachers across the country, especially in the most progressive parts of America.

The critical danger for Republicans in the next decade will be if anything not learning the lessons of 2021 on this issue, leaving them behind to issue-specific think tanks, and sticking with issues more comfortable or historically advantageous to the party and movement conservatism. But if '21, Youngkin, Loudoun County, and running 10 to 14 points ahead are not desired, if the opportunities to chip away at historical Democratic issues like education, health care, and housing are not seized, then the party will merely prolong the state of the country existing between the 40-yard lines or in an intractable political western front–type struggle right at the 50-yard line. Regardless of the particular details of education policy, or if Republicans in the next decade are able to seize an emerging advantage, the fact remains that the emerging Democratic majority is a lost majority as Sean Trende predicted even prior to the 2012 presidential election. The Trende theory of America's political future (up for grabs) has held and the Judis-Teixeira theory has been repudiated even by themselves. A third theory, *The Great Alignment* by Alan Abramowitz,[lxxvi] favored by nearly every PhD and master's thesis in political and social science from 2009 to present, sees our political era as unique in its polarization, specifically in its negative partisanship, that it arose out of the breakup of the New Deal coalition and is largely favored in the academy because the academy is obsessed with racial reductionism, which in turn only promotes more negative partisanship and polarization. The problem with Abramowitz's theory is the problem with much of the media and journalism since Trump's election—it reduces the country down to the obsessions of a thin slice of the electorate: namely predominantly white urban and university progressives and liberals, seen most clearly in the *Hidden Tribes* report from More in Common.

But now with Republicans diversifying and ascending, they'll have to find better ways to lash out and explain away why the country does not want to go all-in on what they're selling. Going into 2008 the country rallied around hope, unity, and trust: three predominant one-word slogans of the Obama campaign. In addition to change, these three words were seemingly the anecdote to a country going in the wrong direction after 9/11. Eight years later, there was significantly less of all three. The millennial generation was always going to end up voting for both parties throughout its lifetime; to think otherwise runs counter to all American political history. And it will largely be those same three words held up by more genuinely populist-leaning and Republican presidential and other candidates that benefit.

On hope, Republicans need look only to author and visiting lecturer to Hillsdale College Wilfred McClay's book *Land of Hope: An Invitation to the Great American Story.*[lxxvii] This text of American history isn't chest-thumping, "U-S-A" chanting jingoism but a thoughtful patriotism reminiscent and asked for by Ronald Reagan's farewell address. And what it is strikes even truer—a synthesizing and necessary course correction to the Howard Zinns of the academy (*A People's History of the United States*), who too quickly and ahistorically frame America as a hopelessly and irredeemably evil country and project in self-governance.

On unity, *most* Americans *like* America in both land and place, and have no problem with its people, fellow citizens, and neighbors. Yet we find ourselves in very divided times. This disunity of 2020 and onward is reminiscent not of the times that led us to a bloody civil war, nor are they even an uncivil war, but rather we are in the times of the sunshine patriot and the Gettysburg Address. The contrast between tearing apart and rioting in the country on one side and Trump's speech at Mount Rushmore, which highlighted the good and great things about this land of hope and heroes, and how Biden has handled similarly difficult times in his presidency, with the dystopian imagery out of *V for Vendetta* and treating his political opponents as threats to democracy, criminals, and terrorists are all most partisans need to know. The country will either rally behind the spirit of 1776 and the country of self-governance put down in our founding charters of freedom, or we'll move on to a successor ideology inspired by neither. Biden was elected on a promise to "return to normalcy," and observers said the "adults were back in charge," and instead, the country in 2022 and 2023 has been brought to the brink socially and culturally, squeezed economically, and closer to the brink of nuclear war than at any time since the Cuban Missile Crisis.

And finally, on trust, the fact that only three institutions in American life register a trust and confidence rating above 50 percent, and none of them have anything to do with the federal government except the military and veterans says a lot too. This is not going to be recovered under the current civic order. But what can happen is in this decade citizen activists and preservers of the American Republic can take up the initiative themselves, just as the founding generation did, and begin building the alternative and parallel institutions that eventually form the core building blocks and influence for the next civic order. This hugging closely what we hold most dear is the best shot for the country, whether it is delivered by the Republican Party as an institution or the party is like it had been in the past many decades, forced into it against the establishment's will, only to become more electable and viable because of it.

That is the story; now here is the evidence. Urban America peaked in their Democratic vote preference in 2012, even though improving nationally, and Republicans bottomed out with a paltry 21 percent performance in major cities. Since that time there have been significant gains in urban America. In the decade since that has risen 11 points to 32 percent. If that rises another 11 or even cracks 40, you have the makings of a long-lasting and durable coalition reminiscent of FDR's in the 1930s but with the greater strength being from rural America, unlike the FDR/New Deal coalition, whose greatest strength was in the cities. Having the greater strength in rural areas, with complementary support from the cities, and holding your own in the suburbs (allowing them to swing here and there with the cycles) is a recipe for long-term dominance within the rules of our electoral system and the American constitutional republic. Whatever the trends and margins in the cities have been or could be in the next decade, these trends pale in comparison to the ones that have already taken place in America's Heartland, where recent deindustrialization and outsourcing has hit the hardest.

The Heartland trends are partly a story of globalization, in which a Trump-led populist appeal around trade, immigration, forever wars, and against the global and coastal elites generally can work well, but the trends actually started even earlier in 2010 and 2012. While Mitt Romney's candidacy fell far short, he cut into margins in all the brightest-red-trending counties above. In a sense, what was a downstream popular movement simply needed someone to take up their cause and move away on key issues from the party of libertarian-influenced economics and muscular preemptive war and toward what the country was actually asking for—first in Barack Obama's candidacy and presidency, and then later in Donald Trump's. The fact that Obama accelerated the Democratic Party toward the postindustrial global economy in his policies while Trump renegotiated NAFTA (USMCA), championed border security and remain in Mexico, and for the first time since Jimmy Carter got the country in no new military conflicts, with 131 casualties compared to the thousands of the two previous administrations, is the difference between Obama's eroding credibility in the Heartland from 2008 to 2012 and Trump's gaining or holding his own in the Heartland (despite numerous battles with institutions and media), only to lose some ground in the suburbs. Whether Romney in '12 or Trump in '16 and '20, or whoever else, the long-term trend is that of a Republican Party continuing to do well in the Heartland of middle America.

Depending on which markers you read, which states you include, the Midwest, where the Republican Party was born, is now the most Republican part of the country again, overtaking the South. These trends are not dependent on Donald Trump either, but rather the issues emphasized and championed. While other candidates would be starting from a clean slate and would seemingly appear to do better, it is of vital importance that the party continue to champion trade deals that work for America's core national interests, stand the line on immigration, and advocate for a peace through strength foreign policy of constructive realism and restraint. While Trump underperformed previous Republican candidates in the South and to a lesser extent the western states, he exceeded the last few candidates in not just the Midwest but also the Northeast. While the favorable trends are less significant than the Midwest, and less noticed because they rarely have resulted in flipping states, they matter for the next decade because if they can continue, then the Republicans have the makings of a far more durable majority. And there is plenty of evidence that some candidates can do well on their own terms, or the more common scenario, a Republican statewide candidate can do well simply because a Democratic one-party state has often proved disastrous for state outcomes. Part of this is the shake-ups and turmoil in the global economy, but the nature of globalization itself has always been highly overrated for much of the Northeast. Prior to midwestern and Great Lakes deindustrialization, the major cities in and round the Beltway deindustrialized first just after the war. In addition to urban rioting in the 1960s and rising crime, this added up to a region that has continually lost people in a relative sense and electoral votes to other regions of the country. In 2016 the Maine Second Congressional flipped, which stayed in 2020, while the state itself and New Hampshire were both fairly close in '16. Upstate New York trended back to its former Republican voting, and in 2021 and 2022 Long Island joined in that trend. Then there is the city itself.

In just eight years New York City has trended nearly 10 percent Republican, more or less in line with the national trend in urban America. With nearly every large city governed by Democrats, and with rising crime, inflation, homelessness, and hosting some of the largest economic inequalities in the country under the nose of a party that goes on endlessly about equality, Republicans could continue to make inroads in New York City and elsewhere by promising commonsense administration, public safety, a choice in education, and providing a counterweight to the totalitarian and scolding tendencies of twenty-first century urban progressives. Only in Manhattan, easily the richest borough, has any part of the city trended Democratic since the 2012 peak. This does not mean New York City itself is about to vote for Republicans again. Rather, the point is instead to say that Republicans are gaining more ground where they do not govern than where they do. And the places where they are losing ground add to the optical and rhetorical story that could be told in the next decade as the country fully transitions—not the transitions of gender ideology, but the transition from the Democratic Party to the Republican Party as America's natural governing party.

Of course, along with both the trends in millennial realignment and major cities becoming about 10–12 points more Republican in the past decade also means a diversifying Republican Party across the board. If these trends keep going, and 2021 and 2022 certainly have provided instances in both polling and, more important, actual confirming election results, what we would also see is continued Hispanic and Asian realignment. To some extent nearly every group is becoming more Republican except college-educated white women, who have continued becoming more Democratic in that time. Driving these realignments are some similar issues, with some distinctions. Hispanic Americans are realigning in part because conservative Hispanics who previously voted for a big-tent Democratic Party are now voting more along ideological lines for the party that is closest to their values—the Republican Party. Similarly, the working-class realignment into the Republican Party is not limited to the white working class either, and 2020 and since have shown this. Meanwhile, while Hispanic realignment is greater in south Florida and southwest Texas than parts of New York City, it's still happening everywhere.

In 2020 Donald Trump's share of the vote doubled to 15 percent in areas of Uptown Manhattan and the Bronx where residents of Dominican descent make up the majority. There was also a uniform shift in Flushing and Corona, Queens, where high populations of Hispanic and Asian voters live. In North Philadelphia, predominantly black and Hispanic, there was a swing toward Trump even in a loss; in Chicago in the minority-majority neighborhoods of Gage Park, Humboldt Park, Little Village, and Pilsen, there were swings toward more Republican voting. Before too long, it's conceivable that the coastal elites are literally the coastal elites with only one exception, the conservative Gulf Coast. It's also conceivable that like previous times in American history, the more heavily urbanized Northeast is again forced into a rearguard action, making its recent trends but an opening salvo to a broader realignment away from one party of power and into the other just as the region had done in the 1930s and 1940s. In both 1932 and 1936, the Northeast remained the most Republican part of the country despite FDR winning in landslides and hailing from New York himself.

The more one dives into the politics and coalitional changes of the two major parties and cultural changes in American society the past ten or so years, the more you can see a window into the future. Unlike popular narrative and conventional wisdom, someone always tends to foresee the unforeseeable, and they're usually an outsider. As President Trump said in one speech: "Don't be afraid of being an outsider, being an outsider is fine, embrace the label, embrace it, because it's the outsiders who change the world, and make a real and lasting difference." Just as FDR championed the "forgotten man," so, too, is that coming to the foray again in our time—whether it gets the convoluted rules and mores of political correctness is no matter. The three phases and waves out of the Third Civic Order and into a new one are nearly complete. The first revolved around the Cold War itself, at a time when American society had stronger and more intact families and communities. While that first wave was shaken culturally over the years, it was not without its triumphs and moments of progress. In one of the most tumultuous years in American history—1968—the country seemed to be coming apart at the seams, yet by the end of that year was an image of the moon from *Apollo 8*, a reading from the book of Genesis, and a window into what American ingenuity and an exceptional nation and people can produce. This is a sentiment not unique to the Republican Party. It was not long ago echoed by the Democratic Party, too, from Bill Clinton's, "There is nothing wrong with America that cannot be solved by what is right with America," to Barack Obama's, "In no other nation in the world is my story even possible." As much as Ronald Reagan's revolution took media bubbles by surprise, it was not too far off from Nixon's "emerging Republican majority" or "I Like Ike," a coalition united by the presence of the Soviet Union and demands of the Cold War. From Ike to Nixon to Reagan the outlook was strong, positive, optimistic, civic-oriented, and forward-looking while inspired by the received wisdom of the past. These were the classic Republicans of the Third Civic Order and their outlook as a counterweight to the dominant party in the system on taxes, regulation, and the size and scope of government, and on the need for a strong defense fit the times.

With the Gingrich revolution in between and an America signaling time and again from 1966 to 1994 that it did not like Democrats holding one-party power, the stage was set for the transition into the second wave. Unlike so many establishment Republicans, Gingrich seemed to understand the Trump phenomenon like few in his cohort did. The great populist revolt if you will, chronicled brilliantly by Salena Zito and Brad Todd, that told a story of a coalition hidden in plain sight, red-blooded and blue-collared, torn by deindustrialization, some former Perot voters, a Reform party that Trump himself got his first ever votes for president under, and of a coalition of rotary reliables, silent suburban moms, and a culture craving respect, feeling left behind by globalization, confused by the endless ideology of the faculty lounge—they took a chance in 2016 on a Trump candidacy they perceived as far more moderate and pragmatic than the media and American elites ever saw. For many, Make America Great Again simply meant making their home towns great again. Articulated best perhaps by Dr. Victor Davis Hanson, national populism was the reaction and necessary bulwark against an encroaching and incremental global elitism that no one ever really voted for or asked for. While Trump's presidency was (for now) to only last one term, the central articulated goal of it is carrying on without direction, an end to the era and philosophy driving globalization. And two years later, globalization sure does look finished.

Instead, what people want is not some grand philosophy but a simple and pragmatic vision of common sense that resembles the country they love and grew up in. The new emerging issues and coalitional changes being added to Republican classic movement conservatism and the national populist revolt are not a retweet but a coalition in transit. In the next decade the continued millennial realignment will produce, albeit slowly and gradually, like the design of a stable and strong town, a deepening and durable populist majority. The new issues will be driven by technology and its role in our lives, the need to produce an economy that is organized around families, around the real needs of American households, and by the everyday experiences whether it's rising crime and public safety or public school indoctrination. The task for Republican leaders in the next decade is to listen to their voters more and to the media and cultural elites less. And the driving force of whether or not they are successful, or whether any party so organized can be is simply: Is it easier to raise a family in this country?

Building alternative and parallel institutions out of the Third Civic Order and in transit to the fourth will not happen overnight. The final three chapters of this emerging populist majority will not promise some great realigning victory in 2022, 2024, or even 2028. Nowhere previously does this book even hold 1932, 1968, or 1980 in such critical election theory esteem. Instead, this emerging and durable trend will be shown across the geography that was the chief inquiry of Phillips, across demography that was the inquiry of Judis-Teixeira, and across ideology that has been the inquiry so often here and elsewhere in so many other places. Intellectually, it'll be more American Compass (Oren Cass, former policy advisor to Mitt Romney and Marco Rubio) and *The American Conservative* (founded by Patrick Buchanan, who it turns out, has been right about mostly everything, a Cassandra of his generation) and less McKinsey, BlackRock, and the chamber. It is also a pragmatic deconstruction of the administrative state, not just because it is a progressive one in design and effect, but mostly because trust and confidence cannot be salvaged or brought back to these institutions. And above all, what's needed is to recover an economy that works for America and Americans first, centered around the real needs of families and households, protecting the national economy and industries, and building the framework for a renewed, reformed, and more confident country again.

CHAPTER 9

THE GEOGRAPHY OF THE EMERGING POPULIST MAJORITY

*T*he *Emerging Republican Majority* put a particular emphasis and organization around geography first, demography second in its organization of American partisan trends and voting history. *The Emerging Democratic Majority* took a demography first, geography second approach. Both mixed ideology throughout. Broadly speaking, both writings organized the United States into the four regions the media did in its coverage of presidential elections in the early television days. On geography, notably, each theory prioritized and organized in the order in which they saw their majority emerging or at least its story evolving. Phillips took a northeast to southern to midwestern to Pacific states approach not just politically but also because it represented the historical founding of the country. The Northeast being a stand-in for the early American colonies and eventually the Union; the South being a stand-in for the former Confederacy, and the western push following the Mason-Dixon line of a Republican Union North (the Party of Lincoln) and the Democratic South (the party of Jefferson and Jackson). These patterns were uprooted only slightly over the course of the century after the Civil War, as Phillips detailed the most exhaustive history of America's ethnic voting patterns that exists to this day.

Whatever is analyzed here will pale in comparison just as *The Emerging Democratic Majority* did. Notably though, both writings were correct for at least one election. Phillips broadly nailed the 1972 through 1988 elections with his book, while Judis and Teixeira were one cycle early in announcing the 2008 professional class and "ideolopolis"-led coalition that would propel Barack Obama to the largest majority for a Democratic winner since LBJ in '64. The major caveats to both though are that the Phillips coalition outside of southern voting patterns going from solidly Democratic to up for grabs later on (in that it was Democratic down-ballot but dependent on a southern candidate up-ballot, and a Republican could be competitive in the South whereas for a century prior they almost never could win more than a state or two and in most states were nonexistent to the point of de facto banned from the ballot) more or less dovetails with the prior Eisenhower coalition. This writing calls it the War Generation Alignment, driven by the experiences of the Second World War and the geopolitical demands of the Cold War with the Soviet Union. In the case of Judis-Teixeira, their prophesied coalition eroded immediately after 2008, and today they write it off as finished, even though the media and culture around them move on like it's gospel. We have no intention of creating such a hornet's nest of broken assumptions.

Like all coalitions, temporary and constantly in motion to varying degrees, the geography of the emerging populist majority is dependent on events and how each party reacts to those events, but will try to control for that by relying heavily on a now even wider sample of American electoral history and past instances while picking up on recent and accelerating trends. What will also change these patterns is people moving from place to place and the impact that has not just on regions but also themselves. The America of post-2002 is certainly more transient than the America of 1969. Therefore locking trends into a straight-line analysis could be even more difficult. But transient America need not be a predictable one either. Not every new arrival to Austin is a progressive Californian that's bringing their politics with them. Not every New Yorker that moves to Florida is adding to the Republican column on day one. In fact, there's some data that suggests that Senator Cruz was able to withstand the challenge from

Beto O'Rourke in the 2018 midterms because of the new arrivals to Texas and had the election been conducted with native Texans, he would have lost. Similarly, there are also trends that suggest those who move to urban areas or big cities from small towns often end up moving back to small towns, especially as they grow their families and raise children.

In the case of Judis-Teixeira, the geographical story of the new majority and demographic inevitability was to be set by the trend-setting California. The Pacific states were the first region of the country analyzed, followed in partisan allegiance by the Northeast, then the Midwest, and the South. Their order of preference got this entirely right. One subtle variation is while the *Republican Majority* had a broad and expansive version of the Midwest, *Democratic Majority* covered it more like a textbook would.

The Geographic Forecasts of *The Emerging Republican Majority* (Phillips, 1969)

Projected Bastions	Contingent Bastions	Battlegrounds	Democratic
Texas	South Carolina	New Jersey	New York
Florida	Georgia	Delaware	Michigan
North Carolina	Alabama	Pennsylvania	Massachusetts
Tennessee	Mississippi	Maryland	Rhode Island
Virginia	Louisiana	Ohio	Connecticut
Oklahoma	Arkansas	West Virginia	Vermont
Kansas		Kentucky	New Hampshire
Nebraska		Indiana	Maine
North Dakota		Illinois	
South Dakota		Missouri	
Montana		Iowa	
Wyoming		Wisconsin	
Idaho		Minnesota	
Utah		California	
Nevada		Oregon	
Colorado		Washington	
New Mexico		Hawaii	
Arizona		Alaska	

Notice the northeastern rearguard action, fully adjusted after being the only holdout states in 1932 and '36 from FDR's landslides. Notice also the bastions of Republicanism including all the states that voted twice for FDR but not a third time, states like North and South Dakota and onward. Nixon, decades before Trump did it, transferred his voting residence from New York to Florida after the 1968 election. The man from small-town California back when it was still "out west" by the end of his life had lived in three of America's four most electorally rich states. Nixon's cabinet, Phillips noted, was also very light on figures from the northeastern establishment while the Democrats replaced Louisiana Senator Russell Long with Edward Kennedy of Massachusetts as Senate whip, a symbolic nod to the new political era. Notably, FDR had actually set out to purge the party of many of these people, just as the party would do post-McGovern in ushering out its working-class coalition for a professional class–led one. Sometimes, voters select the party, but other times parties seek out and try to select their voters. The problem lies in the media and cultural righteousness and scolding lashed out at those no longer following the company line. This is the civic order in action, with media as the court and academia as clerisy. Phillips was remarkably accurate in laying out the next generation or so of American politics. The contingent bastions would prove their contingency by voting for Jimmy Carter in 1976, and Jimmy Carter, while politically flawed in many ways, still knew more than the national Democratic Party brand and establishment, anticipating the increasingly conservative mood of the electorate, and he, not Edward Kennedy, was probably the best bet to head it off.

Largely speaking, this is the political geography that would hold until the 1992 election featured three candidates pulling more than 15 percent of the vote for the first time in eight decades. The only real miss was assuming the Northeast was done voting for Republican candidates, no doubt perhaps a doomer-ism of the Bronx-born Phillips who had grown up in a postwar deindustrializing city, where rising crime and social decay were brilliantly showcased over the course of the 1960s by the twenty-first-century period piece drama *Mad Men*. The Northeast did vote Republican again beyond the battlegrounds three more times to give Nixon and Reagan as big of a landslide as, if not more than, Eisenhower's.

The forecasts and assumptions of *The Emerging Democratic Majority* did not fare nearly so well, but its legacy and stubborn insistence lives on through a media and culture who have likely not read the book itself.

The Geographic Forecasts of *The Emerging Democratic Majority* (Judis-Teixeira, 2003)

(W) = West
(E) = East
(MW) = Midwest
(S) = South

Solid Democratic	Leaning Democratic	Leaning Republican	Solid Republican
California (W)	Nevada (W)	Arizona (W)	Alaska (W)
Hawaii (W)	New Hampshire (E)	Colorado (W)	Idaho (W)
New Mexico (W)	West Virginia (E)	Kentucky (MW)	Montana (W)
Oregon (W)	Missouri (MW)	Virginia (S)[lxxviii]	Utah (W)
Washington (W)	Ohio (MW)	North Carolina (S)	Wyoming (W)
Connecticut (E)		Georgia (S)	North Dakota (MW)
Delaware (E)		Tennessee (S)	South Dakota (MW)
DC (E)		Texas (S)	Indiana (MW)
Maine (E)		Louisiana (S)	Nebraska (MW)
Maryland (E)		Arkansas (S)	Kansas (MW)
Massachusetts (E)			Alabama (S)
New Jersey (E)			Mississippi (S)
New York (E)			South Carolina (S)
Pennsylvania (E)			Oklahoma (S)
Rhode Island (E)			
Vermont (E)			
Illinois (MW)			
Iowa (MW)			
Michigan (MW)			
Minnesota (MW)			
Wisconsin (MW)			
Florida (S)			

Just as Phillips opted for a united and expansive Heartland in support of the political unity and durability of the coming political era, so, too, did Judis and Teixeira opt for an expansive West based around the demographics of California to support their emerging political era. Compared to the Phillips electoral future, which if anything slightly underestimated Republicans at the presidential level, the Judis-Teixeira electoral future by their own admission has been wildly off, but to the latter's great frustration and to the former's as well in some respects. In fact, the focus of Judis's writing since has been on the subject of the revival of nationalism and how much a certain degree of nationalism is needed for a society, otherwise it'll manifest itself in more unhealthy ways, and Teixeira has been writing on his Substack *The Liberal Patriot*[lxxix] alternating between the subjects of Hispanic realignment away from the Democrats and the need for the party to be more supportive of the working and middle classes, and more patriotic again.

Their theory always depended on the Democrats maintaining a big-tent approach. While that may have always been a bit naive as coalitions of everybody in American politics rarely last long because of the inherent nature of coalitional politics, both authors should get credit for honesty and integrity on the manner. The problem lies in the summary and assumptions made in the media and culture largely from people who did not read or understand the book. While there may be no doubt a share of nationalism, as with any ideology, manifesting in unhealthy ways, all across Europe and in America you can see it simply manifesting more so in reaction to the forces of globalization that were never up for a vote or debate. In *The Nationalist Revival* one can see the European psychodrama play out in the vital country of Hungary and the media reaction to Prime Minister Viktor Orbán, who notably governs from the birthplace nation of billionaire hedge fund global left donor George Soros.[lxxx] Whether one calls it Americanism or patriotism or nationalism, the commonality of the protection of the constitutional republic against the forces of globalization and the fear that dates back to Washington's time of avoidance of foreign entanglements cannot be understated as a driver in American life today and the ongoing populist realignments. If the surprising election of Trump may have finally shocked America into grappling with the issues of immigration and trade, Europe, just like with terrorism, had been a few steps or a few years ahead in grappling with these issues.[lxxxi]

Of course, two decades onward from the Judis-Teixeira collaboration reveals an American geographical map now way off. In the early century, they said West Virginia, Missouri, and Ohio would be leaning Democratic; and Florida, Iowa, Wisconsin, Michigan, Minnesota, Pennsylvania, and Maine would be solidly Democratic.

Going the other way, Virginia and Colorado would be better characterized as leaning Democratic than leaning Republican at this point. Our geographical analysis will opt for a mix of both classifications, going through the expansive version of the Midwest, the South, the Northeast, and then the Pacific states in the order from which the emerging populist majority is derived, while opting for closer to the Phillips characterization of bastion states in the coalition, contingent ones, and so forth.

1. The Once and Future United Heartland

In our current political culture, and in the important socioeconomic interests and pocket book realities, I'd like to argue for an even more expansive Heartland, but for purposes of state lines and actual voting and electoral decisions we'll keep it to twenty-three states. However, one could easily add places like Upstate New York, a historical Republican bastion that flirted with Democratic voting under Clinton and Obama, peaking in 2012 before trending back to the Republicans. Upstate New York, along with counties like Hillsdale, Michigan, and Ottertail, Minnesota, have consistently voted Republican dating back to the beginning of the party just before the Civil War. There is also a significant difference that has held in Heartland cities versus coastal cities in their voting patterns with only three notable exceptions: Chicago, Illinois; Saint Louis, Missouri; and recently the Minneapolis-St. Paul, Minnesota, area, whose Democratic-voting trends increased the past two decades and are the only thing that has kept Minnesota from becoming a Republican state as the once strong and balanced state Democratic-Farmer-Labor coalition becomes more like the national party than a local one that included majority voters from the Iron Range, farming communities, and middle-sized towns. The region outside the Twin Cities known as Greater Minnesota has significantly trended Republican in the past two decades. The Iron Range in the north around Lake Superior is perhaps the most notable example of this. The Iron Range was one of the most Democratic voting regions of the country in the middle-twentieth century. By 2016 and 2020 the region went Republican by well into the double digits, a movement of margins only topped by heavily Hispanic areas along the southwest Texas border and Miami-Dade County.

Upstate New York to Greater Minnesota represent political cultures with more in common at this point than either place with its metro region. Upstate New York, even with sizable cities like Buffalo, Rochester, and Syracuse voted Republican by just under or around double-digit levels in the last few statewide elections, and Greater Minnesota posted similar margins. In both places, there is room for significant growth around the issue of turning away from globalization and opting for a reindustrialization and national industrial policy message, a message favored by populist Republicans (and rhetorically populist ancestral Democrats to the extent they still exist) but scorned by libertarian economic leaning Republicans of yesterday. This expanse, called Yankeedom by Phillips and other writers, wraps around the Great Lakes and gives us the core and beginning of a Heartland outside of the Beltway and Great Lakes coastal cities that is historically Republican, increasingly of a populist bent, and who are united by the tragedy of deindustrialization and its downstream societal effects on families and communities. As far as those states seem away from flipping today, both would be feasible under the earlier mentioned scenario of urban America trending another 11 percent over the next decade just as it has in the previous, and the conditions both on the ground (rising crime, homelessness, a cost of living crisis) and transactionally (pushing northeastern and urban capital into a rearguard action) could foreseeably manifest themselves.

The Great Lakes eight states represented in the Phillips book as a quasi-region notably are not wholly in geopolitical orbit.[lxxxii] Just as New York and Pennsylvania are more East Coast and Atlantic-oriented, Wisconsin and Minnesota are more aligned with the farm states economically and culturally. Five decades onward, Minnesota is home to Fortune 500 companies and writers, usually exported elsewhere, that punch far above their weight class and population size. While on one hand the Fortune 500 would bring it further under the yoke of the modern Democratic coalition, the actual electoral results show us that a state that used to be the lone holdout in 1984 is now only a Twin Cities countercultural youth pushback and a competent or average state party away from flipping in the next decade.

The Trump campaign's push to do one last rally in 2016 nearly put the state in tandem with Wisconsin, Michigan, and Pennsylvania. Only the cultural progressivism and de facto one-party city-state of Minneapolis-St. Paul and a well-run party organization could keep it blue in the foreseeable future. In the case of Wisconsin, the birthplace of the Republican Party but also a state with much historical progressive leanings, the current alignment is already *lean* Republican in a toss-up election. This does not mean that toss-up states cannot occasionally produce opposite-party governors and senators in the future; in fact one would expect it in certain cycles. But the long-term trends still stand in Minnesota through Pennsylvania. The "Big Ten" states, if you will, were once easily Democratic in the three-choice elections of the 1990s, got close when just two major options were given in the 2000s, widened in the late decade and early 2010s to double-digit wins for the Democrats even in states like Iowa, and in the ten years since have trended heavily away from the Democrats and toward the Republicans. The core description of the voters switching these margins is not of new arrivals or some theory of "demographics" but rather the Obama to Trump voters who would most often describe their politics as "middle-class," "working-class," "populist," or "patriotic" and "pro-American."

Outside the Great Lakes and Yankeedom zone of the Heartland are the farm states and regions that also cut into parts of both Greater Minnesota and Upstate New York, both large geographic regions. Just as all the states that went for Obama twice and then to Trump either once or twice are Yankeedom states, they are also midland farm states to some extent, some more than others or entirely part of the "Farm Belt" as opposed to the derogatorily and crudely used by the media and culture "Rust Belt" terminology (accurate, but rubbing in the outsourcing and strip mining of communities from coastal and global elite planners). The farm states are where there has been even more erosion and realignment from the Democratic to Republican parties. Notably, the farm state realignment stretches back further into the beginning days of the Third Civic Order than any other at the presidential level. States like North and South Dakota, Kansas, Iowa, and Nebraska all dissented from a third-term for President Franklin D. Roosevelt. Other states like Minnesota, not completely a farm state at all, succeeded in organization and branding, combining what was a de facto third party in the 1920s in the Democrats with the emerging Farmer-Laborites to create the DFL, who has dominated Minnesota state politics under the Third Civic Order just as the Republican Party dominated Minnesota state politics under the second one. Watching a state like Minnesota is critical to understanding how much further and deeper the emergence of the populist-oriented realignment can go. Holding this back is the ineptitude of the state Republican Party in Minnesota versus a state party (DFL) that is one of the best in the country in terms of organization and maximization of vote potential, although there is one very clever thing local Republican activists did recently in the form of a Facebook page called the Republican-Farmer-Labor party. This creation was temporary but invited a cease and desist and copyright infringement claim that only brought more attention to the gimmick. And it works because it is true. Most farmers no longer vote for the Democratic Party, and working-class labor generally is realigning, with union membership itself only slightly lagging behind overall. However, even this has its exceptions. In Ohio, union households voted in majorities for Donald Trump, just as they did in some parts of the Heartland for Ronald Reagan.

The major dissenter and the only state moving in significant margins away from an increasingly populist-leaning Republican Party is Colorado. In 2021 and 2022 nearly every other state that keeps track of registration was trending toward the Republican, whereas Colorado is emerging into a Vermont-west. Just as Vermont has often been an eclectic and dissenting state, settled by many New York City transplants, Colorado has become a popular destination for the progressive-leaning people of the Heartland. This progressive version of smaller-town and nature dwelling is an important distinction and exception to media and cultural characterizations of urban liberals versus rural conservatives.

Overall, the core of the once (under Nixon and Reagan) and future united Heartland is the states that began dissenting from progressive administrative state vision during the war: North Dakota, South Dakota, Wyoming, Kansas, Nebraska, Oklahoma, Idaho, and Utah. Those states have voted Republican in every election since with the only exceptions being the 2008 and 2020 split of the Nebraska Second Congressional District.

The states that have emerged since 2002 were won by Clinton either once or twice. Clinton is our marker here because he is the most identified president with the era of globalization, and at an Electoral College level his coalition was the broadest across the real markers of diversity: geography, demography, and ideology. All these states are not just lost to Democrats twenty years later but look lost easily and lost for good. Missouri, Kentucky, Tennessee, West Virginia, and Montana were not won by Gore (Tennessee was his home state), Kerry, Obama (who got very close in Missouri), Hillary Clinton, or Joe Biden. Finally, for the states that voted for Obama two times and then for Trump states, a statewide version of the pivots: Indiana (who voted for Obama in 2008, back to Republican starting in 2012), Ohio, Iowa, Wisconsin, and Michigan. While Democrats in good years can still make Michigan competitive and to a lesser extent, Wisconsin, the states of the Big Ten are permanently lost. Republicans continue to gain registration advantages, have elected Republican governors and senators in Wisconsin, and as you'll see below, the downstream grassroots advantage at the state legislative levels keeps growing. Iowa's electoral future will be closer to North and South Dakota, just as western Minnesota and southern Minnesota will. Wisconsin, a tipping-point state in 2020, still trended Republican in 2020.

In the future, Nevada out west, Minnesota up north, and New Mexico as a possible extension of the Hispanic realignment, especially along border communities, could be added to this once and future united Heartland with only Colorado and Illinois dissenting. Illinois has a truly big city, so any competitiveness there would need to see some significant (as opposed to the trends without much effort that have emerged over crime, cost of living, homelessness, and so on) movement there, which is the same model for New York and to a lesser extent New Jersey. However, it is conceivable that in a runaway election victory even these states could be added to the Republican column, even though they'd relatively be dissenting states in the Democratic column. In the scenario where Phillips did not anticipate the Northeast being favorable enough in his official forecast to deliver forty-nine-state-level landslides, if a landslide is at all possible in America's electoral future, it'll be a Republican one, most likely a populist-oriented Republican one. However, even absent those landslides using 1988 (forty states won by H. W. Bush, over four hundred electoral votes) as our baseline, the trend line toward an emerging populist future through the Republican Party is on a slow and steady march, marching at quicker pace in some parts of the country, and what is moving against it is simply not broad enough to form a workable coalition as we'll continue to see. And a major part of that trend whether it continues or stalls out will be decided in the Heartland, the same deindustrialized areas that became the target of the media's intrigue and scorn after 2016, relegated to the non-story or ignore pile in most other years when they had "voted right." As American demographer and geography analyst Joel Kotkin points out though, the Heartland could once again have a critical influence on our national identity and serve as a powerful outlet for entrepreneurial energies.[lxxxiii]

Balance of Power (Prior to 2022 Midterm Elections)
The Once and Future United Heartland (Twenty-Three States)

Bold = the core
Italicized = populist realignment
Bold + Italicized = emerging populist realignment
Italicized = future realignment
<u>Underlined</u> = dissenter states

States	Presidency	US House	US Senate	Governor	State House	State Senate
WY	Rep (3 EV)	Rep	Rep	Rep	Rep 51–7–1–1	Rep 28–2
ID	Rep (4 EV)	Rep 2–0	Rep	Rep	Rep 58–12	Rep 28–7
OK	Rep (7 EV)	Rep 5–0	Rep	Rep	Rep 82–19	Rep 39–9
UT	Rep (6 EV)	Rep 4–0	Rep	Rep	Rep 58–17	Rep 23–6
KS	Rep (6 EV)	Rep 3–1	Rep	Dem	Rep 86–39	Rep 29–11
ND	Rep (3 EV)	Rep	Rep	Rep	Rep 80–14	Rep 40–7
SD	Rep (3 EV)	Rep	Rep	Rep	Rep 62–8	Rep 32–3
NE[10]	Rep (5 EV)	Rep 3–0	Rep	Rep	Unicameral nonpartisan league	(De facto Rep 32–17)
MO	Rep (10 EV)	Rep 6–2	Rep	Rep	Rep 116–47	Rep 24–10
KY	Rep (8 EV)	Rep 5–1	Rep	Dem	Rep 75–25	Rep 30–8
TN	Rep (11 EV)	Rep 7–2	Rep	Rep	Rep 73–26	Rep 27–6
WV	Rep (4 EV)	Rep	Split	Rep	Rep 76–24	Rep 23–11
MT	Rep (4 EV)	Rep	Split	Rep	Rep 67–33	Rep 31–19
IN	Rep (11 EV)	Rep 7–2	Rep	Rep	Rep 71–29	Rep 39–11
OH	Rep (17 EV)	Rep 12–4	Split	Rep	Rep 64–35	Rep 25–8
IA	Rep (6 EV)	Rep 3–1	Rep	Rep	Rep 59–41	Rep 32–18
WI	Dem (10 EV)	Rep 5–3	Split	Dem	Rep 61–38	Rep 21–12
MI	Dem (15 EV)	Tied 7–7	Dem	Dem	Rep 58–52	Rep 22–16
NV	Dem (6 EV)	Dem 3–1	Dem	Dem	Dem 26–16	Dem 12–9
MN	Dem (10 EV)	Tied 4–4	Dem	Dem	Dem 70–64	Rep 34–31–2
NM	Dem (5 EV)	Dem 2–1	Dem	Dem	Dem 45–25	Dem 26–15–1
<u>CO</u>	Dem (10 EV)	Dem 4–3	Dem	Dem	Dem 41–24	Dem 20–15
<u>IL</u>	Dem (19 EV)	Dem 13–5	Dem	Dem	Dem 73–45	Dem 41–18

---

[10] Nebraska splits its electoral votes by congressional districts. The Nebraska Second Congressional District went Democrat in 2008 and 2020, both Democrat years at the presidential level, but this has not translated down-ballot or into tough years.

2. The New, Old South

Whether one gives the border states a more expansive definition of the South or an expansive definition of the Midwest, splitting hairs over it is less and less important by the year as both the Midwest and South grow closer together and are distinguished against the coastal regions of the country to the West and East Coasts. What was said in the last chapter, that the midwestern Heartland would supplant the South as the most Republican region in the country, looks like a long shot through analyzing party strength and control today. Two reasons for this are one, a continuation of Heartland realignment, and secondarily, the South becomes a little less Republican in a relative sense. As of now, only two significant strains against a Republican-dominated South exist. One, the Black Belt in the American South runs through South Carolina, Georgia, Alabama, and Mississippi to create majority-minority congressional districts, which existed prior, and runs into the Mississippi River–west counties into Louisiana and Arkansas as well. Two, the growth of government and the professional service class around the DC suburbs in combination with more northern majority-minority counties in Virginia and North Carolina has made both of those states more favorable to the Democrats than in decades prior. While Virginia has shown that it will still vote Republican under the right conditions, North Carolina looks to be much harder to put permanently into their column. Both North Carolina and Florida trended Republican in 2020.

Another big trend is a Great Reverse Migration for black Americans back into the southern United States where home ownership is possible at higher rates, the cost of living is lower, and there are more industrial blue-collar jobs. The deindustrialization that hit the northeast and midwest of Yankeedom was particularly harsh on urban black communities. In Harlem, New York, for instance, over 80 percent of the current jobs are white-collar jobs and under 20 percent are blue-collar jobs. This hollowing out of the urban manufacturing base by planners and business interests has migrated from supporting both parties to some extent to becoming firmly planted within the Democratic Party today. A second place for this migration is into the suburbs, which is one of the reasons Joe Biden did better in a relative sense in the suburbs compared to 2016. This reverse migration to the suburbs and to the South will not be strong enough to change voting patterns in this region though. What is more likely to happen is the South will become less Republican in only a relative sense, possibly being supplanted as the most Republican region of the country. Overall, this loss would be a good thing for the Republican Party though, as it would balance out their geographical coalition. A second big development in the last decade and the next is the status of Florida and Texas. In popular parlance, Florida is trending Republican, and Texas is trending Democratic. While Florida looks about to lose its swing state status, hitting the moment when a cliff-moment is reached in large states and a major party goes from losing competitively to losing by a lot, Texas is not moving nearly as much toward the Democrats as people think. If Hispanic realignment continues, the math for a Democratic Texas just does not add up. What is more likely is that Florida becomes the large state that is the most Republican-voting out of the four, supplanting Texas, which has held that status for decades. This comes as a big surprise to the Democrats so invested in the "demographic inevitability" theory. The title of this section, "The New, Old South," refers to the region overall becoming more competitive and contingent on certain factors just as it was from 1968 to 1972 for Richard Nixon and 1976 to 1980 for Jimmy Carter. This contingency showed up again for Bill Clinton in 1992 and 1996, despite the presence of another Southerner running in Ross Perot and a New England transplant to Texas in President H. W. Bush. Much has been made about Georgia narrowly going for Joe Biden in 2020, but this state, like Arizona, is overrated in its flipped status by ten thousand or so votes. Both Georgia and Arizona voted once for Bill Clinton, just as North Carolina voted once for Barack Obama.

The ten states of the new, old South break down in the core Republican states of Mississippi, Alabama, Louisiana, Arkansas, and South Carolina, which are not going to vote Democratic any time soon. Two of these states voted for Bill Clinton, Arkansas where he was a favorite son, and next door Louisiana, but the Democratic Party has run away from any pretense of a coalitional big tent that could produce such a result again. These five core states are joined by five contingent states in which two of them appear to be trending away from the Democrats in Florida and North Carolina, the latter being more contingent than Florida. The final three contingent states may be trending relatively blue in Texas, Virginia, and Georgia compared to twenty years ago, but all three can and still will be won statewide by Republicans. The down-ballot strength is still there, too, even in the hardest-to-win state of Virginia for the Republicans. While Virginia in any even/neutral year will go Democratic, Texas and Georgia are still a ways away from that status. Out of the two, Georgia is far more likely to reach that status, but it is the state of Texas that Democrats most need to compensate for losses elsewhere, and there is simply a long way to go there still. In the 2022 midterms, the gubernatorial election margin was narrower in the blue state of New York than the still very red state of Texas and far narrower in margin than the nearly 20 percent landslide margin for Republicans in Florida. In the case of Texas, Hispanic realignment and the contingency of the suburbs as a swing and independent check against the party holding power will further limit any further trending possibilities in that state.

Notably, out of the twenty houses in these ten states at the state legislature level, only one house, in the Virginia State Senate, narrowly at a margin of 21–18, is held by the Democratic Party. The new old South represents that middle-ground era existing again in between the days when it was the solid Democratic South for a century after the Civil War and the far less reliably Republican South it has been in the past few decades.

While the South is still a fundamental pillar of the modern Republican coalition, which will most often find itself in the minority or oppositional coalition, this fact is nothing new for the South of either the old or the new. While the early American Republic had a politics dominant from Virginia and the South generally, even when it's been a part of the Roosevelt coalition and later Republican coalitions, it has not been the critical factor in those coalitions. The party of Roosevelt could count on a certain number of electoral votes from the South in a bloc as the Democrats largely could count on since the Civil War. From 1880 to 1932, the leading Democratic states were Mississippi, Alabama, Louisiana, Georgia, South Carolina, Arkansas, Texas, North Carolina, Florida, Virginia, Tennessee, Kentucky, Maryland, Nevada, Oklahoma, West Virginia, and New Jersey.[lxxxiv]

And by the time of George W. Bush, a president from Texas, the South was also the most partisan voting region just as it had been for Roosevelt. On one hand, you could call this the political base from a regional standpoint, but you could also call it a region that will not form the electoral and power balance of whether the coalition wins or loses elections. The region has historically most often been in the Heartland Midwest. And indeed, the relatively strong presidential majority coalition (as opposed to congressional) of Eisenhower through Reagan included strong performances throughout the Heartland. As Phillips noted in the middle of this development, together with the Heartland, the South is shaping up to be the pillar of a "national conservative" party.[lxxxv]

If one could crudely point out the central political idea or ideological word most associated with a region, you could put "conservative" onto the South, "populist" onto the Midwest, "progressive" onto the Northeast, and "classical liberal" or "libertarian" onto the West. Largely speaking these values have held, except for in the coastal parts of both the East and West today. In the twenty-first century, the Gulf Coast is the one coast that stands alone in its opposition to the default politics of its day. But the Gulf Coast increasingly has more allies to form a new elite whereas the East and West Coasts are losing allies from the middle Heartland and throughout much of the country outside of cities, and even in most major cities the position peaked around the mid-2010s.

The New Old South (Ten States)

Bold = the core

Italicized = populist realignment

States	Presidency	US House	US Senate	Governor	State House	State Senate
MS	Rep (6 EV)	Rep 3–1	Rep	Rep	Rep 75–44–3	Rep 36–16
AL	Rep (9 EV)	Rep 6–1	Rep	Rep	Rep 77–28	Rep 27–8
LA	Rep (8 EV)	Rep 5–1	Rep	Dem	Rep 68–35–2	Rep 27–12
SC	Rep (9 EV)	Rep 6–1	Rep	Rep	Rep 81–43	Rep 30–16
AR	Rep (6 EV)	Rep 4–0	Rep	Rep	Rep 77–23	Rep 28–7
FL	Rep (30 EV)	Rep 16–11	Rep	Rep	Rep 78–42	Rep 24–16
NC	Rep (16 EV)	Rep 9–5	Rep	Dem	Rep 69–51	Rep 28–22
TX	Rep (40 EV)	Rep 23–13	Rep	Rep	Rep 83–67	Rep 18–13
GA	Dem (16 EV)	Rep 8–6	Dem	Rep	Rep 103–77	Rep 34–22
VA	Dem (13 EV)	Dem 7–4	Dem	Rep	Rep 52–48	Dem 21–18

3. The Northeastern Rearguard Action

The Northeast, whether derogatorily referred to as closer to the Beltway or more closely identified with the beautiful scenery of Greater New England, has since the founding been in a give-and-pull relationship with the South. As the South becomes more Democratic, or slightly less Republican, so, too, will the Northeast become more Republican or less Democratic. This can already be seen in the trends since 2012 when the regional Republican Parties more or less bottomed out across the board. Today though, out of the twenty-two houses of the eleven state legislatures, four of them are held by the Republican Party, both houses of the state legislature in Pennsylvania and both houses of the state legislature in New Hampshire. Unlike much of the southern state legislatures, a good midterm cycle or a presidential cycle with coattails could easily yield even more gains. The party is within striking distance in Maine for both houses, and in New Jersey, although

New Jersey holds their elections in odd years. At the gubernatorial level, New Jersey Republicans seemed almost taken by surprise at how close they came to pulling off a surprise win in a state that Joe Biden easily won by double digits. In 2021 they picked up six seats in the General Assembly and a state senate seat famously won by trucker Ed Durr who spent less than a hundred dollars. This upset victory is incredibly symbolic of the coalitional possibilities of an emerging populist majority run through the Republican Party that can succeed across the country, including in areas thought uncompetitive for Republicans, which may very well be true for the country-club-set image of the party, but those days are long gone, and Republicans would be wise to fully embrace this gift.

In fact, running against Beltway politics, increasingly the core image of the Northeast, is the heart of modern American populism. This Beltway in some respects has expanded with the growth of the federal government and the professional services wrapped around them to create the academy to professional-class consensus most identified with the party of government, the Democratic Party. If Republicans allow four or five more trillion-dollar bills to be spent as they have in the past twelve years, whereas before there were zero in American history, they risk the continued expansion of this professional-class coalition through Virginia and perhaps elsewhere. Indeed, if the Democrats were smart and less arrogant today about their right to rule, they'd sign on to not just a growth in government, but they'd also move entire departments and agencies to other parts of the country to try and replicate what has happened in Virginia. This growth in government is seen at not just the federal level but the state and city levels, too, where growth in the civil service has created the budgetary problems in the city of New York, who has become most dependent on Democrats winning the presidency once a decade to reinforce its fiscal mismanagement. There are instances of this growth being stopped in its tracks, notably by Governor Scott Walker in Wisconsin. However difficult it may be for Republicans to make inroads with public employee unions in major metropolitan areas, this is not true generally of the more heavily unionized Northeast region of the country.

While public unions will prove difficult to impossible, and union leadership will not fill any Republican campaign coffers with few exceptions, union membership is another story. What happened in Michigan with Reagan Democrats and in Ohio with Trump union households can happen everywhere for at least seventeen of America's top thirty unions by membership. These unions are generally relegated to the skilled trades, security, and some transport. But this theory of the case would be more in line with the nature of lasting coalition building, which generally involves taking the path of least resistance and taking advantage of what your opponents are giving you. The Democratic Party has continually gone out of its way to move working-class people out of its coalition and hasn't exactly done much to appeal to middle-class suburbia either.

The suburban trend is if anything driven by the politics of optics and what the Republican Party has given them as an opportunity the other way. Demographer Joel Kotkin was quite optimistic about the future of America's suburbs a decade ago[lxxxvi] but now is alarmed at the trend of policies aimed at hollowing out single-family housing and other measures that increasingly are driving the middle income American and global middle class to the point of extinction.[lxxxvii] This has already happened largely in urban America, especially along the Beltway, creating a sort of *Downton Abbey*-coalition of upstairs and downstairs for the Democratic Party, the sole governing party in these large cities like New York, Boston, and Philadelphia. And increasingly it's not just a Democratic majority governing the increasingly low voter turnout and civic participation cities but a progressive majority. However, the optics of presiding over the most economically unequal parts of the country will continue to provide new path of least resistance opportunities for populist-inclined Republicans who put in the effort.

In large part, the 11 percent trend in urban America since 2012 is with little effort and organization made there. It is a naturally occurring trend upset of major party efforts. If investments are made in better organization, more targeted efforts, and grassroots outreach to communities, then much more could be possible. In some cases spending no more than Ed Durr did on his campaign, for example, could work, as many communities across major cities have already trended 5, 10, 15 percent or more in the last decade. The Republicans have the making of a coalition that is broad, deep, and lasting. And it is a coalition where victories in places like Maine, New Hampshire, New Jersey, New York, Connecticut, and even Rhode Island, which trended Republican in 2016 more than nearly every state in the country, could happen again and happen faster than people think. This middle-out, pro-working, and middle-class coalition with a set of policies to address the real economic and social needs of families and households would put the "Labor" in the newly branded (cease and desist be damned) Republican-Farmer-Labor party—or if need be, the Republican-Veteran-Trucker party. It is through this coalitional framework, something old, something new, something borrowed, and something blue that the Yankees could get their groove back again.

As Phillips pointed out and argued well throughout the New Deal era, the Northeast and the South have maintained a changing position with regard to one another and the Republican Party. With the two never seeming to be going in the same direction[lxxxviii] as the Democrats have improved their position in the South relative to the Reagan and Bush eras, it would follow from this history that it has peaked in the Northeast in the modern era and will begin to come back to the Republicans. The leading political position the Northeast had from the Civil War to the Great Depression era got pushed into a rearguard action by the 1930s and '40s before adjusting over the next few decades. Could this be what is happening again? Not just to the Northeast but to the "left coast" as well? This is certainly the behavior of the current default and governing coalition in America, recommending adding states, senators, and packing the court in a way reminiscent of the Republican coalition of the second half of the 1800s, adding new states out west to maintain its pre-McKinley coalition in the electoral college, which for two decades was fairly tenuous. This same feature is happening to the current Democratic Party of the late Third Civic Order.

The Northeastern Rearguard Action (Eleven States)

Italicized = emerging populist realignment
Underlined = dissenter states

States	Presidency	US House	US Senate	Governor	State House	State Senate
ME[11]	Dem (4 EV	Dem 2–0	Split	Dem	Dem 80–67–4	Dem 22–13
PA	Dem (19 EV)	Tied 9–9	Split	Dem	Rep 112–90	Rep 28–21–1
NH	Dem (4 EV)	Dem 2–0	Dem	Rep	Rep 213–187	Rep 14–10
NJ	Dem (14 EV)	Dem 10–2	Dem	Dem	Dem 46–34	Dem 24–16
NY	Dem (28 EV)	Dem 19–8	Dem	Dem	Dem 106–43–1	Dem 43–20
CT	Dem (7 EV)	Dem 5–0	Dem	Dem	Dem 97–54	Dem 31–9
RI	Dem (4 EV)	Dem 2–0	Dem	Dem	Dem 65–10	Dem 33–5
DE	Dem (3 EV)	Dem	Dem	Dem	Dem 26–15	Dem 14–7
<u>*MA*</u>	Dem (11 EV)	Dem 9–0	Dem	Rep	Dem 129–30–1	Dem 37–3
<u>VT</u>	Dem (3 EV)	Dem	Dem (Ind caucus Dem)	Rep	Dem 93–45–7–5	Dem 21–7–2
<u>MD</u>	Dem (10 EV)	Dem 7–1	Dem	Rep	Dem 99–42	Dem 32–15

4. The Left Coast

The last region in the geography of the emerging populist majority, even more so than the Beltway elites and Northeast, is the West Coast, or the left coast, setter of all the hip trends. "The left coast" will also be pushed into a rearguard action, but that action could very well be relegated to the

---

[11] Maine also splits its electoral votes by congressional districts. The Maine Second Congressional District went Republican in 2016 and in 2020, one a lean-Republican year, the other a lean-Democrat year at the presidential level, and this *has* translated down-ballot.

larger dissenter state of California, whose Republican past will likely never return. While Washington and Oregon have trended Democratic and in the progressive orientation for years, it's the increasing professional, tech industry, and cultural left coalition of Portland and Seattle that will re-create the trends happening all across the country of an outstate voting against the metro urban core. Washington and Oregon for years trended along with Minnesota and Wisconsin, reflecting an original Yankee and northern settling pattern, but have since split and gone in two directions overall; 2004 was the last time either state was within 5 percent. In the short and medium term, these states will not realign or be a part of the emerging populist majority, but there is a good chance of an additional congressional seat or two out of them. At the state legislature level, they also do not show nearly the Democratic-heavy orientation as many of the Northeast states have. An emerging populist majority that delivered a forty-five-state landslide victory would include Oregon and Washington eventually, leaving only California, Hawaii, Massachusetts, Vermont, and Maryland as the dissenting states.

The only true core part of the six Pacific states is Alaska, who is an eclectic part of the core. Alaska has been trending relatively Democratic in many ways, but in reality its politics reflect the peripheral nature of all the states at the distant edges of the United States. The Alaskan Independence Party is a quasi-third party, which only a few states have in the above 5 percent nature, and it has a coalition majority in the state house rather than a Republican one. Regardless of its trends, Alaska has a ways to go before it would flip, although any state with a lower population always has the possibility to trend far more quickly with enough new arrivals or different voter turnouts and electorates emerging. That being said, as eclectic and confusing as Alaska's recent Republican politics have been, the only other Republican-leaning state in the Pacific, Arizona, will look to solidify their Republican standing in the decade to come. Unlike Georgia, Arizona's 2020 win for Biden was far more situational. While Arizona does have two Democratic senators, it has a Republican governor and state legislature.

If broader Hispanic realignment continues along the border, that and its status as a popular destination for retirees will help offset any arrivals from progressive Californians seeking affordability or the growth in any professional-class-heavy business and industry.

The Pacific coast from Eisenhower to Reagan featured a far different political culture that mirrored the development and settlement patterns from the East by and large, with San Francisco being more Catholic, more pro-Labor, anti-prohibition, and more Democratic from the start with Los Angeles being more protestant, anti-Labor, for prohibition, and more Republican.[lxxxix] That relative split from history has more or less been totally wiped out as California offers a grim picture on what a one-party progressive Democratic state would look like.

It is in the West Coast that a Republican future or a populist future looks the roughest and tallest climb, yet even there the same factors in rural counties and small-town areas remain. California farmers have been alienated, as represented by academics and historians like Dr. Victor Davis Hanson. In Oregon, with no hope of reversing the trend of state politics from the West Coast, a dozen or so eastern Oregon rural and small town counties have started a movement to join the state of Idaho. This action would require approval from the state legislatures of Idaho and Oregon, and also from Congress. Actions like this and similar movements from Virginia, Colorado, and Illinois of counties far away from the centers of power and the capital represent the most bold part of the so-called "national divorce." Contrary to media and elite hysterics, the operative part of this divorce refers not to some sort of neo-secessionist impulse but rather a growing realization that Washington, DC, and many state capitals do not have the people's interests in mind and have let power go to their heads at the expense of constitutional rights and freedoms. The idea that this would be anything other than the alternative and parallel institutions and drive mentioned frequently in this book is mere rhetorical browbeating or mischaracterization. What was once a culture war, essentially won by progressives, has either been reignited or entered the spiritual and philosophical realm over reality itself. And at the legal and legitimate authority realm, the burden of proof is on the progressives, whether down-stream activists or upstream institutions, to argue convincingly for their desired system—which is some version of a unitary state from DC with the states and counties as inferior actors in terms of not just resources but rights as well.

But the unitary system preferred by the progressives and seen most often on the western coastal cities and in the Beltway has the burden of proof, not the grassroots movements of America First populists or movement conservatives who rarely differ in their desire to see a federal system of power divided between separate branches of government and between federal, state, and local governments themselves.

One can see versions of both "progressive federalism" and "conservative federalism" at play in the past decade. The difference between the two is that at its most benign level with conservative federalism—whether from COVID restrictions or Second Amendment sanctuary counties across nearly every state—the counties themselves are aligned with the Constitution and Bill of Rights that were written with the intention of declaring what the government of the United States of America and state governments *cannot* do. Whereas the progressive federalism of sanctuary cities has infringed and usurped authority that is the prerogative of the federal government (immigration).

Rather than the neo-secessionism detractors say exists in the Biden era, what is really happening goes back to the founding—a spirit of and a renewal of *federalism*, which is also our best way out of this long national crisis. Not just federalism between the federal government and the states, but also within the states themselves, when that state government is infringing on constitutional rights. After all, it was first and foremost the actions of state governments of the Jim Crow Democratic South that stained the legal legacy of the Tenth Amendment of the US Constitution, turning it into a mere "truism"; and on COVID restrictions and the Second Amendment, the Supreme Court is again siding against states infringing on the constitutional rights of American citizens just as the southern Democrats of that era had done.

Contrary to our moment, what this book has tried to do is take existing and real trends and foretell a new and emerging era in American political history. And in the remaining decades of the twenty-first century, it is far more likely that the dissenter states come from a "People's Republic of California" than from a coalitional backbone that desires a return to tradition and greater societal stability, and is made up of parents, married people, and families to a greater degree. This coalition also has a faith makeup and independent self-reliant streak that make the doldrums of losing an election cycle or two easier to take, whereas the progressives of the left coast, whether successor ideology and activist in inclination or an establishment technocrat, have made politics and the ups and downs of their party and ideology central to their identity. This is exactly the sort of mindset that is far more likely to break away if a project that one is deeply passionate about and committed to fails to materialize.

The Left Coast (Six States)

Bold = dissenter states
Italicized = future realignment potential at the
peak of the emerging populist majority
Underlined = the only core Republican state in the region

States	Presidency	US House	US Senate	Governor	State House	State Senate
CA	Dem (54 EV)	Dem 42–11	Dem	Dem	Dem 59–19–1	Dem 31–9
HI	Dem (4 EV)	Dem 2–0	Dem	Dem	Dem 47–4	Dem 24–1
OR	Dem (8 EV)	Dem 4–1	Dem	Dem	Dem 37–23	Dem 18–12
WA	Dem (12 EV)	Dem 7–3	Dem	Dem	Dem 57–41	Dem 28–21
AZ	Dem (11 EV)	Dem 5–4	Dem	Rep	Rep 31–29	Rep 16–14
AK	Rep (3 EV)	Dem	Rep	Rep	Coalition 21–19	Rep 13–7

Beyond clawing back a semblance of a competitive Republican Party in major cities and urban America, and the coalitional benefits of that opportunity, urban America will still be a Democratic-leaning place even at its peak, just as major cities have been throughout most of American history. For all these trends and brush strokes, it's important to note there will be exceptions. Within the next cycle perhaps, Republicans will be able to elect mayors and win a majority in major cities like Miami, Florida, and Las Vegas, Nevada. The suburbs will be battlegrounds and vary greatly from cycle to cycle, but from within the 40- or more accurately 45-yard lines. Mostly, the suburban identification with the urban core will determine whether they lean Democratic (if identification is present) or Republican (if identification is absent). An example of this can be seen in Westchester County going from a Republican bastion of the country club variety to a 65 percent and plus Democratic bastion where the Clintons reside. One could argue that it's the true seat of globalization or the late Third Civic Order's dukes and earls, just as the Upper West Side represented a de facto seat of silk-stocking Republicans in the Second Civic Order. What will really give the Republicans their continued core—both of its populist orientation and its big city equivalent but also its long-term structural power and emerging, lasting majority—is the fact that it is continuing to grow in dominance in small towns and rural America. This fact is particularly seen in the county-by-county level presidential results.

County-Level Presidential Results Since 1932

Election	Democratic Counties Won	Republican Counties Won	Electoral College Vote Aligned
1932	2,723	373	Yes
1936	2,636	459	Yes
1940[12]	1,950	1,144	Yes
1944	1,754	1,340	Yes
1948[13]	1,640	1,193	Yes
1952	995	2,104	Yes
1956[14]	896	2,143	Yes
1960[15]	1,186	1,891	No
1964	2,275	826	Yes
1968	684[16]	1,849	Yes
1972	131	2,980[17]	Yes
1976[18]	1,711	1,403	Yes
1980	900	2,213	Yes
1984	333	2,781	Yes
1988	820	2,294	Yes
1992[19]	1,519	1,582	No
1996	1,526	1,587	No
2000	674[20]	2,439	Yes
2004	583	2,530	Yes
2008	875	2,238	No
2012	693	2,420	No
2016	490	2,622	Yes
2020	538	2,574	No

[12] Third Civic Order is locked in with a precedent-breaking third term and onset of America's entry into the Second World War.

[13] Third-party southern Democrat candidate Strom Thurmond won 265 counties.

[14] Unpledged wins in thirty-two counties.

[15] The 1960 election, classified earlier as a "crossroads" American election, was also the first election where the Democratic Party was able to win the presidency without needing to win a majority of counties.

[16] Third-party American Independent Party candidate George Wallance (Democratic governor of Alabama) wins in 578 counties.

[17] Nixon's 1972 county-level total is a high-water mark for either major party in American electoral history.

[18] This is the last time Democrats won a majority of US counties.

[19] Third-party independent candidate Ross Perot won fifteen states. This is the last time any third-party candidate won a county. Despite a 6 percent win and a clear electoral majority, Democratic winner Bill Clinton did not receive a majority or plurality of county-level wins.

[20] Democratic county-level performance totals have never recovered from the post-Clinton drop-off. This is the biggest indictment of any possibility of a successor ideology or through the institutional civic order winning and controlling the future of American politics. Land power matters in both war and in politics.

Democrats can be in denial about this all they want, but it will become increasingly harder and harder to pull off an Electoral College inside straight while winning five hundred counties or fewer. In addition, what happens at the county levels and state legislative levels as seen above has its effects on the congressional level as well.

Congressional-Level Presidential Results Since 2000

Election	Congressional Districts Won (Dem.)	Congressional Districts Won (Rep.)	Electoral College Vote Aligned
2000	209	226	Yes
2004	175	258	Yes
2008	234	195	Yes
2012[21]	168	213	No
2016	199	230	Yes
2020[22]	137	205	No

This mismatch between the aspirations and goals of the formerly emerging Democratic majority and the electoral realities and the lack of future possibilities their coalition is creating is slowly and steadily creating a country where the Republicans will emerge and replace the Democrats as America's natural governing party if they seize the opportunity and develop and communicate a positive, optimistic, and common-sense-driven agenda for America's future. To find out who has the advantage in even the close electoral contests we've been having the past few decades, one need only look to the trend lines in the tipping-point states throughout American history.

---

[21] Incomplete results, accessed at USElectionAtlas.org.
[22] Incomplete results, accessed at USElectionAtlas.org.

Close (Less Than 2%) Tipping-Point States
in Presidential Election History

Election	State	State Margin	National Margin	Winning Candidate
1844	New York	1.1%	1.5%	Dem.
1876	South Carolina	0.5%	-3%	Rep.
1880	New York	1.9%	0.1%	Rep.
1884	New York	0.1%	0.6%	Dem.
1888	New York	1.1%	-0.8%	Rep.
1916	California	0.4%	3.1%	Dem.
1948	California	0.4%	4.5%	Dem.
1960	Missouri	0.5%	0.2%	Dem.
1976	Wisconsin	1.7%	2.1%	Dem.
2000	Florida	0.0%	-0.5%	Rep.
2016	Pennsylvania	0.7%	-2.1%	Rep.
2020	Wisconsin	0.6%	4.4%	Dem.

Throughout America's history, especially when the two major parties were engaged in a seemingly endless battle near the 50-yard line, where the tipping-point state broke in the Electoral College often made all the difference. In securing another few decades of Republican dominance, the McKinley and Theodore Roosevelt coalitions featured a New York that broke strongly for the Republicans after years of being the tipping-point state in the country. In both the proto-civic order years of Wilson and the post-FDR years, the state of California proved to be the tipping point for an emerging Democratic Party as it rose to America's natural governing party status. California's status as trendsetter is not baked in but was set in motion from this status as a large state that went all-in on a new direction for the country. California did it again during the Cold War, as it was the home state of Richard Nixon and elected Ronald Reagan twice as Governor before the Gipper carried California twice in 1980 and '84 presidential elections. Its thriving defense industry and the days of a more moderate and more Republican-friendly Hollywood helped reinforce the "Republican president, Democratic Congress Cold War era" status for the War Generation

Alignment. Just as the defense and aerospace megalopolises of the emerging Republican majority and the ideopolises of the emerging Democratic majority became synonymous with those eras and theories, so, too, will the tipping-point states of the populist and relatively more traditional Heartland of the country become forever associated. The small towns and rotary reliables of the Great Revolt feel remarkably different whether in victory or defeat than the perpetually divided and hysterical culture found on the megacity and overdeveloped coastlines. The zeitgeist has been introduced, and contrary to the notions of the culture and media, we're likely at the beginning of something rather than at the end of a movement that goes the way of the Federalists, the Whigs, or the historical populists.

In the past two decades, Florida, Pennsylvania, and Wisconsin proved to be the tipping-point states. All three of these states appear to have either broken in the Republican direction or are soon heading there. And once they do, only increasingly hard-to-grasp dreams of a blue Texas or running the table with states like Michigan, North Carolina, and Georgia could occasionally produce the 2020-type narrow victory that Joe Biden got, except this time they would not have the congressional majorities to go along with it.

From the pushback during the war itself to Nixon barnstorming the country in the 1966 midterms and his victory during the crossroads election of '68 to Reagan and Gingrich and now to Trump and the possibility of a twenty-first century Grover Cleveland recapture of the White House or one of the various other viable candidates who take up the mantle, so long as the party continues to build in the direction of national populism, a return to tradition, and an embrace of the patriotic core of the American Heartland, the 306 electoral votes that Trump received in 2016 could soon be the floor in the decades to come, rather than the ceiling.

The Geography of the Emerging Populist Majority

Italicized = won by B. Clinton once or twice

Bold = won by Obama once or twice

<u>Underlined</u> = dissenter state realigned in the other
direction or trending relatively away

Bold + Italicized = the five hold-outs to the forty-five-
state peak of the emerging populist majority

Core	Emerging / Realigned	Future Realignment	Dissenters
North Dakota	*Montana*	Nevada	<u>Colorado</u>
South Dakota	*Kentucky*	Minnesota	<u>Illinois</u>
Wyoming	*Tennessee*	New Mexico	<u>Virginia</u>[23]
Idaho	*Missouri*	Maine	<u>Georgia</u>
Oklahoma	**West Virginia**	New Hampshire	***Vermont***
Utah	**Indiana**	New Jersey	***Massachusetts***
Kansas	**Ohio**	New York	***Maryland***
Nebraska	**Iowa**	Connecticut	***DC***
Arkansas	**Wisconsin**	Rhode Island	***California***
South Carolina	**Michigan**	Delaware	***Hawaii***
Alabama	**Pennsylvania**	Oregon	
Mississippi	**Florida**	Washington	
Louisiana	**North Carolina**		
Alaska	Texas		
	Arizona		

---

[23] While Virginia is one of the two Obama-era states that realigned from Republican to Democrat, unlike Colorado, Virginia has shown that it can be competitive in the right environment and with the right candidate, and indeed this is a running theme across nearly all fifty states with the exception of California and Hawaii. There are certainly challenging states for Republicans, but the party is ultimately competitive in more states than Democrats are, and it is the Democrats whose coalitional realities do not match their governing ambitions and hopes for future political dominance.

CHAPTER 10

THE DEMOGRAPHY OF THE
EMERGING POPULIST MAJORITY

I t is said that a trend shown in the past is a fact, while a future trend is but an assumption. Before moving from geography to demography, a moment of humility is necessary. These trends can change. As of this writing, they look most likely to change not through Democrats following the sincere and good advice from the cowriter and popularizer of "demographic inevitability" but through a lack of will on the part of the Republican establishment to actually fight for its voters. Like in the past, it's more likely than not that the establishment will not fight, will resist a populist surge, but simply lose and become overwhelmed by it. Before Trump was unelectable, Ronald Reagan was considered unelectable. Before there was Bill Kristol and Liz Cheney, there was Nelson Rockefeller. Just as it is with any challenge to a civic order, the focus must be on the dominant party in the system first, not the answering one.

In his Substack *The Liberal Patriot* newsletter, Ruy Teixeira laid out three things Democrats would need to do to buck this increasing trend: one, Democrats must move to the center on cultural issues; two, Democrats must promote an abundance agenda; and three, Democrats must embrace patriotism and what he calls "liberal nationalism." This is all sensible and good advice that would work if followed. The problem is any American

THE EMERGING POPULIST MAJORITY

who has spent any amount of time around urban progressives knows that this is a lost cause, especially numbers one and three. On two, an "abundance" agenda could in theory become a bipartisan program of a future and emerging populist majority. However, in areas dominated purely by progressives, no abundance agenda will be achieved because of the significant gap between progressive aspirations and goals and economic realities on the ground. One and three though speak volumes for how much the last six years have already accomplished in changing the conversation. It would have been unheard of eight years ago to wipe away the bipartisan globalization and neoliberal to neoconservative consensus; now it looks increasingly on its deathbed.

In *The Emerging Democratic Majority* it was posited that Democrats had a solid blue wall of 267 electoral votes that stemmed from every state Gore won from the Clinton coalition of 1992 and 1996.[xc] From there a new floor was established for the new millennium commanding a following not just from the adjusted eastern establishment but also the Far West in California and the Midwest, on to the metropolitan areas like the North Carolina research triangle and Florida's high-tech and tourist areas. And this thesis seemed to play out nearly perfectly in the 2008 presidential election just as Phillips's thesis had proven prophetic years prior. American politics has changed dramatically since the first Obama midterm, and it has changed in an accelerating direction that is steadily favoring the rise of national populism in a patriotic fusion with traditional conservatism. While our last chapter showed how much climbing and emerging have already taken place across geography, a lot more has taken place across demography both in terms of American realignment from Democratic to Republican (or to Independent/unaligned) and to a lesser extent, from Republican to Democratic (or to Independent/unaligned) that does not show up nearly as much because of the heavy Democratic tilt and starting point of major cities. These changes fall into two categories: the old gaps and the new. The old more familiar voting gaps have been closing in recent years either from one side coming to the other or both sides. Meanwhile, the new gaps that are emerging are part of the reason the polling industry has been a mess for about eight years. The unintentional reason that pollsters have trouble getting elections right lately is because they no longer know how to model the electorate to account for these new gaps and are stuck in the universe of the old gaps and paradigm that is closing.

The Old Gaps Are Closing

Favorable demographics based around current voting trends and drawing a straight-line analysis into the future lies at the heart of why it was always a reach that any sort of "emerging Democratic majority" existed. It also makes sense why it was relied on by the media and culture of the progressive world. An onward and upward, straight-line analysis by and large is their view of history—linear. Whereas the conservative or traditional view of history tends to be more cyclical or seasonal. In addition, coalitions of everybody are harder and harder to keep intact. In 2020, Democrats won their lowest share of the black vote since 1980, their lowest share of the Hispanic vote since 2004, and their lowest share of the Asian vote since 2008. The gap in college education as a stand-in for social class also is showing signs since the 2020 election and, somewhat seen in that election, of appearing across race and ethnicity. Republicans have been making gains with Hispanics, whose ethnic voting patterns look to have more in common with European-based ancestry and immigration than the history of the black vote, which Democrats rhetorically tried to connect them to with their "people of color" language. The problem with such sloganeering as a stand-in for identity politics appeals is that it's shallow, divisive, and increasingly dehumanizing. This in combination with economic advancement under the Trump years and economic inflation and crisis under the Biden years is and will continue to accelerate working- and middle-class flight out of the Democratic Party for Hispanic voters, who will increasingly vote more like noncollege-educated and working-class white voters.

There is a secondary reason Hispanic voters will continue to realign. As President Ronald Reagan long ago predicted, their ideological bent and values will eventually come to be a better fit in the Republican Party. This may have not emerged over the years for a variety of reasons, the appearance of Democrats being better on the economy, a significant difference in community outreach and living patterns in tandem with the rules of America's electoral system, but the increasing cultural left bent of the Democratic Party over gender ideology, critical race theory, in tandem with the economic devastation brought by progressive and liberal Democratic preferences on Covid-19 and the climate will increasingly push Hispanic Americans out of the Democratic Party and into Independent and Republican voting patterns. Even if Hispanics come to constitute a swing vote along with Catholics and Asians as American demographer and geopolitical consultant Peter Zeihan has suggested, that alone would change the voting and coalitional calculus dramatically for Democrats. There is evidence to suggest it could get worse than that for Democrats, and herein lies the emerging populist coalition through the Republican Party even more so.

Since the 2020 election, an election in which Hispanics voted 6 percent more Republican than in 2012 and 6 percent less Democratic, continued realignment along border towns and counties has commenced, which elected Mayra Flores in a special election in Texas's Thirty-Fourth Congressional District, a district that has elected Democrats since the Civil War. Although Flores went on to lose in the November midterm election, she is running again for this now-toss-up seat along the border. Two other Hispanic women are Republican nominees in south Texas, and according to Trump's Hispanic Outreach Advisor Steve Cortes, this trend extends beyond just Texas and beyond south Florida as well. While the accuracy of polling has been called into question for many cycles now, the misses have almost universally been in one direction. According to the overall rarely accurate (but in one direction) *New York Times* poll, Democrats now have just a 3 percent advantage with Hispanic voters, down from 45 percent as recently as 2018. Hispanic voters leaving the Democratic Party for the Republican one are driven by both culture and economics, making the realignment more lasting so long as the Democrats continue their progressive bent across the country. The trend and candidacies are not merely limited to communities with larger share of the population states like Texas and Florida but stretch into Virginia and Indiana as well. After the 2022 midterms, Republican Diego Morales became the only Hispanic secretary of state in the nation for either party. This increasing diversity in candidacies for Republicans does not mimic the cynical appeals of Democrats' identity politics approach but is based around appeals to patriotism and populism, and ultimately offers the American electorate a second chance to build a diverse America around the constitutional republic and founding charters of freedom since it appears the Democrats' vision of "diversity is our strength" is but a slogan after all.

Asian voters on the other hand have a slightly different trajectory. In common with Hispanics, they share a desire for an economy of upward mobility. Like the Phillips work on ethnic voting, it is again more accurate to look at voting by country of national origin, which means the future trajectory will have more in common with white European-based immigration than anything else. Asian voters from Vietnam have every bit the experiences with the terrors of communism as do Cuban Americans. For a time, Asian Americans overall voted Republican in the 1980s and 1990s. It is tempting to say that they, with their higher rates of college education, will follow the trajectory of college-educated white Americans, but that newer gap that is widening is poorly understood as we'll see in a moment. To the extent that Asian Americans return to their historical home of the GOP, crime waves in major cities, race and education issues at the university down to K–12 levels, and runaway cultural progressivism that shows no signs of humbling itself will continue to drive Asian Americans out of the Democratic Party and into the Republican Party, even if to possibly a lesser extent. Since 2012, however, Asian voters have become 10 percent less Democratic and 10 percent more Republican. While Asian voters are historically more Republican than Hispanic voters and have trended more Republican since 2012 (10 percent compared to between 6 and 8 percent), it's possible that given the increasing populist dynamics going on throughout the country that the next ten years will see more Hispanic realignment than Asian. Another reason this might be so is the share of the electorate itself. While Asian immigration is the fastest growing in the country, the share of the electorate is at 4 percent. In 2020, the Hispanic share of the electorate equaled the black share of the electorate at 13 percent, while the white share of the electorate was at 67 percent.

Since the election of Donald Trump, America has gotten less progressive and liberal across the board, even according to liberal pollsters like Morning Consult. Five years ago, 54 percent of black Americans identified as somewhat liberal, liberal, or very liberal. In 2022 by the same methodology just 33 percent of black Americans identify as such. While Morning Consult has a questionable track record in its predictive electoral capabilities, comparing it to itself to track these trends can be helpful. For Hispanics, the same 18 to 22 percent reduction is seen. In 2017, 55 percent of Hispanics identified as somewhat liberal, liberal, or very liberal, and today just 37 percent do. Throughout that same time period, white Americans became 9 percent less liberal by this poll, which can be explained by being more ideologically dispersed to begin with. In many ways what is happening is the ideological disbursement that has for decades been seen with white Americans is now becoming the case with Asian, black, and Hispanic Americans, and the ideological voting patterns are traveling increasingly to the party affiliation level and voting patterns. More conservative Hispanics are voting Republican, similar to how conservative white voters, who once gave Jimmy Carter a large enough share of the vote to nearly be the last Democrat to win white voters, increasingly became in the 1980s and 1990s. Throughout that same time period black Americans became more conservative (from 15 to 18 percent), Hispanic Americans became more conservative (21 to 23 percent), and white Americans became more conservative as well (30 to 33 percent). However, the largest gains were seen by the moderate self-identification, a possible consequence of increased polarization.

The Phillips theory and research on the long-term trends and the evolution of ethnic voting in American political life still holds, and it's not unique to European-based immigration waves. Or at minimum, the patterns emerging whether realigning on appeals to patriotism, populism, nationalism, or conservatism are far closer to those historical trends than the historical trend the ruling Democrats wished was true—dividing America up by white versus non-white or connecting non-white voters into a "people of color" category cringingly reminiscent of the language of past segregation. While the immigration politics of the past may have been the origins of American identity politics in much of the northern establishment, today immigration politics that used to travel through the city and Ellis Island crosses at the border, and the assumption that legal immigrants have cultural solidarity with illegal immigrants has been yet another miscalculation by the Democrats. No one much appreciates the person who cuts in line or doesn't pay ever at the dinner table. While Hispanic and Asian voters may be realigning to a lesser extent in places like New York City, this is because there have not been any substantive efforts by local organizations and the state Republican Party until recently. In 2022 Congressman Lee Zeldin lost the governor's race to Democrat incumbent Kathy Hochul by single digits, 6.4 percent, against a one-party Democratic city and state that continues to preside over even worse local and state outcomes than the national brand has presided over. As the Republican Party grows more populist, and more diverse, the Democratic Party has grown slightly more white, but this is only in a relative sense. Democrats have not won the white vote in over four decades, and as we'll see in a moment, no amount of gains with college-educated white voters will make up for the margins they're losing from their former base that they've long since abandoned.

Black Americans meanwhile are also contributing to this emerging populist majority and are realigning, albeit to a lesser extent. After reaching peak Democratic vote percentage in 2008 and 2012, black voters have trended 7 percent Republican as well, in line with everyone else. How much further can this go? Whether it grows or stays or even reverses, the black share of the electorate is the same as it was ten years ago, and nearly the same as it was when Ronald Reagan was president. As prominent black conservatives have noted, more black babies are aborted in New York City than born. This is an intolerable statistic and increasingly, the demographic version of the rearguard action the Northeast and state of California will be pushed into is the increasingly toxic relationship between white progressives and the black community. Nearly every issue facing the black community in urban America is an internal party revolt against white liberal Democrats. Gentrification and housing issues are an internal party conversation, and while it is fair to say Republicans and conservatives are not participating in that conversation, they are also not included in it. The relative and so-called conservatism of the real estate industry is called into question by the fact that most of the urban real estate industry in operation votes Democratic, unlike its suburban and rural counterparts. Issues with policing and the "defund the police" movement are also an internal conversation, but the resulting consequences of increasing crime rates and the erosion of the rule of law from the rioting of 2020 and policies like bail reform have become the concerns of Republicans and in part are powering urban Republican rebirth.

No matter the vote margins achieved, the elevation of black conservatives should be done frequently by a populist-conservative fusion for the benefit of the country writ large and the Republican Party's special role standing tall as a leadership party during some of America's most divisive and fraught historical moments. Standing against the evils of slavery, communism, and lately abortion has defined the party since its inception. This moralistic impulse has always suited the Republican Party well, and it can suit its populist-infused incarnation as well, at least far more than an increasingly secular but overly righteous, moralizing, and scold-laden Democratic Party, especially in its progressive youth wing.

The gender gap is another old gap the media and culture have promoted since time immemorial that is closing. In 2012, the gap between men and women was more or less the same in 2020, after growing in the previous elections. It had closed in particular compared to 2016. This was true of both married and unmarried men and women. For married men and women it has closed from between 11 and 12 percent to between 4 and 5 percent. This dovetails to the increasing holding of the civilizational line quality during a crisis for American families and households. While COVID no doubt created much marital stress and some divorces, those who got through the long, hot summer and "dark winter" of these years emerged stronger and with a renewed sense of familiar purpose. For unmarried men and women, the gap also closed from a gap of between 13 and 15 percent in 2016 to between 9 and 10 percent four years later. While the overturning of *Roe v. Wade* was predicted to provide a massive surge across America, there is little evidence to support this, but some evidence that it helped Democrats turn out more voters along the margins in the fall of '22. In opinion poll after opinion poll, abortion rarely makes the top three issues driving voters to the polls, and where it is felt strongest was in voters already against Republicans and already turning out to vote in the past. In the medium and long term, which has been a more primary focus of this book, it appears to be net-favorable for the Republicans given the increasing American family dynamics in favor of the Republicans. Over the next few decades, red America will see increasing birth rates while blue America will see suppressed birth rates because of abortion policy being at the state rather than the national level. This will further grow a gap in preference in family formation that is already present, which will increase the desperation in Democratic partisans to ideologically propagandize in schools, while in turn increase a push for universal school choice in Republican households and probably many moderate Democratic ones as well, where an increasing unease with the progressive worldview and dogma is also emerging. This difference in families could reach a peak of two kids by 2030 and will further reinforce future Republican advantages and the emergence of a populist majority future. There are one of two choices: either economies in three-kid red America will continue to grow and meet demand, or household travelers will move and venture into one-kid blue America, which in tandem with the local population will continue the relative realignment there.

The millennial traveler story has been one of movement into large cities and the ideopolises of the emerging Democratic majority but now has become a reverse migration and movement back to smaller and midsized home towns for many, or movement closer to home as millennials start their families. Of the few professional-class millennials who made the jump from the "aspiring" professional-class status that masqueraded as the left-populism of Bernie Sanders, those families and households are trending far more conservative and patriotic as they seek to batten down the hatches of their homes, fighting back against increasing crime and COVID-19 policy insanity, and will be unabashedly "mama and papa bears" whether moderate or more politicized when it comes to their children and schools. By 2030 school choice will have gone from victories in states like Arizona to the law of the land in a majority of states around the nation, with calls to make it universal. Elder millennials, those between the ages of about thirty and forty right now, are increasingly Republican after starting from a 34 percent gap of more Democratic than Republican in 2008.

This can be seen ideologically too. The same aforementioned Morning Consult poll has the eighteen to thirty-four age range getting 13 percent less liberal in the last five years, from 47 percent to 34 percent. While this has not yet equaled a growth in conservatism, the chief beneficiaries were don't know/no opinion and a 5 percent growth in moderates from 22 to 27 percent. Millennials were supposed to be the most Democratic voting generation since the baby boomers, who themselves have voted Republican majority multiple times, just as every generation in American history has. Like their mostly boomer parents, millennials, too, will vote for Republicans at least once in their lifetimes, possibly as soon as the 2024 through 2032 time frame, and possibly more than once as well. The age and generation gap overall is yet another gap in American politics that has closed. In 2008, those aged eighteen to twenty-nine voted 66 percent Democratic, 32 percent Republican. This gap of 34 percent compared to +8 in the Republican direction for seniors at the time has closed dramatically, both by younger voters becoming relatively less Democratic and older voters becoming relatively less Republican, too, in the most recent election possibly due to coronavirus factors that will be situational and less salient going forward. Unlike white millennials, who voted for Democrats by 10 percent in 2008, white Generation Z has already started off voting Republican by 9 percent. If there is any sort of generation gap by race anywhere else, it works in the opposite direction. For black Americans, those older than sixty voted 4 percent more Democratic than black Americans between the ages of eighteen and twenty-nine, and 14 percent more Democratic than black Americans between the ages of thirty to forty-four. For Hispanics and Asians, the voting by age and generation trends followed more closely to white Americans with younger trending relative Democratic, and older trending relative Republican.

The final much-talked-about gap that is closing is urban and rural polarization itself. This is not because of anything happening in rural America, which is continuing to trend away from the Democrats, but rather because urban America is trending away from the Democrats in a relative sense and toward the Republicans. In 2008 the Democrats were still able to only lose the rural vote by 8 percent; by 2020 that range was at 15 percent, and it bottomed out at 30 percent (62–32) in 2016. Biden did slightly better with seniors, rural voters, and in the suburbs, while doing worse with the middle class, in urban areas, and with minority voters across the board. The urban-rural polarization closing is another great opportunity for a populist-led Republican Party, as what the Democrats identified with, globalization and deindustrialization, has created "extraction zones" in small-town rural areas while creating "sacrifice zones" in the much earlier deindustrialized and more urbanized areas of the Northeast. A policy platform of reshoring and reindustrializing, opting for a pro-worker, pro-consumer, pro–Main Street small business, and pro-family economic agenda would go a long way toward finishing off a realignment just half underway.

There is already a critical mass of people fed up with and ready to leave the Democratic Party, but the jury is still out on whether the Republicans can forge together a coalition that can last through the tough midterms and presidential cycles while cresting higher and higher for the waves. If it is to accomplish this, closing these old gaps is only one-half of the equation, with the other half being paying attention to the new signals within the American electorate. Despite the much-spoken-about handwringing over January 6 from Democratic-aligned media, or major city rioting in the summer of 2020 in Republican-aligned media, this latest version and outburst of frustration with public authority is also nothing new but just a new generation's expression of it. For instance, boomers of all ideological stripes in the past can be easily attracted to lawlessness,[xci] especially in pursuit of a higher purpose. Millennials and Gen Z, whether in their woke variety or based variety, are increasingly repeating that story through modern issues and lenses. In this sense, the generational gaps, too, are closing, with boomers returning to their youthful politics relative to yesterday, and millennials and Gen X especially closing in from the other direction.

The New Gaps Widening

The one gap that has reached the attention of the media and society and been discussed ad nauseam is the college-education gap, more fairly characterized as a "credentials" gap perhaps. This gap thus far has only shown up in white America and can be best described as a consequence of the heavy left- and liberal-leaning bias of academia. But it does capture the realignment better than any single variable in American life and in some ways functions as a corollary to the still-widening old gap of the role faith and religion plays.

In 2020, college-educated white voters, who still comprise a lower share of the electorate than noncollege-educated white voters, went Democratic by 3 percent. By contrast, noncollege-educated white voters went Republican by 35 percent. This gap of 38 was nearly nonexistent just twelve years prior in 2008, when Republican John McCain lost every single educational category but was *closest* to winning those with a bachelor's degree (50–48). The postgrad Democratic lean has long been there, but the bachelor's degree had not been as present in the past.

The trends and lean of the country in 2008 compared to 2016 and 2020 is well-documented at the college education levels. Educational attainment and credentials as a crude stand-in for social class was spoken about often as white college educated and white noncollege educated and the pollsters still follow along these lines. However, the new and increasing driver of the overall college gap is this factor now plays out across every racial group.

For a slice of the electorate that is still over a third that is an almost insurmountable number, spread across a geographically wide territory, associated negatively with globalization, which is associated now with the Democratic Party. If the Democrats want to wage a final war against their former base, that's one thing, but they are not winning enough white college-educated voters, or any other voter group for that matter, to make up the difference anymore. This more than anything is why the emerging Democratic majority is not only un-emerged, it is utterly finished. The best electoral outcome the Democrats can hope for in the future is similar to 2020 but likely downgraded in the Senate and to some extent the House.

And this social class realignment should not be entirely surprising; it would be more surprising if it did not happen. Throughout American political and electoral history, the interests of the white working class and upper-middle class have never been going in the same direction or been in the same coalition. The upper-middle class, outnumbered but still carrying far more weight in numbers than the super-wealthy who can be found in either party in any era, was heavily Republican during the FDR and New Deal eras but today is increasingly one of the most reliable voting groups for the Democrats. Meanwhile, the white working class that was heavily Democratic in the FDR and New Deal eras today is increasingly heavily Republican. The professions and educational credentials associated with the occupations and professions show this contrast well.[xcii]

Therefore, this education-as-crude-stand-in for social class dynamic can also be seen through extension to occupation itself. Consider the most common donors to both Biden and Trump throughout the 2020 presidential cycle below:

Most Common Biden Donors	Most Common Trump Donors
Professors	Homemakers
Social workers	Disabled
Nonprofit employees	Welders
Librarians	HVAC professionals
Lawyers	Ranchers
Writers/Authors	Truckers
Therapists/Psychologists	Plumbers
Teachers/Educators	Machinists
Creative directors	Construction workers
Public relations professionals	Electricians
Researchers, general	Farmers
Deans and higher education professionals	Police officers

Extending the analysis to employees and by businesses and organizations who employ them reveals an even more one-sided picture of the social class dynamic.

Most Common Biden Donors (Employers)	Most Common Trump Donors (Employers)
Columbia University	NYPD
University of Pennsylvania	US Marines
Harvard	US Military
University of Washington	
University of California	
Google	
Facebook	
Nike	
NIH (National Institutes of Health)	
Deloitte	

Notably, in terms of actual size of organization (top one hundred employers) no one else donated to Trump in majorities. Yet despite this two-to-one overall fundraising advantage, Biden and the Democrats still found their modern-day landslide victory and emerging, forever majority elusive. None of these common donor types are surprising; however, they do back up lots of claims. For instance, the argument against Dr. Fauci from downstream Republicans and non-Republicans alike was not that his science was bad or incompetent, but that he was a compromised bureaucrat whose funding depended on his political support for the Democratic Party. The Judis-Teixeira thesis was right about the nature of coalitions being cities rebuilt and built anew, with old cities sometimes popping up again from a bygone coalition. They were also right about a constituency being at the leading edge of the coalition. For the coalition they titled "George McGovern's Revenge,"[xciii] urban professionals and the professional social class were the leading constituency for this twenty-first-century majority. And it is with this coalition that the hammer will fall the hardest in the years and decades to come.

Along the way they subscribed to a "party systems" theory popular with political scientists, historians, and legacy media journalists that credit Jacksonian Democrats, Lincoln Republicans, McKinley Republicans, New Deal Democrats, conservative Republican majority, and their new Democratic majority with a few transitions in between as marking the critical elections of American politics and party coalitions.[xciv] But both in their own text and in the broader literature discussed here there is little evidence for critical elections and party systems other than their use as a narrative in retrospect, broadly set up to serve the conveniences of the present-day coalition. Yet in their discussion of this meta-worldview and narrative is a very interesting comment that makes the tables above on professions, donors, and where modern interests lie so revelatory: "From Andrew Jackson through Franklin Roosevelt and Bill Clinton, Democrats have defined themselves as the party of the average American and Republicans as the party of the wealthy and powerful."[xcv] If this is still true in the early

2020s, all the professionals and ordinary citizens in the tables above must be mightily confused.

Symbolically, to this very day the Democrats still are "America's Natural Governing Party," but if Americans at a rate of seven or eight out of every ten say that government is taking the country in the wrong direction, if they've said it for years, and if the response and answer from that government is more of the same, and from and by the same elites, then we're right back in Thomas Jefferson's dilemma about the need to institute a new government, or a *new civic order*, a little farther out west, or in this case, in a more populist, more national, more patriotic, and more respectful of tradition direction.

The aforementioned parental and family gap that is two-to-one Republican to Democratic provides the long-term reinforcement and is driving a good part of the millennial realignment around marriages, mortgages, and children. While single millennials may very well hold to their Democratic loyalties, their frustration and dependence on that party will eventually overwhelm their spirits, and nearing forty, they will simply give up the fight as a more pastoral, parent-driven America seeking a civic and cultural renewal emerges.

This "party of parents" the Republican Party has already turned into will continue to put pressure on the stagnating, declining in fundamental outcomes and enrollment, and increasingly cornered public school system. From the 2019–20 school year to the 2020–21 (post-COVID) school year, enrollments in public schools across the country reached modern records. As public school enrollment continues to decline, it will be replaced by the alternative and parallel institutions already building as we speak across counties and states throughout the country, not unlike the Depression-era laboratory of democracy reforms that began in the states first.

The "Old Gap" That Does Continue to Grow Is One of Religion

But to less an extent than before largely because Republicans, too, have become less religious and less connected to faith life. For the party, this means a somewhat waning influence of not just evangelicals but of protestants broadly who have seen the largest declines in worship and involvement with church organizations the past decade and a half. Meanwhile, more organized and centralized historical churches and denominations have held much stronger. The Protestant share of the electorate has shrunk by 11 percent since 2008, but the Catholic share of the electorate has shrunk by just 2 percent. However, the Protestants who are leaving are of the Democratic variety, making the margins by which Republicans are winning Protestants even wider now, while Catholics, too, are also more Republican than 2008. In 2024, it's entirely possible that Republicans will win the Catholics period as they did in 2016. In church attendance an even clearer picture emerges. Of those who profess no religion, now 22 percent of Americans, Democrats win those voters by a margin of two to one. This means not only that the future of the Republican Party is still religious and faith observant, and the future of the Democratic Party increasingly less so, and the faith-based appeals that are attempted will sit awkwardly, but it also means that the future of organized US religions is more Orthodox, more conservative and traditional, and more Catholic. All of whom have more children than nonreligious people. Whether it is the gaps that are closing, the new ones emerging, or the old ones still growing, almost all these changes favor Republicans, and while all trends can and do reverse eventually and go back again, the fact remains that what is transpiring now in the growing coalition versus coalition environment that makes up US party politics and elections, taken to their (illogical and impossible) realignment extremes, means a Republican Party that wins every state but three and a Democratic Party that loses substantially in every region of the country. Now this of course will not happen, but a Democratic Party that does not understand the electorate that actually exists is a party without a future rather than one with an emerging majority. The actual demographics of America in 2020, even if everyone turned out at their professed and wished-for 100 percent turnout, look something like this:

Demographic Group	White, noncollege	White, college	Black	Hispanic	Asian/other
Share of Electorate (%)	43.2%	24.7%	12.5%	12.6%	7.0%
Current Status	Republican	Republican in '16, Democratic in '20	Democratic	Democratic	Democratic
Long-Term Trend	Republican	Slight Democratic	Republican	Republican	Republican

America at this crossroads still has many potential futures, and the elites of this country may prefer to gaslight into a country united against noncollege-educated white Americans who make less money on average than Nigerian Americans and Filipino Americans. However, a much preferable realignment for the country and the American constitutional republic is a diversifying, pastoral, familial, and patriotic return to tradition and a civic renewal that builds a middle-out economy based around the real needs of households rather than Washington bureaucrats, stays out of unnecessary wars abroad, and commits itself to building a more unified and shared vision for the land of hope. But that new consensus, for a new vision to run dominant throughout American life, requires grappling with the contrasting visions and their origins themselves. As Thomas Sowell discussed in *A Conflict of Visions*[xcvi] and *Intellectuals and Society*,[xcvii] the anointed vision is the vision of American elites who propose solutions and security in theory and dependency in actuality. Eventually, a more humble vision of a restored constitutional republic in spirit and in law, and a public policy regime that understands the nature of trade-offs rather than quick and easy solutions, can begin to peel back the veil and bring the country out of the long crisis and crossroads, and into something far more humble and workable.

CHAPTER 11

THE IDEOLOGY OF THE EMERGING POPULIST MAJORITY

A nother confession of humility: Is this the only possibility for America's political future? Of course not. However, the alternative to the final days of the Third Civic Order—more popularly known in the past few decades as the neoliberal-neoconservative establishment consensus or the "center holding" in 2012 parlance—if it is not an emerging populist majority, is also decidedly away from the establishment, even if it may use the long march through (discredited and distrusted) institutions to fait accompli.

Increasingly, partisan Democrats say Republicans are a threat to "our democracy," and Republicans say Democrats have moved on from the federal constitutional republic, which is what we are and were designed to be. How can both of these things be simultaneously true? Regardless of where one stands in this struggle rhetorically and factually, what is becoming clearer is America's "constraining" philosophies of liberalism and conservatism in a traditional sense have failed and are failing while ceding that ground to America's "movement" philosophies of progressivism and populism. While both liberalism and conservatism have a vital role in upholding the freedom and ordered liberty of the Constitution, it was also conservatism that had an evolving and constraining role to play in the maintenance of tradition.

Today, both have failed at these roles, and increasingly both flailing constraining philosophies are dependent on the movement-based ones that have reformist roles. Both establishment progressive neoliberalism and a preference for globalization and neoconservative or *Conservatism, Inc.* and a tendency toward globalization prefer the constraining nature of the status quo, whereas populists of either rural or urban variety and progressives of the mostly urban variety prefer that their ideological imprint move America into a new golden age by their own differing definitions. In the case of the populists, this golden age is a renewal, a rebirth, a return; for the movement progressives it's right now and then tomorrow as the next best option. Traditional conservatives as a constraining philosophy are ill-equipped to face down today's progressives in the same way traditional status quo liberals are ill-equipped to face down either movement-based American ideology. In this sense, the real alternative to the emerging populist majority and a broad coalition across rural and urban and across demographics is not the current establishment but a postnational and postliberal progressive successor ideology. And this alternative should decidedly scare many Americans who value either freedom or tradition, or both.

Successor Ideology Foundations

On one hand, the successor ideology completes Woodrow Wilson's dream of moving the American government beyond the constraints imposed by the Constitution. Even if today's devotees to intersectional wokeness would denounce Wilson as a racist and southern Confederate sympathizer, they share with him an indifference toward constitutional restraints, an elitist and scolding top-down preference for their own hegemony over American society, and an obsession with race, and they are ultimately pro-war, not anti-war. In the face of the first major land war in decades on the European continent, the anti-war left has all but disappeared, but its successor ideology foundations can be found in that same decade of tumultuous change and upheaval.

In a real sense, the origin point of today's left lies still in the Port Huron statement of 1962, a seminal moment of the New Left but also a call for a reform not of the Republican Party but of the Democratic Party. This is more evidence of the dominant party paradigm from within a civic order. In 1962, the Democratic Party was the party of the southern Dixiecrats. And the New Left was un-American at its core, revolutionary and idealistic at best and at worst violent in its tactics as seen by the excesses of the 1960s with urban rioting and terrorist acts from the Weatherman. The events taken up by the younger millennials and the older cohort of Gen Z, or zoomers, largely the children of baby boomers and older Gen X, have on the left been born out of this direct line from the Port Huron statement downstream and the academic "long march through the institutions" upstream. Of course, the real origin story of the New Left and New Politics theorists was the university itself. Save the party, save the nation, save your soul: the New Politics slogan since the 1968 Dump Johnson movement with its ideals rooted in the founding slogan of Students for a Democratic Society, which preached something called a "participatory democracy." The prophecy from this generation now entering its elder years and seeing its younger selves in new cohorts was that in a society where the average age was falling every year and more and more young people were going to college, conservatism could only but yield diminishing returns.[xcviii]

In truth, despite more and more people finishing and attempting college than ever before, conservatism itself and the Republican Party generally show no signs of going away and are in a stronger position than the assumptions of New Politics then and its various revival attempts today whether through the system or outside it. The real lesson of the sixties[xcix] is that liberals get in the biggest political trouble—whether instituting open housing, civilian complaint review boards, or sex education programs— when they assume reform is inevitable in tandem with its twin partner called progress. One can draw a straight line not in the fundamental assumptions of an onward and upward progressive triumph and future but in its origin myths of faulty assumptions. Society is getting younger? No, almost every country in the West is getting older; birth rates and family formation rates are down. More people going to college erase conservatism? Yes, more are attempting and finishing college today, but it has had the opposite effect. Conservatism regularly outpaces progressivism or liberalism in ideological self-identification whether one looks at Pew Research or Gallup research or newer outfits like More in Common. If populism was regularly included, it likely would too. Additionally, the college gap has merely contributed to turning the conservative and populist fusion into a more closely linked project united by patriotism, Americanism, and the founding and spiritual recovery of tradition and the American Republic at its core, while turning the progressive and liberal project into a law of diminishing returns, creating significant aristocratic imitation tendencies and biases and turning that coalition into an upstairs-downstairs one that holds nearly all American institutions but is incapable of delivering satisfying outcomes or leadership to the country. No amount of hoping for the eighteen- to thirty-four-year-old demographic to save it has worked out for the Democratic Party since the sixties. It was in much better shape electorally before it started trotting out that line. Another assumption of the sixties generation being forgotten but lived again today was the power being in the cities now. While progressivism remains viable and competitive and influential on college campuses and in major cities, that is about the only place it is, and this fact is highly resented by the rest of the country, a reality a populist-conservative-patriotic fusion will perpetually benefit from whether or not strategically competent.

The *Hidden Tribes* report labels this younger generational cohort "progressive activists," but in the past few years it has reawakened many of the boomer traditional liberals to its side as liberalism itself has moved firmly into postliberalism and in many respects postnational status. From within the dominant party of the civic order, there is no substantial and workable pushback from the liberal class, as it has been replaced by deeper authoritarian and totalitarian tendencies. The Never Trump allies of 2020 have more or less added to this reality, as you see the neocons reborn with gusto through the Democratic Party, even if their influence may be situational and both sides are essentially using one another.

Much of America's polarization is driven by the Hidden Tribes of the "progressive activists" and the also skewing-younger "devoted conservatives." In 2016, 94 percent of "progressive activists" voted for Hillary Clinton, while 98 percent voted Democratic in the midterms two years later. They have now reached and surpassed the near 100 percent levels of "devoted conservatives" who voted 97 percent for Trump in 2016 and 96 percent Republican in the '18 midterms. The traditional liberals and traditional conservatives have intense partisanship but at lesser levels than the emerging generations who were thought to come into American life with greater consensus than those of the "consciousness revolution" but instead have had a delayed, more abstract, and considerably less coherent version of it, although possibly less violent in the long run due to the absence of the Vietnam War and societal skin in the game.

Where the Democratic coalition is particularly vulnerable via the Hidden Tribes characterization of the electorate is within the politically disengaged and moderate tribes: patriotically driven and lower income in the case of the disengaged, and civic-minded and busy raising families in the case of the moderates, eschewing the relatively younger extremes and even the older ones in the form of the traditionals. A Republican populist-leaning and -led coalition could either be a Trump return via a Grover Cleveland impression or Trumpism without and after Trump, which the media has said is impossible. This is a case of wishcasting. Not only is it possible and probable, it likely represents an even larger victory down the road due to the maturation of these longer and steady trends and the continued arrogance and refusal to understand the country they demand to lord over from the coasts in the case of media, culture, and intellectual elites. The permanent political class was increasingly despised by the country before Trump, during Trump, and will still be after Trump.

Again and again, the signal from the electorate over the long run has been "change" rather than "more of the same," and the party of "change" and the party that is "of the future" increasingly is not the Democratic Party.

In theory the successor ideology can *still* win, but it'll be very hard to do it through the Democratic brand right now. Most likely, it'll need to consistently trick an electorate that has mostly caught wise and either do a heightened march through institutions like the cultural Marxists did or move into full totalitarianism. Either route seems likely to split the country into some form of the much-talked-about but seldom-understood national divorce. The national divorce does not mean the country will split in two; it means what is already in part happening—that one side has given up on talking to the other and vice versa and is therefore retrenching within institutions in the case of the dominant ruling party or building alternative and parallel institutions in the case of the opposition party of the civic order. The reason why it is much safer for the country and more likely to be acceptable to the losing side is the inherent freedom of the constitutional order itself. The progressive successor ideology would like a unitary state run from Washington, with subordinate districts in the form of the states, whereas the emerging populist majority would opt for the humble and federal constitutional republic, which divides and shares power between the national, state, and local governments and the people, and separate but coequal branches of government, the executive, legislative, and judicial with final interpretation of the law vested in the US Supreme Court. Losing the court and having *Roe* overturned ended the long era of the liberal class treating the court as a super-legislative body that would pass through its goals when Congress would not.

When Democrats talk about "our democracy" they mean either the Third Civic Order or ensuring their successor ideology replaces it. When Republicans, such as this author on Substack, echo Ben Franklin in saying, "a republic if we can keep it," we mean preserving the American constitutional republic, and in order to do that we need to do some open-heart surgery at this point. The result of the progressives losing out would be in large part protection still for whatever they hold dear that is enshrined within the Constitution, and if they wanted to go their own way within a state or city, a reborn and true Tenth Amendment would allow that more than many powers currently held. Meanwhile, a real, free, and patriotic America losing out completely would simply not live under the rule of the progressive activists in the twenty-first century, and it is unlikely the progressives would have the talent and resources to compel compliance from them. It would instead be a national version of what happened during the COVID lockdowns in New York City and elsewhere; the restrictions remained, but they were regulations on paper. People stopped following them, businesses that were deputized stopped enforcing them, and most went their own way, ignoring the scolding Karens and busybodies at every turn in open defiance. Much has happened in America since the 2018 midterm elections, but here is a speculation on where those tribes stand to help inform where an emerging populist majority may be taking the country.

The *Hidden Tribes* Report from More in Common (UK), 2018

	Progressive Activists	Traditional Liberals	Passive Liberals	Disengaged	Moderates	Traditional Conservatives	Devoted Conservatives
2018	8%	11%	15%	26%	15%	19%	6%
2022–23[24]	20%		7%	38%		30%	

The Postliberal Progressive Activists

It's possible that even lower than 20 percent now constitute the progressive activists and traditional liberals folded together. A key defining aspect of this tribe is how utterly unpersuasive they are in the public square and how dependent on political correctness, media and cultural monopoly or dominance, and cancel culture they are. The always small and institutional

---

[24] The Tribes of *The Emerging Populist Majority*.

governance neocons are folded into this group, too, but could just as easily be cast aside by postliberal progressives. This tribe is increasingly authoritarian and believes in a rights and ordered liberty regime for themselves but not for their opponents, unless their opponents can be driven into the wilderness and tamed. This tribe is the opposite of the populists and the emerging populist majority, which is nationalist and patriotic. The driving feature of the postliberal progressive activists is statist yet denigrating of American culture, history, and philosophy of governance. This is why progressive activists make for a natural coalition with globalists and pro-globalization interests, even though ostensibly they have many contradictory values on paper. The progressive activists are not only postliberal, they are also postnational.

The New "Buckley" Conservatives

Torn between two tribes is a diverse and broad group united by an unwillingness to join either proposal out of the Third Civic Order. This tribe will ultimately become the new conservatives in a William F. Buckley standing athwart history yelling "stop" sense. Composed of civic moderates, independents, some passive liberals who never opted in and followed the progressive bend, holding to classical and traditional liberalism, and other more disengaged and unpoliticized citizens will make up the difference on whether the emerging populist majority governs with unified governance or split governance. The occasional setback, the slowdown and stop, will come from this group. And when they are on board, it is because they trust the direction the populist-patriotic-conservative fusion is on rather than feeling the need to temper it and opt for split governance.

The Traditionals

The traditionals are the older classic conservatives closer to the Reagan variety. The difference between them and the populists is age, tactics, energy, and generational experiences. And what keeps them from being the new Buckley conservatives is the fact that what they believe in is actually coming into reality in their lifetime. This tribe in the past is best described as the skeptical Trump voter in 2016 who was pleasantly surprised by the outcomes, even questioning the style and methods to get there. Ultimately, aware of the unrelenting pressure from the progressives and the *Brave New World*, *1984*, and *Animal Farm* hybrid, this group is more driven by the size and scope of government, taxes, and regulation over trade, tech, and forever wars.

The Populists

The populists are the vanguard of the movement, organization, and the new counterculture. More than half of them are realigned, newly politicized, and ancestrally Democratic. What unites populists, especially in the face of universal scorn from elites, is a sense of patriotism and love of country. Unlike questions over the size and scope of government, populists are driven more by who is running the government and country, and our institutions, and specifically the fact that they are mismanaged at best, and American citizens are being intentionally wronged at worst. The populists are more ideologically flexible at the policy level but unrelenting at the principle and visionary level. But perhaps the best summation comes from the American Legion pamphlet *Americanism*.

In transitioning to a party of parents, of Main Street, of uninformed service members, perhaps it's notable to focus once more on the past, as much of this book of America's political future has done. One, the Republican establishment, and indeed the establishment overall, has consistently resisted populist and outsider onslaughts. Many times, it has gone to great lengths to stop them. Yet once they lose out, that populist wave from the outside becomes part of the newly formed establishment. Perhaps some drop off, but others adjust. It is no matter how it reacts, for almost all major change has come from the grassroots, citizen-level. The top-down party has rarely engineered great victories. This is true of either party really. In revisiting the many waves and transits out of the Third Civic Order, or challenging it, we're reminded of just how much that is with us today that Americans by their electoral and small "d" democratic choice never signed up for at all.

First, we have the beginning prior to, during, and after the war—the foundational period itself. In 1938 FDR and the Democrats lost seventy-nine seats (seventy-two in the House, seven in the Senate) after a double-dip recession and court-packing schemes failed. During the first full year in the war, Republicans picked up fifty-three seats (forty-five in the House, eight in the Senate) in 1942. Four years after that, in the first midterm after the Second World War, Truman and the Democrats lost sixty-four more seats to the Republicans (fifty-four in the House, ten in the Senate) as Congress flipped for the first time in sixteen years. It proved to be short-lived, and if anything gave the Republican Party a false sense of security and confidence for the 1948 campaign that saw one of the most impressive presidential comebacks of all time. Republicans and their standard-bearer, Thomas Dewey, did not campaign hard enough at all.

Two decades later, after a '64 landslide victory, a media now fully realigned to the ruling civic order and an intellectual class even further ahead predicted its own forever majority for LBJ and the Democratic Congresses. Instead of a New Deal, it was going to be a Great Society. In the first election to render a verdict on the Great Society, fifty seats (forty-seven in the House, three in the Senate) were picked up by Republicans. Indeed, the coalition that came to pass was predicted and forecasted with near total accuracy by Kevin Phillips, and although Phillips himself grew disillusioned with the Republican coalition by the early twenty-first century, having underestimated the evangelicals within the emerging coalition forged much more by the Cold War itself, this is not entirely surprising given his Bronx-born and -raised roots.

The coalition that is ultimately a populist revolt against the globalization and the tragedy of deindustrialization—personified by Trump's shocking victory, the most shocking victory since Truman in '48 and FDR in '36—has greater unity and higher intraparty support in a party coalition that is steadily diversifying and growing again faster than their opponents for the first time since the Reagan years. Prior to Trump, this wave saw seventy-two seats picked up in the Tea Party midterm of 2010 (sixty-three in the House, nine in the Senate) and then six more Senate seats in 2014 before achieving the first Republican trifecta in non-9/11 times in more than eight decades. And despite all the unified effort to engineer a blue wave in 2018 from a unified intellectual, political, cultural, and media class, only twenty-three seats of this blue wave materialized. Democrats picked up twenty-six in the House to flip it but lost three in the Senate. The incredible durability of a rural-strong, middle-class, and Heartland-led coalition is increasingly proving its mettle in both good years and difficult, challenging times. And along the coast, where the elites in tandem with Davos and the World Economic Forum plan a future where we'll all own nothing and be happy, a new zeitgeist and new counterculture have emerged for the punch-back, upon which it's possible that the Yankees may indeed get their groove back. So long as these forces remain ascendant, there is hope yet for the American constitutional system, our freedom, faith, traditions, families, and our flag and the republic for which it stands.

One need only look to the recent and increasingly gaslit bias of historians' rankings of presidents to understand the epitome of late Third Civic Order clerisy and gatekeeping. For instance, consider that Dwight D. Eisenhower was the last Republican nominee the *New York Times* has endorsed for president, and that prior to 1912, they typically endorsed the Republican candidates. Consider the *Washington Post*'s ownership the last half decade by one of the world's richest men and founder of Amazon, Jeff Bezos. "Democracy Dies in Darkness" was the slogan trotted out during that time, and the phrase "our democracy" is now used as a pejorative toward its speaker's disingenuousness. While it was entirely plausible in 1948, in 1958, and even in 1988 especially to make the claim that this country enjoyed a balance between its two party coalitions so as to make its party politics functional, today it enjoys no such balance. Increasingly, the elites, administrative bureaucracy, and institutions are of one world-view on one side, and the people and grass roots are on the other.

Whereas in the late nineteenth century populism was a precursor to a Democratic coalition that would triumph over elite and professional opponents and synthesize with progressive reformist forces, so, too, is populism today a precursor to a future triumph as it synthesizes and makes allies with the forces of conservatism, patriotism, and tradition. Nor was populism totally a project run through the Democratic Party over a century ago. Rather, it existed in fusion as both an ally and critic of both parties depending on which party was dominant in the region. Indeed, our best precursor for a sane future whether one prefers the "democracy" word or the "republic" word may very well be during the 1880s and '90s when southern highland Republicans briefly made cause with lowland poor whites and with blacks. It was a capital "P" Populist-GOP alliance. Republicans won some local successes in this brief and forgotten era, capturing the North Carolina governorship even; however, Bourbon Democrats triumphed and then enacted poll taxes to disenfranchise Republican or Populist-leaning poor whites and blacks alike.[c] What this coalition had in common was the narrative of the underdog against entrenched power. Despite being out funded and tragically legally disenfranchised at the ballot box, the growing populist movement must ensure that a modern version of the Bourbon Democrats not take hold. Whether through Jim Crow, poll taxes, or in welfare state urban politics today the history of black vote manipulation by the Democrats runs strong, and Republicans in an emerging populist majority should take every opportunity to remind people of this history.

Neither the incumbent nor the Democratic-allied institutions and administrative state enjoy the narrative advantage of being the underdog, the common person, or "normalcy." Indeed, some would argue that it was an irony of history that the narrative existed in the first place. In his article "The People vs. the Democratic Party" Michael Walsh submits that the Democrats' real history is a history in which "lust for power, not a concern for the poor and dispossessed, looms large."[ci]

Despite having all the financial and power advantages in the world, its coalitional health has been steadily fading with only brief recoveries in good cycles. Meanwhile, the steady climb upward out of oppositional status is happening for a coalition that first could only win the presidency but now can win and usually wins Congress, and controls a majority of the states themselves and the Supreme Court for the first time in decades. Think of the coalitions in this country as lake beds, and you want to assess their health. You want your lake, your coalition, to be deep and broad to the point where the water fills up to the shoreline. The deep or shallow nexus is the reliability and intensity of your voting base to turn out and remain committed to the party coalition and cause. Additionally, the broad or narrow nexus is the raw percentages and numbers of voters, and it is either growing and broadening or it is narrowing. And because the alternative to the emerging populist coalitional majority is not so much a continuation of the status quo of the administrative state but a successor ideology of postliberal and postnational progressives going through those institutions, you assess the health of all three potential coalitions.

Coalitional Health

	Democrat Administrative State Coalition	Successor Ideology Coalition	Republican Emerging Populist Majority Coalition
Geography	Deep, but narrow and narrowing	Deep in cities, not broad	Deep, broad, and broadening
Demography	Shallow, broad, but narrowing	Shallow and narrow	Shallow and narrow, but deepening and broadening
Ideology	Shallow, and narrowing	Deep and narrow, and deepening, not broadening	Deep, broad, and broadening

The status quo of the administrative state coalition has long been deep but narrow and narrowing across geography, perhaps its biggest weakness and a key driver of the push to add Supreme Court justices, states, and senators, and so on. These are not the moves of a confident coalition or a king who wears the crown comfortably anymore. Additionally, despite the broad demography that formed the backbone of the Judis-Teixeira thesis, it's becoming clearer that it is shallow and slowly peeling off in many areas and gaining almost nowhere as this book has argued. Finally, a once "big tent" coalition ideologically has increasingly narrowed and become the politics and cultural preferences of urban progressive activists and professional-class liberals. There are simply not enough large cities, across enough states, that are actually gaining in votes by number or percentage, even in those cities, to support this type of coalition. Even the relative gains in the suburbs would have to speed up considerably to reinforce the status quo, and considering where those gains are—largely tied to the existence of a large metropolitan core—even that is often a redundancy.

We could then turn to the *real* alternative to the emerging populist majority, the successor ideology itself. How likely is it that the Astoria, Queens; Brooklyn DSA Left; San Francisco; Portland; Seattle; or Chicago progressive illiberal left challenge continues to grow its coalition rather than suffer a backlash? Has there been even one victory in a swing district for this younger, more credentialed but less educated and experienced upstart movement? No. For the time being it appears as if the Democratic-led administrative state and the successor ideology need one another and are dependent on being against a Republican coalition of some variety, to the point of casting them as villains and enemies of the state itself, to survive. The kayfabe-esque presence of President Trump on Twitter made him the perfect heel to bring the successor ideology into more power and influence over the weakening Democratic coalition, providing it with a much-needed boost, but it was also at great cost and exposure. However, any Republican will be cast as an existential threat no matter what, and the *why* is more important; these coalitions genuinely are held together by negative energy at this point rather than positive energy to survive. And survive it will in the short and medium term. All of what is said here is in flux and far more gradual than the work of grand pronouncements of past works. This work promises a growing populist and grassroots future, not necessarily a Republican one. Yet Republican it will be because of these gradual trends. And it will have little to do with Donald Trump, Mitch McConnell, Ron DeSantis, or any other political leader or figure, and much to do with the trends and energies that make any elected figure possible or any outcome improve along the margins. Elections do matter; they matter quite a great deal in making life just a bit more tolerable, just a bit better, but they are no substitute for what turns around a country at its core or what makes a human life succeed. In this sense, our societal need that you can hear all across social and legacy media to fulfill our aspirations through the inner workings and horse race of politics, parties, and elections is doomed to fall short and miss the mark. The next election will not be the most important of our lifetime, but every once in a while, it is. We just won't know it until later. We suspect, much like this thesis, the most important moments have already occurred.

The most important election of our lifetime so far was in 2016, and its outcome set in motion at least a preview and a vision of what the next era in American politics would be. And contrary to the dark and dangerous rhetoric the media claims it to be, in the long run this next era and its associated vision will be decidedly positive, optimistic, and hopeful. In 2020, according to More in Common's work, two-thirds of Republican voters cast their ballots for something rather than against something, whereas two-thirds of Democrats cast their ballots against something rather than for something. One could write this off as the work of mere incumbency, but 2020 was not a typical election. There was not really an incumbent versus a challenger candidate so much as the incumbent still was the "change" candidate that Obama first campaigned as, then Trump represented against Clinton. And his opponent, now the current president, a man who had been in elected office nearly interrupted since 1972, was the "return to normalcy" candidate, or restoration candidate if you will. And indeed, Joe Biden's lifespan itself epitomizes the entire length of what we've termed a "civic order" and why it is unnatural for it to last any longer than that. Slowly but surely the vision of the country first articulated by Woodrow Wilson is getting discredited in its institutions beyond the point of return. Trillion-dollar bills have been passed, but people will not remember them. There is no relationship between the people and these spending bills like there is between Social Security and Medicare, and little to no relationship has been established with policies like the Affordable Care Act either. One hundred years later, after World War I saw the second great mobilization of the American system, this time ushered in by a liberal academic with a deep belief in strong government, that war became an excuse to take over virtually the entire economy from the railroads to the telephone system and a host of other activities.[cii]

Yes, Biden was the return-to-normalcy candidate, but whatever that means does not last much longer. Increasingly, many are realizing there is not much normalcy to the Biden administration either. Despite being an incumbent, Donald Trump still was the "change" candidate in 2020, and he was one who, even after serving for a full term, was still treated as an outsider by the entire political establishment and elite that considers itself entitled to rule. Whether or not Trump becomes president again, he has exposed the actions of those who actually run the country, and his singular term as president has started a ticking clock on the final days of their default governance. In 1920, just as in 2020, the economy went into a steep slide, and in response to that slide the default governance of the day, the status quo, took place, and the slide subsided in 1920 a year later. This forgotten depression, never marking itself on the public memory, stands in contrast to the lingering economic issues of today of a devalued currency, indebted society, and secular sluggish growth too dependent on consumer spending on goods and services. But make no mistake, in those days just over a century ago, even though debilitated by a stroke, Wilson represented the precursor of what was to come. He was the "change" candidate just as much of the Progressive Era was the change and reform from the prior status quo.

This "incumbency-as-the-change-candidate" is unusual for American presidential elections and probably has not happened since the days of Theodore Roosevelt, whom the *New York Times* was decidedly against in its 1904 endorsement, in an era where it usually endorsed Republicans, America's natural and default governing party of that day. Simply put, 2016 was the most important election of our lifetime because it was the difference between an alternative vision being articulated from the status quo of uniparty real and relative managed decline and two choices of more of the same: forever wars, growing central government, endless cultural division, and bewilderment and bemoaning about continued "division." It was the difference between whether *Roe v. Wade* continued to be the law of the entire land and the return to the constitutional order laid down by the founders rather than the winds of the yearly opinion polls. Just as the 1912 three-way electoral split that resulted in Woodrow Wilson becoming president was the most pivotal election to the eventual development of the progressive administrative state that moved beyond the Constitution and beyond the republic to the degree it can get away with, so, too, will the 2016 electoral result that has already passed become that for what is to come. At this point, the biggest danger lies in "unity" before its time for a new consensus to come. A forced unity is far worse than one that takes work and effort and happens gradually over many events, years, and elections. Slowly but surely, America has moved from a macro national conversation of "yes versus yes, but bigger" and "yes versus me too" to one of "yes versus yes, but slower" and "yes versus no." The key now, and the key to the success of the emerging coalition, will be to articulate a "yes versus no, and over here now."

***

By the presidential election of 2032, America will be as far away from the end of World War II as Abraham Lincoln's Gettysburg Address was from the Declaration of Independence. In our four score and seven years ago moment, we face an America that will be as divided and at a crossroads as the one Lincoln faced in 1863. Yet we suspect we will once again emerge a victorious nation, with boundless potential for prosperity and possibility, in our land of hope. Lincoln himself led the country through that crisis by thinking seriously about the American founding and American Revolution. He had to get to the heart of the story and retrieve the moral arc that made it so compelling.[ciii]

The emerging populist majority did not need to be Republican. It could have conceivably been either party. And that the current party is and stands to benefit was not the main purpose of this writing.

In the years to come time will tell whether the Republican Party understands the populist and patriotic majority that powered it to the impossible upset of 2016, the midterm wave we just experienced, and the likely recapture of the White House to come in 2024.

Time will tell whether the code can be cracked on reversing real and relative American decline and ushering in a new era of cultural and civic renewal. And time will tell whether the American family unit can be preserved not just as a sociocultural entity but also centered in an economy organized around the real needs of American households, with a national industrial policy rather than a global one.

One thing is for certain though: populists have the energy, they are the zeitgeist, and increasingly they have the ideas. And the party that accepts that energy and those ideas will rightfully govern for a long, long time.

In our storied past America succeeded because of common sense; a common philosophy, culture, and history; and a respect for the common people (self-governance) to chart their own destiny. This is how and why it can succeed again. And we must succeed again; there is nowhere else on Earth to go.

EPILOGUE AND REACTION TO THE 2022 MIDTERMS

This book was not about some Republican forever future that started in 2022 or will start in 2024. If anything, our thesis strongly rests on the long game of persistent and ongoing trends, American political history, and a bit of creative thinking forecasting how parties will react to the challenges of the twenty-first century. The '22 midterms were disappointing if you were a Republican partisan and a pleasant surprise if you were a Democratic partisan; it's that same conventional wisdom that continues to miss the forest for the trees. What actually happened was a blue wave in purple battleground districts—which is reflective of the money, institutional, and civic order (America's default party) advantages Democrats have—and a red wave in most of red AND blue America.

Most of what this book covers continued to present itself and, in many respects, accelerated in 2022.

The Republican Party continued to become the party of parents, continued a steady and gradual realignment of Hispanic and Asian Americans, occurring faster in some places that had previously been slower like New York and swinging back a bit compared to 2020 in places like Texas. The Republican Party continues to be the beneficiary of younger Americans realigning around marriages, mortgages, and children. And the party continues to be more competitive where US elections are technically and constitutionally held—in the states.

While the House margins were disappointing due to Democrats narrowly and strategically tailoring to win every jump ball, the House flip continues a trend where Republicans have now won four of the last seven national popular votes in the House, and continues a trend where the electorate says "no thanks" to unilateral Democratic governance. Since the baby boomers got into power, America said "no" to Democrats after two years in 1994, "no" to Democrats after two years in 2010, and "no" to Democrats after two years in 2022. Going back further, after giving slim margins to Jimmy Carter and a Democratic Congress in 1976 with an eclectic and ultimately unrepeatable coalition, America said "no" to unilateral Democratic-run America in 1980 by giving Ronald Reagan over four hundred electoral votes, then over five hundred electoral votes. Since the end of the Second World War the American electorate has given six presidential landslides to the Republicans and one to the Democrats in 1964. Republican one-party mandates have fared only marginally better, which brings us the stalemate of our times—slowly budging...

In the Senate is where Republicans should be most disappointed. Outspent by Democrats and abandoned by the establishment, the populist wing of the Republican Party consistently shows up for the establishment, but the establishment does not show up for them. Mitch McConnell, who cannot break 30 percent in favorability and has long been the most unpopular politician in the country, in tandem with the media has worked to try and blame President Trump and anyone associated for the underperformance. Nowhere does the long American stalemate continue the strongest than in the halls of the Republican establishment. Yet even in the Senate, the underperformance is not permanent; 2022 was a neutral environment for the US Senate map, and 2024 will not be. In two years, Democrats will have to defend Senate seats like West Virginia, Montana, and Ohio, and have no realistic opportunities for pickups. Regardless of the outcome of the presidential and House elections, the Senate is almost a lock to flip, and when it does, the Democrats will not win it back again in our lifetimes. This is the long, slow, and persistent advantage that formed the majority of the thesis in *The Emerging Populist Majority*.

The Democratic Party continues to be a dead end for civic moderates, veterans and current military service members, and increasingly for black Americans. It is increasingly no longer a big-tent party and is growing less demographically diverse on top of the already-existing erosion along diverse geographical and ideological lines. Yet it also continues to be America's natural governing party with near monopolies over institutions: academia, culture, media, entertainment, and technology. That these built-in advantages and a party establishment who fears their activist base yet can effectively rig their primaries to avoid them cannot produce a lasting majority tells us that the American people have no interest in handing the keys over to a party whose progressives continue to expand their ambitions and lust for power and control over others as if they are members of a coalition receiving 1936 and 1964 landslides.

What the midterms did guarantee though was that Joe Biden is going to be unchallenged for a second term and that we may get the election in 2024 we were going to have but for COVID in 2020. Regardless of whether Trump or DeSantis or anyone else is the candidate, the emerging issues that formed the backlash to globalization seen in Brexit and in the 2016 US presidential election are still with us and being synthesized with the old party and the emerging party of parents. The anti-populist streak from the coastal and global establishment will continue to lead to well-funded smear campaigns on a populist ascendency, but it will not wash away the realities under our feet and in our streets and at our dinner tables. Standing in the way and slowing down a country trading off long game-winning field goals every two to four years is a Republican establishment that has not won an election since 2004 and has been dependent on patriotic and populist energy in their grass roots to go through the channels of the party. There is no political future for the neoconservatives or the party of the establishment. The strategy and tactics must evolve and change with the coalitions that have emerged and shown promise and room for growth. Until ballot harvesting and mail-in election laws are properly codified, challenged, and the rule of law in elections is reestablished, the Republican Party must target the very voters so critical to the margins in 2016 and keeping the margins very close in 2020 across America's vast Heartland, often from the working class and often from rural and exurban America where outsourcing and deindustrialization has hit communities the hardest the last few decades.

For a new and lasting coalition to emerge through the legal vessel that is the Republican Party, which could have conceivably gone through the Democratic Party as well, a strength and durability must exist through all three prongs of diversity: geography, demography, and ideology. The facts show the Republican Party is much closer to this triumph than the Democrats are, who are getting further away from their "demographic inevitability" coalition. While the Republican Party must hold the line on immigration, education, and elections, the emerging populist majority and any possibility of a rebound for American and Western civilization will turn on the maintenance and protection of families.

The most relevant outcome of the '22 midterms had nothing to do with the top line results. Instead, it had to do with the fact that the Republican Party won married men by 20 percent, married women by 14 percent, unmarried men by 7, but was wiped out with unmarried women by 37 percent, at least partly driven by the overturning of *Roe v. Wade*, which will only contribute to the partisan parental and family gap across America. Demographics are still destiny, and increasingly the new demographics favor the Republican Party even when it underperforms in a midterm election.

One of these coalitions can save civilization and renew the country around a set of core values and principles and a shared national identity; the other cannot. Millennials who are realigning around marriages, mortgages, and children started off voting more Democratic than Gen Z, yet both in tandem with Gen X and their children embody a shared destiny upon which the twenty-first century will turn. The United States of America is one of the only powerful countries on Earth that is not scheduled to demographically fall apart completely in the coming years. Because baby boomers were a large enough generation, who also had enough children—mostly millennials—the future of America will depend politically, economically, and culturally on whether over 50 percent of millennials have children and become parents, and whether over 55 percent of Gen Z, a smaller generation, have children and become parents. Therefore, the party that encourages and makes it easier to raise a family in this country and in our communities will rightfully and righteously govern for a long, long time.

On one side, America can take the path of Congresswoman Alexandria Ocasio-Cortez, who morally questions whether it is right to bring children into this world and onto the good Earth because climate change is supposed to wipe us all out in a decade. Or America can take the path of renewal. We can grow up, pick ourselves up, and hold the line through the not-so-roaring twenties, commit to forming and raising families, and a populist-conservative-traditionalist-patriotic-national fusion through the only viable party for it—the Republican Party—commits to a pro-natal, pro-family, and pro-America agenda both culturally and economically to bring about a renewal we can only now dream of. These dreams, rather than from our fathers and mothers, are from our grandfathers and grandmothers, and from our founders.

AFTERWORD

BY STEVE CORTES

America's political and cultural future will be forged by populists and led by the young adults now rising to positions of prominence across our society. This rising generation has endured childhoods and young adulthoods marred by successive financial crises, seemingly endless wars, and a country dominated by increasingly concentrated political and economic power structure. That ruling class power paradigm works against the interests of most Americans but especially the young.

Whether this upstart populist backlash eventually dominates from the left or from the right remains a very open question. Thankfully, thought leaders and activists like Troy Olson and Gavin Wax stand at the forefront of a patriotic populist nationalist movement on the right, ready to resurrect America culturally, politically, and economically.

I first learned of their good work during the ludicrous assault on the wonderful Teddy Roosevelt statue that stood for decades outside the American Museum of Natural History in New York City. That magnificent work of public art, the *Equestrian Statue of Theodore Roosevelt*, displayed the twenty-sixth president of the United States advancing on horseback with the assistance of two guides, one black and one American Indian.

Tragically that statue was removed to appease political correctness, along with scores of other cultural and historical masterpieces that were torn down across America during the George Floyd summer of rage in 2020. The statues fell either by violent brute force or by processes dominated by woke communist intimidation. These desecrations flowed from the mayhem of those 2020 Black Life Matters riots that mimicked Pol Pot and the Khmer Rouge in declaring American history as dead. The leftists also channeled the Afghan Taliban in vandalizing and removing cherished monuments that honored heroes like Christopher Columbus and Abraham Lincoln.

But young patriots like Olson and Wax stood up against this madness and protested peacefully but forcefully at the Manhattan landmark, arguing to preserve this inspiring tribute to one of America's truly great leaders. Their group, the New York Young Republicans, earned national media attention for their bravery and persuasive presentations. As a Chicago talk radio host at the time, I summoned Gavin to appear on my program to discuss these events and was immediately impressed at the commitment and knowledge of this young man.

Thankfully, he and Olson now provide that wisdom to wider audiences through this insightful and badly needed book, *The Emerging Populist Majority*. They may not have successfully saved the Teddy Roosevelt statue, but they may well save our nation through helping to persuade the American citizenry to awaken, rise up, and reclaim the levers of power in our republic. Why will young people drive much of this populist surge in America? In large part, because the policies of the ruling class that have so broadly damaged America have inflicted particular pain upon the young.

For example, citizens under the age of forty in 1998 held a 13.1 percent share of all national wealth. By 2021, that total was more than cut in half to only 6 percent. Getting more specific by age grouping, today millennials only own 4.6 percent of all national wealth. For comparison, when the boomers were the same age as millennials are now, back in the late 1980s, as young people they then commanded 21.6 percent of national wealth, nearly five times the present rate.

Clearly the intense concentration of economic and political power has resulted not only in an overall third world–like disparity in prosperity but also a systemic generational one. This economic repression of the young results directly in worrisome societal and cultural trends, including a decades-long plunge in birth and marriage rates, concurrent with more recent soaring rates of suicide, other deaths of despair, and the use of psychiatric pharmaceuticals.

As America acts more like an oligarchy and less like a republic, young citizens pay an especially acute price. But what are the mechanisms to reclaim that republic, to wrest control back from the abuses of Big Business in cahoots with Permanent Washington? Clearly, only a populist vision can facilitate the needed reforms, such as trust-busting versus harmful and pernicious corporate monopolies and oligopolies. Only a true populist movement can insist on onshoring to bring productive capacity back to the shores of America.

Speaking of America's boundaries, the ruling class uniparty occasionally gives lip service to border protection and controlled migration, but in reality, the DC cabal has united with C-suite executives for decades to allow, and even incentivize, nearly unchecked mass illegal trespassing into our homeland. Only a populist surge will demand not just law-and-order regarding border enforcement but also an even more muscular vision of American sovereignty. The populist nationalist must demand far stricter legal immigration practices, perhaps even a total moratorium on migration until better protocols and filters can be established.

For decades, real wages, meaning incomes adjusted for inflation, have been stagnant or falling for working-class laborers in America. The Trump term brought a notable and very welcome respite, with real wages surging into 2019 for all categories but especially for the previous laggards, like those with only high school diplomas.

But because of the Chinese Communist Party Virus, the global economy was smashed by Beijing's epidemiological dirty bomb. In America, leftist politicians massively exacerbated this already troublesome pandemic through utterly tyrannical lockdowns that brazenly abused power and relied on quackery rather than real science. This economic and political calamity harshly interrupted the nascent progress for workers under President Trump. Now, due to the mismanagement of the Biden regime, real wages now plunge into an all-out tailspin, further crushing the prosperity and confidence of the masses. But patriots like Olson and Wax step into this breach to offer keen analysis and fresh proposed solutions to reestablish economic abundance and diffused political power. They work toward a society that again cherishes family, promotes public virtue, and prizes aesthetic beauty.

These young firebrands reject the crass calculus of the ruling class Brahmins who simply want to personally profit while overseeing the managed decline of America. This growing cadre of like-minded young patriots brings vigor and creativity to campaigns and to public policy. In this regard, they indeed channel the energy and skills of the great Teddy Roosevelt, one of the greatest New Yorkers and Republicans to ever live.

To that end, this book, *The Emerging Populist Majority*, provides an important blueprint for patriots committed to saving this great republic.

BIBLIOGRAPHY

Baime, A. J. *Dewey Defeats Truman: The 1948 Election and the Battle for America's Soul.* Boston: Houghton Mifflin Harcourt, 2020.

Barry, John. *The Great Influenza: The Story of the Deadliest Pandemic in History.* London: Penguin Books, 2004.

Berg, A. Scott. *Wilson.* New York: Berkley Books, 2013.

Brown, David S. *The First Populist: The Defiant Life of Andrew Jackson.* New York: Scribner, 2022.

Dionne, E. J., Jr. *Our Divided Political Heart: The Battle for the American Idea in an Age of Discontent.* New York: Bloomsbury, 2012.

Frank, Thomas. *Listen, Liberal: Or, Whatever Happened to the Party of the People?* New York: Metropolitan Books, 2016.

———. *The People, No: A Brief History of Anti-Populism.* New York: Metropolitan Books, 2020.

———. *What's the Matter with Kansas? How Conservatives Won the Heart of America.* New York: Picador, 2004.

Friedman, Thomas. *Hot, Flat, and Crowded: Why We Need a Green Revolution–And How It Can Renew America.* New York: Farrar, Straus and Giroux, 2008.

———. *The World Is Flat: A Brief History of the Globalized World in the 21st Century.* London: Penguin Books, 2005.

Gingrich, Newt. *Trump and the American Future: Solving the Great Problems of our Time.* New York: Center Street, Hachette Book Group, 2020.

Gurri, Martin. *The Revolt of the Public and the Crisis of Authority in the New Millennium.* San Francisco: Stripe Press, 2015.

Hemingway, Mollie Z. "Trump vs. the Media." In *Saving the Republic: The Fate of Freedom in the Age of the Administrative*, ed. Roger Kimball, p. 73. New York: Encounter Books, 2018.

Judis, John B., and Ruy Teixeira. *The Emerging Democratic Majority.* New York: Scribner, 2002 (paperback edition 2004).

Judis, John B., *The Nationalist Revival: Trade, Immigration, and the Revolt against Globalization.* New York: Columbia Global Reports, 2018.

Kimball, Roger, ed. *Saving the Republic: The Fate of Freedom in the Age of the Administrative.* New York: Encounter Books, 2018.

Korda, Michael. *Ike: An American Hero.* New York: Harper Perennial, 2008 (hardcover ed., 2007).

Kotkin, Joel. *The Coming of Neo-Feudalism: A Warning to the Global Middle Class.* New York: Encounter Books, 2020.

———. *The Next Hundred Million: America in 2050—How the Addition of One Hundred Million Americans by Midcentury Will Transform the Way We Live, Work, and Prosper.* London: Penguin Books, 2010.

Marcus, David. *Charade: The Covid Lies That Crushed a Nation.* New York, Nashville: Bombardier Books, 2021.

McCullough, David. *Truman.* New York: Simon & Schuster, 1992.

McClay, Wilfred M. *Land of Hope: An Invitation to the Great American Story.* New York: Encounter Books, 2019.

Meacham, Jon. *The Soul of America: The Battle for Our Better Angels.* New York: Random House, 2019.

O'Neill, William L. *American High: The Years of Confidence 1945–1960.* New York: The Free Press, Macmillan, 1989.

Pearlstein, Rick. *Before the Storm: Barry Goldwater and the Unmaking of the American Consensus*. New York: Nation Books, 2009 (paperback ed., 2001).

———. *Nixonland: The Rise of a President and the Fracturing of America*. New York: Scribner, 2008.

———. *Reaganland: America's Right Turn 1976–1980*. New York: Simon & Schuster, 2020.

Phillips, Kevin. *The Emerging Republican Majority*. Garden City, New York: Doubleday Anchor Books, 1969.

Rodden, Jonathan A. *Why Cities Lose: The Deep Roots of the Urban-Rural Political Divide*. New York: Basic Books, 2019.

Rove, Karl. *The Triumph of William McKinley: Why the Election of 1896 Still Matters*. New York: Simon & Schuster, 2015.

Shlaes, Amity. *Coolidge*. New York: HarperCollins, 2013.

———. *The Forgotten Man: A New History of the Great Depression*. New York: Harper Perennial, 2008.

———. *Great Society: A New History*. New York: Harper Perennial, 2019.

Smith, Jean Edward. *FDR*. New York: Random House, 2007.

Sowell, Thomas. *A Conflict of Visions: Ideological Origins of Political Struggles*, revised edition. New York: Basic Books, 2007.

———. *Intellectuals and Society*. Revised and enlarged edition. New York: Basic Books, 2011.

Strauss, William, and Neil Howe. *The Fourth Turning: An American Prophecy: What the Cycles of History Tell Us About America's Next Rendezvous with Destiny*. New York: Three Rivers Press, 1997

———. *Generations: The History of America's Future, 1584 to 2069*. New York: HarperCollins, 1991.

Stoll, Ira. *JFK, Conservative*. Boston: Houghton Mifflin Harcourt, 2013.

Trende, Sean. *The Lost Majority: Why the Future of Government Is Up for Grabs–and Who Will Take It*. New York: Palgrave Macmillan, 2012.

Vance, J. D. *Hillbilly Elegy: A Memoir of a Family and Culture in Crisis*. New York: Harper, 2016.

Walsh, Michael. "The People vs. the Democratic Party." In *Saving the Republic: The Fate of Freedom in the Age of the Administrative,* ed. Roger Kimball, p. 333. New York: Encounter Books, 2018.

Widmer, Ted. *Lincoln on the Verge: Thirteen Days to Washington.* New York: Simon & Schuster Paperbacks, 2020.

Zeihan, Peter. *The End of the World Is Just the Beginning: Mapping the Collapse of Globalization.* New York: HarperCollins, 2022.

Zito, Salena, and Brad Todd. *The Great Revolt: Inside the Populist Coalition Reshaping American Politics.* New York: Crown Forum, 2018.

ENDNOTES

i   Richard Brookhiser, *James Madison* (New York: Basic Books, 2011), 98–117.

ii   Ibid., 103.

iii   Wilfred M. McClay, *Land of Hope: An Invitation to the Great American Story* (New York: Encounter Books, 2019), 94.

iv   Jon Meacham, *The Soul of America: The Battle for Our Better Angels* (New York: Random House, 2019), 31.

v   David S. Brown, *The First Populist: The Defiant Life of Andrew Jackson* (New York: Scribner, 2022), 302.

vi   Ibid., 367–68.

vii   Ibid., 1.

viii   Rick Perlstein, *Nixonland: The Rise of a President and the Fracturing of America* (New York: Scribner, 2008), 42.

ix   Ibid., 43.

x   Martin Armstrong, "The Long Depression—the First Great Depression," *Armstrong Economics* blog, July 16, 2015, https://www.armstrongeconomics.com/history/americas-economic-history/the-long-depression-the-first-great-depression/.

xi   Victor Davis Hanson, "Dueling Populisms," *Defining Ideas* (April 12, 2018), Hoover Institution, https://www.hoover.org/research/dueling-populisms.

xii   Thomas Frank, *The People, No: A Brief History of Anti-Populism* (New York: Metropolitan Books, 2020), 13.

xiii   A. Scott Berg, *Wilson* (New York: Berkley Books, 2013), 743.

xiv   Thomas Sowell, *Intellectuals and Society* (New York: Basic Books, 2009), 309.

xv   Karl Rove, *The Triumph of William McKinley: Why the Election of 1896 Still Matters* (New York: Simon & Schuster, 2015), 378.

xvi   Amity Shlaes, *Coolidge* (New York: HarperCollins, 2013).

xvii   Sean Trende, *The Lost Majority: Why the Future of Government Is Up for Grabs–and Who Will Take It* (New York: Palgrave Macmillan, 2012), 156.

xviii   Ibid.

xix   Shlaes, *Coolidge*, 208–09.

xx   Ibid., 291.

xxi   Ibid., 297.

xxii   Thomas Frank, *What's the Matter with Kansas? How Conservatives Won the Heart of America* (New York: Picador, 2005), 89.

xxiii   Rick Perlstein, *Before the Storm: Barry Goldwater and the Unmaking of the American Consensus* (New York: Nation Books, 2009, paperback ed.), 158-9.

xxiv   Joseph Campbell, *The Hero with a Thousand Faces* (New York: Pantheon Books, 1949).

xxv   William Strauss and Neil Howe, *The Fourth Turning* (New York: Three Rivers Press, 1997), 3.

xxvi   Jean Edward Smith, *FDR* (New York: Random House, 2007), 479.

xxvii   Amity Shlaes, *The Forgotten Man: A New History of the Depression* (New York: Harper Perennial, 2008), 383.

xxviii   Michael Korda, *Ike: An American Hero* (New York: Harper Perennial, 2008), 656.

xxix   David McCullough, *Truman* (New York: Simon & Schuster, 1992), 586.

xxx   A. J. Baime, *Dewey Defeats Truman: The 1948 Election and the Battle for America's Soul*, (Boston: Houghton Mifflin Harcourt, 2020), 139.

xxxi   William L. O'Neill, *American High: The Years of Confidence 1945-1960* (New York: The Free Press, Macmillan, 1986), 97.

xxxii   Ibid., 179.

xxxiii   Ira Stoll, *JFK, Conservative*, (Boston: Houghton Mifflin Harcourt, 2013), 4.

xxxiv   Abraham Lincoln, "What is conservatism? Is it not adherence to the old and tried, against the new and untried? We stick to, contend for, the identical old policy on the point in controversy which was adopted by 'our fathers who framed the Government under which we live'…." Cooper Union Speech, February 27, 1860, abrahamlincolnonline.org, https://www.abrahamlincolnonline.org/lincoln/speeches/cooper.htm.

xxxv   O'Neill, *American High*, 4.

xxxvi   American Legion, "Pillar 3: Americanism," August 7, 2012, https://www.legion.org/pillars/211656/pillar-3-americanism.

xxxvii   Frank, *What's the Matter with Kansas?*, 28.

xxxviii   Perlstein, *Before the Storm*, 140.

xxxix   Amity Shlaes, *Great Society: A New History* (New York: Harper Perennial, 2019).

xl   Ibid., 307.

xli   Trende, *The Lost Majority*, 158.

xlii   Rick Perlstein, *Reaganland: America's Right Turn 1976-1980* (New York: Simon & Schuster, 2020).

xliii   Frank, *The People, No: A Brief History of Anti-Populism*, 217.

xliv   Ibid., 218.

xlv   Frank, *What's the Matter with Kansas?*, 242-43.

xlvi   Thomas Frank, *Listen, Liberal: Or, Whatever Happened to the Party of the People?* (New York: Metropolitan Books, 2016), 59.

xlvii   E. J. Dionne Jr., *Our Divided Political Heart: The Battle for the American Idea in an Age of Discontent* (New York: Bloomsbury, 2012).

xlviii   Jonathan A. Rodden, *Why Cities Lose: The Deep Roots of the Urban-Rural Political Divide* (New York: Basic Books, 2019).

xlix   Ibid., 9.

l   Perlstein, *Reaganland*, 269.

li   Mollie Z. Hemingway, "Trump vs. the Media," in *Saving the Republic*, ed. Roger Kimball (New York: Encounter Books, 2018), 78.

lii   Frank, *The People, No: A Brief History of Anti-Populism*.

liii   Ibid., 14.

liv   Ibid., 17.

lv   Thomas Friedman, *The World Is Flat: A Brief History of the Globalized World in the 21st Century* (London: Farrar, Penguin Books, 2005), 385–86.

lvi   Peter Zeihan, *The End of the World Is Just the Beginning: Mapping the Collapse of Globalization* (New York: HarperCollins, 2022).

lvii   Friedman, *The World Is Flat*, 374.

lviii   Thomas Friedman, *Hot, Flat, and Crowded: Why We Need a Green Revolution—And How It Can Renew America* (New York: Farrar, Straus and Giroux, 2008), 9.

lix   Trende, *The Lost Majority*, 196.

lx   Jonathan A. Rodden, *Why Cities Lose: The Deep Roots of the Urban-Rural Political Divide* (New York: Basic Books, 2019), 83.

lxi   Chris Matthews, Commentary during the MSNBC Election Night broadcast of the 2016 US Presidential Election, https://www.youtube.com/watch?v=ShKIGsex4XI.

lxii   J. D. Vance, *Hillbilly Elegy: A Memoir of a Family and a Culture in Crisis* (New York: Harper, 2016), 262.

lxiii   Stoll, *JFK, Conservative*, 203.

lxiv   Salena Zito and Brad Todd, *The Great Revolt: Inside the Populist Coalition Reshaping American Politics* (New York: Crown Forum, 2018), 8.

lxv   Ibid., 9.

lxvi   Ibid., 18.

lxvii   Strauss and Howe, *The Fourth Turning*, 247.

lxviii   Trende, *The Lost Majority*, 155.

lxix   Martin Gurri, *The Revolt of the Public and the Crisis of Authority in the New Millennium* (San Francisco: Stripe Press, 2015), p. 341.

lxx   Victor Davis Hanson, *The Dying Citizen: How Progressive Elites, Tribalism, and Globalization Are Destroying the Idea of America* (New York: Basic Books, 2021).

lxxi   John M. Barry, *The Great Influenza: The Story of the Deadliest Pandemic in History* (London: Penguin Books, 2004), 461.

lxxii   David Marcus, *Charade: The Covid Lies That Crushed a Nation* (New York, Nashville: Bombardier Books, 2021), 264–65.

lxxiii   Trende, *The Lost Majority*, 181.

lxxiv   Ibid.

lxxv   Ibid.

lxxvi   Alan I. Abramowitz, *The Great Alignment: Race, Party Transformation, and the Rise of Donald Trump* (New Haven: Yale University Press, 2018).

lxxvii   McClay, *Land of Hope*.

lxxviii   Both Virginia and North Carolina were listed as leaning GOP but very competitive in *The Emerging Democratic Majority*.

lxxix   Ruy Teixeira, *The Liberal Patriot*, https://www.liberalpatriot.com/p/the-democrats-hispanic-voter-problem-dfc

lxxx   John B. Judis, *The Nationalist Revival: Trade, Immigration, and the Revolt against Globalization* (New York: Columbia Global Reports, 2018), 109–10.

lxxxi   Ibid., 94–96.

lxxxii   Kevin P. Phillips, "The United Heartland," in *The Emerging Republican Majority* (Garden City, New York: Doubleday Anchor Books, 1969).

lxxxiii   Joel Kotkin, *The Next Hundred Million: America in 2050—How the Addition of One Hundred Million Americans by Midcentury Will Transform the Way We Live, Work, and Prosper* (London: Penguin Books, 2010), 114.

lxxxiv   Phillips, *The Emerging Republican Majority*, 187.

lxxxv   Ibid.

lxxxvi   Kotkin, *The Next Hundred Million*.

lxxxvii   Joel Kotkin, *The Coming of Neo-Feudalism: A Warning to the Global Middle Class* (New York: Encounter Books, 2020).

lxxxviii   Phillips, *The Emerging Republican Majority*, 184–6.

lxxxix   Phillips, "The Pacific States," in *The Emerging Republican Majority*.

xc   Judis and Teixeira, *The Emerging Democratic Majority*, 4–5.

xci   William Strauss and Neil Howe, *Generations: The History of America's Future—1584 to 2069* (New York: HarperCollins, 1991), 313.

xcii   Trende, *The Lost Majority*, 168.

xciii   Judis and Teixeira, *The Emerging Democratic Majority*, 37.

xciv   Ibid., 14.

xcv   Ibid., 15.

xcvi   Thomas Sowell, *A Conflict of Visions: Ideological Origins of Political Struggles*, rev. ed. (New York: Basic Books, 2007).

xcvii   Sowell, *Intellectuals and Society*.

xcviii   Perlstein, *Nixonland*, 507.

xcix   Ibid., 509.

c   Phillips, *The Emerging Republican Majority*, 191–3.

ci   Michael Walsh, "The People vs. The Democratic Party," in *Saving the Republic*.

cii   Newt Gingrich, *Trump and the American Future: Solving the Great Problems of our Time* (New York: Center Street, Hachette, 2020), 330.

ciii   Ted Widmer, *Lincoln on the Verge: Thirteen Days to Washington* (New York: Simon & Schuster, 2020), 353.

ACKNOWLEDGMENTS

We owe a debt of gratitude first and foremost to the forerunners of this subgenre that fuses political science and American history. First, we'd like to mention the Kevin Phillips book *The Emerging Republican Majority* from the late 1960s that encountered much discussion and confusion over its contents. Every thirty years it has been said the punditocracy and commentariat burst open with a new wave of books foretelling America's political future with an oracle-like sense of certainty, yet this is largely driven by the partisans that read into it too deeply. To both John Judis and Ruy Teixeira, whose intellectual humility today we hope to repeat in the years to come if what has been written here does not come to pass. Finally, a nod to the contrary tradition from Sean Trende that cautioned against grand realignment and forever-majority pronouncements in general. While the title of this book nods to the former, we hope much of its contents points to the latter. The future is always up for grabs.

Additionally we'd like to thank the Raheem Kassam and Steve Cortes for writing the foreword and afterword to this book and for the clear articulation of what is transpiring in American life and in the broader world. To our readers and those who gave constructive criticism and feedback along the way, we give our thanks to Matthew Tyrmand, Zachary Kangas, Nathan Berger, Jacqueline VanMoer, and many others.

And to the many other writers and sources that were incorporated throughout this book—with particular note to journalist and writer Salena

Zito and Brad Todd for exhaustively doing the investigatory work to bring the stories of those from deindustrialized America to the forefront without judgment—we are grateful. For it is in our view that our national civic and economic renewal must come from the Heartland regions moving outward. In the years to come, we hope policymakers and citizens alike will expand this realignment and continue to frustrate and confound those who see the future as already written as a story just for them rather than all of us in the land of hope.

Finally, we'd like to thank the team at Post Hill Press for taking a chance on us and quickly realizing the potential of this book not just for the election cycle to come but also for its potential staying power as a positive and constructive contribution to a genre that all too often is misunderstood and mischaracterized.

ABOUT THE AUTHORS

 **TROY M. OLSON** is a post-9/11 army veteran, lawyer by training, family man, writer, the sergeant-at-arms for the New York Young Republican Club, and chairman of the Veterans Caucus. In addition to a JD, Troy has an MA in international relations and has a background in politics, campaigns, law, writing, and real estate. Troy has been published by The Daily Caller, and you can find his regular writings on his Substack where he writes about public policy, geopolitics, and American political realignment. Troy was born and raised in Detroit Lakes, Minnesota, and is based out of New York City, where he lives with his wife, Jacqueline, and his son, Theodore.

 **GAVIN M. WAX** is a New York–based conservative activist, commentator, columnist, and operative. He serves as the seventy-sixth president of the New York Young Republican Club, the oldest and largest Young Republican Club in the country, and he is a frequent guest on Fox News, Fox Business, Newsmax, One America News, and Real America's Voice News. Gavin's articles have been published by *American Greatness*, *American Thinker*, The Daily Caller, *The Federalist*, Foundation for Economic Education, *The Hill*, *Human Events*, The Mises Institute, *The National Pulse*, Newsmax, *Newsweek*, RealClearDefense, RealClearPolicy, RealClearPolitics, and *Townhall* among others.